D1353120

NEW MEDIA CULTURES

Series Editor: Steve Jones

New Media Cultures critically examines emerging social formations arising from and surrounding new technologies of communication. It focuses on the processes, products, and narratives that intersect with these technologies. An emphasis of the series is on the Internet and computer-mediated communication, particularly as those technologies are implicated in the relationships among individuals, social groups, modern and postmodern ways of knowing, and public and private life. Books in the series demonstrate interdisciplinary theoretical and methodological analyses, and highlight the relevance of intertwining history, theory, lived experience, and critical study to provide an understanding of new media and contemporary culture.

Books in this series . . .

TUNE IN,
LOG ON

Soaps, Fandom, and
Online Community

Nancy K. Baym

NEW MEDIA
CULTURES

Sage Publications, Inc.
International Educational and Professional Publisher
Thousand Oaks ■ London ■ New Delhi

For information:

Sage Publications, Inc.
2455 Teller Road
Thousand Oaks, California 91320
E-mail: order@sagepub.com

Sage Publications Ltd.
6 Bonhill Street
London EC2A 4PU
United Kingdom

Sage Publications India Pvt. Ltd.
M-32 Market
Greater Kailash I
New Delhi 110 048 India

Printed in the United States of America

Library of Congress Cataloging-in-Publication Data

Baym, Nancy K.
    Tune in, log on: Soaps, fandom, and online community / by Nancy K. Baym.
       p.   cm.— (New media cultures)
    Includes bibliographical references (p.) and index.
    ISBN 0-7619-1648-2 (cloth)
    ISBN 0-7619-1649-0 (paperback)
    1. Soap operas—Social aspects—United States. 2. Soap operas—Electronic discussion groups. I. Title. II. Series.
    PN1992.8.S4 B39 1999
    791.45′6—dc21   99-6435

This book is printed on acid-free paper.

00 01 02 03 04 05 06 7 6 5 4 3 2 1

Acquiring Editor:	Margaret H. Seawell
Editorial Assistant:	Renée Piernot
Production Editor:	Sanford Robinson
Production Assistant:	Karen Wiley
Typesetter:	Lynn Miyata
Indexer:	Mary Mortensen
Cover Design:	Candice Harman

Contents

Acknowledgments

This book is the end result of nearly a decade of work that many people have influenced and inspired along the way. Rex Clark introduced me to the social worlds of the Internet in 1990. When I wrote my first paper on this subject in 1991, Nina Baym and Peggy Miller saw immediately that this was "my project." Many people on the rec.arts.tv.soaps (r.a.t.s.) newsgroup who read that paper encouraged me to pursue the work. Despite my doubts, I figured that when your mom, your dissertation director, and your respondents all want you to keep at it, they probably are right. They were, and I am grateful for their guidance. Many people gave helpful comments including Peggy Miller, Barbara O'Keefe, Ellen Wartella, Cheris Kramarae, Henry Jenkins, Larry Grossberg, Mary Ellen Brown, Robert Sanders, Brenda Danet, and several anonymous reviewers. Julie Snow, Susan Barnett-Lawrence, Rex Clark, Yves Clemmen, Carine Melkom-Mardorossian, and Christine Levecq all have made face-to-face soap viewing much more fun over the years. Stan Kerr of the University of Illinois and Lyle Kipp helped with computing accounts and programming. Mark Huglen helped to code data. In addition to opening my eyes to the Net and watching my soaps, Rex Clark wrote the database I used to handle all these data and had countless conversations about the research with me. Our beautiful son, Zane, kept my priorities obvious. My editor and friend, Steve Jones, deserves extra special thanks for patiently remaining convinced that there was a good book here, for working to amplify my voice rather than inserting his own, and for being the only editor out there who is as big a Nick Rudd fan as I am. I never would have written this book without his unwavering encouragement. Thanks also go to Margaret Seawell and Renée Piernot at Sage Publications. The quotations from Liccardo's (1996) and Susman's (1997) articles in Chapter 1 are excerpted from *Soap Opera Weekly*. Thanks go to Mimi Torchin, editor-in-chief of that fine magazine, for this and her general encouragement (despite her qualms about the Net). Ann Limongello at ABC found photographs of the characters for me to use. Many thanks also go to the colleagues and students at the University of Illinois and Wayne State University who have helped to make my career a pleasure.

Some of the ideas and paragraphs in this book have appeared previously in earlier articles published in the *Journal of Folklore Research* (1993), the *Journal of Computer-Mediated Communication* (1995), and *Research on Language and Social Interaction* (1996) as well as the following books: *The Cultures of Computing* (1995) edited by Leigh Star, *Cyber-Society* (1995) and *CyberSociety 2.0* (1998) edited by Steve Jones, and *Theorizing Fandom: Fans, Subcultures, and Identity* (1998) edited by Cheryl Harris and Alison Alexander.

Dozens of people from r.a.t.s. and rec.arts.tv.soaps.abc have generously participated in this study and provided ongoing excitement and encouragement. This book is for them. I hope I have done them justice.

Introduction:
Three Tales of
One Community

M y daily routine in graduate school went something like this. When I was done teaching, taking my classes, and doing the readings or whatever else had to be done that day, I curled up on my couch, rewound the videotape, and (making liberal use of the fast-forward button) watched my soaps. Later, I turned on my computer and logged on to rec.arts.tv.soaps (r.a.t.s.), a Usenet newsgroup distributed through the Internet. Once "there"—in my tiny study nook with the computer before me—I read the many messages that had been posted about my soaps, sometimes sending my own. The r.a.t.s. newsgroup transformed my understanding of computers; for the first time, I saw them as social tools. The more time I spent reading and posting to r.a.t.s., the less the collection of written messages seemed like lines of glowing green text. I saw in them instead a dynamic community of people with unique voices, distinctive traditions, and enjoyable relationships. Reading r.a.t.s. began to influence me as I viewed the soap opera. I began to think of how those others would react, the types of discussion each episode would provoke, and what I might have to add.

1

Soap viewing had become the base on which witty, sociable women and men had built an interpersonal realm rich with strong traditions and a clear group identity.

When I began to think of r.a.t.s. as a "community," I gravitated toward that term primarily for its warm, emotional resonance. When I decided a few months later to add scholarly inquiry to my recreational use of r.a.t.s., I was led by the question of how people who rarely (if ever) met face-to-face, whose participants came and left, and who seemed to have such a limited communication medium managed to create not just a social world but a social world that felt like community? The case of r.a.t.s. demonstrates the types of communicative practices through which online places come to feel like communities and gives us grounded ways in which to think about the much theorized but underexamined phenomenon of online community. The tale of r.a.t.s. as an online community is one of three this book has to tell.

Early research on computer-mediated communication (CMC) generally identified its defining feature as anonymity and the consequences of that anonymity for social interaction as negative. More recent work has continued to focus on anonymity, stressing the novel opportunities to develop alternative identities or to enhance the ones we already have. It certainly is true, at least so far, that race, rank, physical appearance, and other features of public identity are not immediately evident. Neither are emotional reactions such as laughter or expressions of disgust. Gender, although generally apparent, is not always known with certainty. Scholars who focused on the lack of contextual cues and feedback in task-oriented communication (Baron, 1984; Kiesler, Siegel, & McGuire, 1984) argued that because of this enhanced anonymity, participation becomes more evenly distributed across group members. Consensus becomes more difficult to achieve when everyone is willing to talk. Anonymity also was taken to remove social norms and to increase *flaming* or antagonistic attacks on other users. Recent work has been less damning of online social potential, sometimes celebrating its liberating possibilities (Stone, 1995; Turkle, 1995) and other times investigating its ability to make people seem more likable (Walther, 1996).

Although the term *virtual community* has become common parlance, thanks in no small part to Rheingold's (1993) book, when one goes to the scholarly literature in search of what makes an online group a community and how online community works, one tends to find instead autobiographical accounts of online life (e.g., Cherny & Weise,

1996) or ideological arguments about whether these groups are "real" communities or good or dangerous for offline communities (Porter, 1997). Speculation abounds, but comprehensive frameworks grounded in empirical evidence about what happens within online communities still are in short supply. This book is an effort to fill that void, offering ways in which to think about online communities that are grounded in close study rather than in personal reflection.

The second story in this book is about r.a.t.s. as an audience community, in particular a soap opera fan community. Online communities have formed around thousands of topics; r.a.t.s. is one of the many hundreds formed around the mass media. Much like online communities, audience communities have been better discussed and theorized than documented. The cultural studies work that has examined (often soap opera) audiences and the more recent research into fandom or fan culture have built a strong case for the importance of audience interaction about mass media. This work leads us to understand the mass media in the context of the everyday lives of interconnected individuals. However, audience researchers rarely have ventured into the spontaneous interpersonal communication in which people perform their identities as audience members (Nightingale, 1996) and, hence, have given us too little insight into how the mass media are appropriated for interpersonal purposes. Looking closely at what r.a.t.s. participants do as they discuss the soap, and how they build relationships with one another and identities for themselves in the process, forces us to rethink our understanding of what it means to be a fan, especially as more audience members go online to discuss the mass media and to create fan Web sites.

I came to r.a.t.s. as a soap fan who had long recognized the social significance of my engagement with soap operas. From its beginnings, my soap watching had been situated within social relationships. In many cases, watching soaps or discussing them with housemates and acquaintances was integral to the development of our friendships. I became a soap fan at 15 years old, when I took a luxurious summer foray into the working class with my first job as a hotel maid. I was trained by an older woman who had worked there for years. For 2 weeks, we worked together. The official skills she taught included making beds with "hospital corners," getting pillows into their cases with ease, and using clever tricks to make bathtub faucets sparkle. My unofficial socialization included an explanation of all the characters on *General*

Hospital, their relationships, and their current story lines. The entertainment came in handy in the repetitive job of room cleaning, but I also quickly discovered another advantage of watching: It gave an academic brat like me something easy yet involving to discuss with the people who worked there year-round, people with whom I seemed to have little in common.

Given that I have a modicum of self-respect, I also came to r.a.t.s. prepared to think favorably of soaps and their fans. Any soap fan knows, however, that not everyone conceptualizes soaps as worthwhile or soap fans as intelligent. The pervasive stereotype about soaps and their viewers (which I will critique in Chapter 1) ensures that no one has to justify dismissing soap operas as mindless melodrama or imagining that they appeal primarily to vulnerable women living vicariously through them. Before I became a fan, I too assumed that soap operas were for other, less intelligent (or affluent) people. As a child, the only soap viewer I knew looked after the children around the corner while their parents worked. My earliest soap opera memory is the opening screen of *As the World Turns* flickering in the children's living room; I remember thinking that this woman must be lazy if she was watching the soaps. The class difference between this domestic laborer and me, combined with my meager understanding of domestic labor, surely enhanced my sense that soaps were for other, lesser people. I have since discovered that as Jensen (1992) would argue, the soap fans are not Them but rather Us (see also Jensen & Pauly, 1997). We all are members of audience communities of one sort or another, although some of the materials around which we organize might be granted higher social status. Instead of asking what is wrong with people that would make them want to watch soaps, the far more interesting question is how audience members, in this case soap viewers, "use the mass media to structure and articulate our relations with one another and to make the world intellectually meaningful, aesthetically pleasing, and emotionally compelling" (Jensen & Pauly, 1997, p. 163).

Audience communities and online communities co-opt mass media for interpersonal uses. Grappling with the social nature of these new types of community requires understanding them not just as online communities (organized through a network) or as audience communities (organized around a text) but also as communities of practice organized, like all communities, through habitualized ways of acting (Hanks, 1996; Lave & Wenger, 1991). Viewed in this way, the limits and possibilities of computer networks and mass media texts are preexisting contexts that become meaningful only in the ways in which they are invoked by participants in ongoing interaction. The focus is on how networks and texts are transformed into socially meaningful fields through interaction that is ongoing and patterned in subtle yet community-constituting ways. From a practice perspective, the key to understanding online and audience communities is to focus on the communicative patterns of participants rather than on the media through and in response to which members coalesce. Thus, the third story this book has to tell is that of r.a.t.s. as a community of practice. The remainder of this introduction provides an orientation to each of these three ways of looking at r.a.t.s. by providing a structural overview of Usenet and r.a.t.s., an abbreviated account of what we do and do not know about audience communities, and a theoretical and methodological orientation to communities of practice. I close with an overview of the research in which the remainder of the book is grounded.

The Structure of Usenet and rec.arts.tv.soaps

Had I gone online in 1984, I could have been among the first to participate in r.a.t.s. In 1990, when I did go online, r.a.t.s. was one of a few thousand newsgroups distributed through the Usenet computer network, which piggybacks onto the Internet. When it was developed during the 1970s, the network's original function was to enable computer scientists to share programs between North Carolina and California (Raymond, 1991). As it became Usenet, it quickly outgrew both that narrow population and narrow function, distributing thousands of primarily recreational discussion forums. Although less famous than the World Wide Web, America Online's chat rooms and folders, or the interactive real-time conversation spaces known as multi-user domains (MUDs) and multi-user domains object oriented (MOOs), Usenet is arguably the oldest, largest, most widely accessible, and most widely used network for interactive online discussion. The scholarly research into Usenet (and other forms of computer-mediated communication) has been scattered across multiple disciplines and takes a wide variety of approaches. One of this book's ambitions is to build a holistic model of interaction in Internet groups that can integrate this disparate research. Rather than pulling this literature together into an unwieldy review, I will draw on others' findings throughout the book and focus in this section on the more basic background of what newsgroups are and how they work.

Soap viewers were among the first to appropriate the Internet for recreational use, but they were not alone in flocking to Usenet.[1] By 1993, Usenet linked at least 3 million users at more than 100,000 sites across the United States and throughout most of the world (B. Reid, 1993). Although no one seems to be able to keep track of the Internet's growth, there surely are exponentially more sites today. During the early 1990s, nearly all Usenet sites were mainframe computers at universities or colleges, computing and software companies, and scientific laboratories, both government and private. Since then, the growth in commercial Internet service providers, especially America Online, has led to millions of individuals accessing Usenet through personal accounts at a cost of approximately $20 (U.S.) per month.

Like much online activity, the precise history of soap opera discussion on the Internet is not well documented. The r.a.t.s. newsgroup is one of Usenet's oldest groups and was one of the first (if not *the* first) Internet sites specifically dedicated to soap operas. It began when it split off from the general television newsgroup, then called net.tv. As the few original participants who still were there when I arrived told the group's history (something they did only when asked), the non-soap fans became annoyed at the excessive soap opera discussion, and the soap opera fans moved to create their own group, which was named net.tv.soaps. The earliest record of the group is a traffic report from late October 1984 that reported that during the 2 weeks prior to that date, the group had distributed 11 messages (Adams, 1992). The "rec.arts" was substituted for "net" in 1986 as newsgroups multiplied and the hierarchical system used to name them expanded.

The most popular of Usenet's groups always have been those that discuss recreational and social issues. This is demonstrated by statistics gathered by Brian Reid through 1994 and posted to Usenet. In the 20 most *read* discussion groups in March 1993, for example, his figures show that a quarter of the messages (4,629) were in groups discussing social issues ranging from political activism to Indian culture. Nearly a fifth of the messages were in groups discussing sex. If figures on readership tap users' curiosities, then figures on the number of messages each group generates tap users' creative investments. In the highest *volume* discussion groups, half of the messages (24,983) were about social issues such as Indian culture, abortion, homosexuality, and guns. Another two fifths of the messages (20,025) in these high-traffic groups were in fan groups that discussed sports, television shows, and movies.

As is apparent to anyone who remembers how recently no one had heard of it, the Internet has grown tremendously. To see the figures on Usenet's growth, however, still is stunning. Consider these statistics collected by Rick Adams about the messages passing through uunet, one of the larger networks through which Usenet runs. In the fall of 1984 when r.a.t.s. began, there were only 158 groups and a mere 303 daily posts in all groups combined. When I arrived in 1990, Usenet was huge, distributing about 1,231 newsgroups that contained a daily average of 6,055 posts, nearly 20 times more than was the case 6 years earlier. Since 1990, the Web has become the most visible aspect of the Internet. However, the Web has scarcely inhibited Usenet's growth, and indeed, it probably has boosted it given that Usenet can be accessed through the Web. In 1997, statistics on the size of Usenet from an Internet service provider called Erol's (1997) indicate a daily average of 682,144 posts, 113 times as many as in 1990 and 2,251 times as many as in 1984.

The r.a.t.s. newsgroup never has been one of Usenet's most read groups, generally ranking between 200th and 300th among groups in estimated readership (B. Reid, 1993). However, from its modest beginnings during its first 4 years, r.a.t.s. traffic has expanded exponentially. Consider the number of posts to r.a.t.s. in consecutive 2-week periods 1 year apart over a 10-year period, as shown in Table 0.1. By the fall of 1993, so many messages were passing through r.a.t.s. each day that printing them would have taken nearly a $1\frac{1}{2}$-inch-thick stack of letter-sized paper. By 1994, the traffic on r.a.t.s. had grown to be so unmanageable that it was further subdivided into three groups: rec.arts.tv.soaps.abc, rec.arts.tv.soaps.cbs, and rec.arts.tv.soaps.misc. These three offshoot groups now carry a biweekly average of as many as 6,104 posts (2,744, 1,568, and 1,792 average messages, respectively) (*tile.net*, 1997). Although soap opera discussion obviously continues to thrive on Usenet, the three groups that once comprised r.a.t.s. account for only about 0.06% of Usenet messages.[2] Because most data on which this book is based were collected prior to the split, I will speak of r.a.t.s. throughout the book.[3]

There is no consensus on how many Usenet groups exist now, but there are at least 30,000, each of which is identified by topic. The

TABLE 0.1   Biweekly Numbers of Posts to rec.arts.tv.soaps, 1984-1993

2-Week Period Ending . . .	Number of Posts in rec.arts.tv.soaps
October 23, 1984	11
October 22, 1985	8
October 22, 1986	32
October 22, 1987	68
October 27, 1988	231
October 22, 1989	427
October 8, 1990	696
October 23, 1991	1,037
October 23, 1992	1,685
September 8, 1993	2,412

SOURCE: R. Adams, news.lists (newsgroup).
NOTE: After 1994, these types of statistics no longer were collected.

contents of each newsgroup are electronic letters called *posts* or *articles*. These are contributed by individuals from personal accounts. With the exceptions of some site restrictions and some moderated groups, these articles can be any length and are not censored prior to distribution. These posts are the sole constitutive elements of a Usenet group. Without messages, there is no newsgroup. Until DejaNews (http://www.deja.com) began archiving Usenet on the Web in 1995, the only places any messages were stored were the accounts and hard drives of ambitious individuals.

In the simplest sense, there are two ways in which to interact with any newsgroup including r.a.t.s. *Lurkers* read without ever contributing or contributing only rarely.[4] *Posters* write messages. People lurk and post through programs called *newsreaders*, which keep track of which articles already have been read, allow people to edit what they will read, and allow people to reply to posted messages and to create new lines of discussion. Anyone with access to Usenet and the minor expertise it requires can read the recent contributions to a newsgroup or add one's own. One consequence of this is that the groups cannot exclude anyone with access from participating; except in moderated groups, there are no group participants with the power to exclude others. However, as many have noted (Healy, 1997; E. M. Reid, 1991; Rice, 1989; Robins, 1995), users are largely preselected by external social structures. Furthermore, as we will see in Chapter 6, groups may use social pressure to drive out undesirables.

When people read newsgroups, they see only the articles that have arrived at their sites since they last read. Participants need not be online simultaneously; they can read and respond at different times. Thus, the temporal structure of all Usenet newsgroups is that of an ongoing asynchronistic meeting (Hollingshead & McGrath, 1995). Messages are stored at each site for a time period left to the sites' system administrators to decide, usually no longer than a couple of weeks. Until the old messages are removed, readers can check in at their convenience to read or respond to what messages have arrived. The asynchronous structure of r.a.t.s. distinguishes Usenet from the real-time Internet interaction that takes place on Internet relay chat (E. M. Reid, 1991), MUDs, and MOOs (E. M. Reid, 1995; Stone, 1995; Turkle, 1995).

Although people often experience Usenet interaction as akin to talk, one of the ways in which this asynchronous online interaction is very different from talk is that posts, the equivalent of conversational turns, appear to the newsgroup reader as a list rather than as a temporally situated sequence. The potential for conversational chaos is not hard to see; imagine a party in which everyone wrote their utterances and set them up in a row. It would seem nearly impossible to create coherent threads of conversation, let alone attribute messages to particular speakers or link them to particular prior turns. Usenet and the newsreader programs used to access it provide a number of structural features that help to organize the groups and minimize this type of chaos. Two particularly important elements of the structure are the headers and the quotation system. Here is a sample post:

```
From
news.cso.uiuc.edu!ux1.cso.uiuc.edu!howgard.redkin.aps.
net!allik!
herdfine.university.EDU!nntp.university.EDU!walter!far
gate
Sat May 8 20:07:18 CDT 1993
Article: 100045 of rec.arts.tv.soaps
```

```
Newsgroups: rec.arts.tv.soaps
Path:
news.cso.uiuc.edu!ux1.cso.uiuc.edu!howgard.redkin.aps.
net!allik!herdfine.university.EDU!nntp.university.EDU!
walter!fargate
From: fargate@herdfine.university.EDU (Susan Fargate)
Subject: Re: AMC: Tad/Ted
Message-ID:
<1993May5.024010.6295@gordon.university.EDU>
Sender: news@gordon.university.EDU (Sir Headlines)
Organization: Science Dept, University.
References: <1993May3.231122.28337@IRO.UMontreal.CA>
<13669006@pccupp.cap.pc.com>
Date: Wed, 5 May 93 02:40:10 GMT
Lines: 25
```

In article <136690006@pccupp.cap.pc.com>
Beth@pccupp.cap.pc.com (Beth Hunter) writes:

>Hi Everyone,
>
>I'm still way behind on AMC (getting less as my
>post-work activities schedule is lighter in
>May), but am I missing something here? Are we
>supposed to beleive that Ted Orsini looks
>exactly like Tad Martin?????????
>
>The Ted Orsini story was based on the fact that
>Nola's kid disappeared as a child. It would not
>therefore be a requirement that the guy (our
>tadski) who shows up on her doorstep look
>exactly a certain way, similar coloring should
>be enough.
>Obviously, I'm missing something, since the
>writers wouldn't actually expect me to beleive
>anything as unlikely as them being identical.
>Right? :-)
>
I agree Beth, but the Erica-turned-30 storyline was
enought to convince me that "believability" is not a
prerequisite for a storyline. It bugs me because it
is hard to get swept up in any sort of suspense
knowing that your hypotheses (based on logic) are

```
bound to fall short of the writers' whims, but then
again, I have been watching for 14 years so it must
not bug me too much!
--
Susan Fargate    fargate@herdfine.university.EDU
```

The headers provide information about the message's route through the sites, the newsgroup(s) to which it has been sent, the sender of the message, the subject, a unique identification number, the machine and organization of origin, other posts referenced in the message, when the post was sent, and its length. Other lines, such as summary lines, can be added at the time of posting. Headers automatically accompany every post; it is impossible to send a post *without* headers, although some newsreaders allow one to read without seeing all header lines.

The lines labeled "From" and "Subject" are perhaps most important in creating a sense of conversational coherence because newsreaders index these two to create their menus. The from line identifies the sender. Although fake and anonymous addresses can be used, in general, providing the sender's e-mail address helps to make the sender accountable for his or her behavior in that it allows others to send e-mail directly to a sender who offends. Especially prolific posters emerge as personalities in any newsgroup. Thus, their names in the from line invoke implications for those familiar with the contributors. This familiarity allows regular readers to form expectations about the messages and select which ones to read. Readers can go straight to the posts from those they like or can skip posts from those they dislike. They can even create *KILL files*, which cause their newsreaders to automatically eliminate messages from selected individuals. The subject line also is a major organizational resource for Usenet social situations. Chosen by the sender, or automatically replicated in responsive posts, the line is intended to make explicit the message's topic (although the topics may change sooner than the subject lines in ongoing discussions).

The opportunity to title posts gives rise to labeling practices that help to structure the group. For example, one of the most basic organizational problems for r.a.t.s. is that very few people follow every soap opera, yet all soap operas are discussed in the same group. Thus, although the newsgroup's concern with the general topic of daytime serials defined the external boundaries of the group, that concern was too broad to meet the separate interests within the group. To negate this problem, participants created a conventionalized system to segment the

TABLE 0.2   Participation in rec.arts.tv.soaps by Soap Opera in
                10-Month Period

Soap Opera	Number of Posts and Percentage	Number of Posters and Percentage
All My Children	8,665 (27)	481 (21)
Days of Our Lives	7,537 (23)	308 (13)
The Young and the Restless	3,436 (11)	276 (12)
As the World Turns	2,972 (9)	192 (8)
Santa Barbara	2,531 (8)	162 (7)
Guiding Light	2,390 (7)	234 (10)
General Hospital	1,779 (6)	228 (10)
Another World	1,133 (4)	154 (7)
One Life to Live	874 (3)	131 (6)
The Bold and the Beautiful	551 (2)	104 (4)
Loving	385 (1)	62 (3)
Total	32,253 (100)	2,332 (100)

NOTE: Percentages are in parentheses. Percentages do not add to 100 due to rounding.

group by using the initials of each soap opera in the subject line. For example, a post about *All My Children* (*AMC*) might carry the subject line "AMC: Carter and Natalie," whereas one about *Days of Our Lives* (*DOOL*) might read "DOOL: Update for Thursday."

Because people tend not to read posts about soap operas they do not watch, r.a.t.s. is in many ways not a single group; instead, it comprises nearly a dozen subgroups, each of which discusses one serial (and each of which has its own personality). In 1992, when I collected most of my data, *AMC* and *DOOL* discussion constituted about half of the messages. Table 0.2 summarizes the distribution of posts and posters in terms of which soap operas they discussed, based on an analysis of subject lines during 10 months of r.a.t.s. posts.[5] Thus, the discourse on r.a.t.s. is made coherent in part through the use of headers that segment the messages by soap opera and then by sender and topic.

Another essential Usenet resource for creating conversational coherence is the quotation system used to reference previous messages, demonstrated in the post quoted earlier. When a post is a reply (usually indicated in the subject line with "Re:"), many newsreaders automatically insert a line immediately below the headers that provides the identification number of the prior post and explicitly attributes authorship to that quotation based on its from line. Quoted words are marked with angle brackets (>) in the left margin, just as they are in most e-mail software. This ability to embed previous messages within a new post allows posts to be chained together in an ongoing interactive thread of discussion.

The interaction within Usenet messages is a novel hybrid between written, oral, interpersonal, and mass communication. Like writing, there is no body movement, vocal tone, rate, or volume. However, some nonverbal cues are available as writers on Usenet, like those in other forms of writing, exploit "aspects of graphic form such as spelling, punctuation, typography, and layout for expressive purposes" (Danet, 1993). Participants are temporally separated, as they are in writing. As a result, Usenet writers cannot assume that all readers will have read the messages to which they are responding or that all readers will be able to tell to which message Usenet writers are responding. Usenet's quotation system, which allows writers to replicate whole or partial prior turns within their own messages, helps to mitigate the potential noncoherence of Usenet discourse by explicitly marking topics and creating an orientation to specific previous messages.

Despite the similarities to writing, r.a.t.s. participants experience their own interaction as "talk." The comment of one r.a.t.s. participant that she likes r.a.t.s. because "I enjoy having some people to talk about the show with" (Gail, 1991 survey)[6] exemplifies the naturalness with which people apply a talk metaphor to online language use. Although r.a.t.s. participants do describe themselves as "reading" rather than "listening," they characterize their own messages as "sharing" or "expressing" and never as "writing." Like speech, Usenet is interactive and contextualized. Writers can assume whom many of their readers will be and that they will share many referents, will be reading within a few days, and will be able to respond. Like interpersonal communication, messages may be built off the comments of particular individuals, have consequences for one-on-one relationships, and be highly personalized. However, like mass communication, Usenet interaction always is written for a large audience and is affected by and affects the writers' public images and the image of the group as a whole. This overlap between interpersonal and mass communication provides the potential for otherwise disconnected individual voices to establish a community. The story I tell of r.a.t.s. as an online community is about how participants draw on these structural resources to create the practices, norms, relationships, and identities that come to define the group.

Audience as Community?

Although it might surprise some to see so much soap discussion occurring in a medium usually associated with more masculine pursuits, it will not surprise anyone familiar with research on soap audiences that soap viewers are eager to talk about the shows. There is an eclectic and sometimes irreconcilable range of approaches to audience research (as evidenced in Hay, Grossberg, & Wartella, 1996). Most every research tradition that has been applied to soap audiences, however, has resulted in the finding that much of the appeal of soap operas is interpersonal. Quantitative survey work in the social scientific tradition has found that the chance to interact with other viewers is one of the genre's main appeals. Cantor and Pingree (1983) claim that many soap opera fans use soaps as means for social interaction by "talking and thinking about them with family and friends" (p. 145), a finding supported in college student populations by Compesi (1980), Perse and Rubin (1989), and Rubin (1985). College students who expect to be able to socialize while watching soaps and afterward are more likely to look positively on the viewing experience (Babrow, 1987, 1989). Rubin (1985) argues that whereas viewers of many genres discuss shows together, soap viewers cite this as a motivation significantly more often than do others. Using qualitative interviews, Whetmore and Kielwasser (1983) argue that postviewing and previewing interaction are as important to fans as is the actual viewing of the soap. Because of the value of this talk, they argue, the soap opera audience becomes interconnected. They, and scholars within what has come to be known as the ethnographic approach,[7] argue that people often start watching soaps so that they can participate in the soap talk communities in their homes and at work (Brown, 1994; Hobson 1989, 1990). Harrington and Bielby (1995) found in a survey of 706 soap fans that 96% talked with other fans on a regular basis. Of these, 37% talked regularly with 4 or more fans and 3% talked on electronic bulletin boards. In Blumenthal's (1997) smaller sample of 91 female soap viewers, she found that 82 talked about soaps with others. Of these, 74% discussed them with family, 62% with friends, 28% with coworkers, and 23% with acquaintances. In sum, soap fans almost always talk about soaps with other fans, and it appears that they are more likely to do so in more intimate relationships.

Research originating in the British cultural studies tradition argues for the importance of viewing conditions (Morley, 1989). At the same time that this approach was being developed in Britain, Radway's (1984) groundbreaking work on American romance readers, *Reading the Romance,* argued that what women fans made of romance novels could be understood only by looking at how they used the books in the local contexts of their reading. Within this domestic context, Radway argues that reading these seemingly patriarchal texts in fact functioned as a form of resistance through which women made time for themselves in homes where they were expected to care for others. Much soap research has followed this situational approach to examining interpretation. Hobson (1989) discusses how, for many women who watch soaps at home, viewing is embedded in the activities of cooking and feeding their families (see also Geraghty, 1991). Ang (1985) and others have looked at the viewing practices of the elderly, who often are socially isolated and, as a result, focus far more of their attention on the show during viewing than do busy mothers. Many working people, such as me and those on r.a.t.s., videotape soaps and watch them ritualistically in the evening or on weekends. These types of viewing practices influence the meanings taken from soaps (Ang, 1985).

Despite the interest in situated viewing, there has been surprisingly little effort to empirically document soap opera discussion or to engage the issues this discussion raises. What work there has been falls short on numerous grounds including, above all, limited data. Hobson (1989), for example, discussed the shows with six women who worked and talked about the soaps together and then interviewed one other woman about television talk at her workplace. Liebes and Katz (1989) put together focus groups to watch and discuss a single episode of *Dallas.* Williams (1992) discussed soaps herself with one fan. Brown (1994) conducted interviews and observed several small groups of soap opera fans. Although the findings are highly provocative, this methodological reliance on the focus group interview rather than on the observation of spontaneous and naturally occurring fan talk has obscured how this talk is used to negotiate relationships among viewers as well as between viewers and shows.

Three exceptions to this are a study by Lemish (1985), who observed a group of soap fans who gathered in a public location ritualistically to watch their soap together. She articulated the social roles that these fans developed vis-à-vis one another and the show. The studies by Harrington and Bielby (1995) and Blumenthal (1997) used participant observation, interviews, and surveys to examine fans in the context of other fans. Harrington and Bielby (1995) address "how fanship and fandom are shaped by the cult of celebrity and by fans' relationship with the entertainment industry" (p. 5), whereas Blumenthal (1997) focuses on providing a feminist analysis of soap viewing. Both discuss the sense of community that can emerge among soap fans, but it is not their focus. Harrington and Bielby (1995) compare soap opera fan club events to family reunions, pointing out that "authentic social relationships develop among fans, and these potentially long-term friendships, organized around intimacy and mutuality, cement the subculture even further" (p. 58).

Following Radway (1984), both Harrington and Bielby (1995) and Blumenthal (1997) argue that soaps have the potential to empower women. However, whereas romance novels create a private space for their readers, soaps create a social space, enhancing women's social bonds to one another. Blumenthal argues that as women watch soaps together and discuss them, they use them as a chance "to engage in sisterhood—women's community-building" (p. 103). Blumenthal identifies a phenomenon I will elaborate in my analysis of r.a.t.s., that is, the use of soaps to develop a community ostensibly organized around soaps but also functioning as a community in which traditionally female concerns and values are honored.

The issue of audience community has received its fullest treatment in work on fandom, exemplified by Jenkins (1992) and Lewis (1992). By elaborating the complicated networks of video- and audiotape traders, fan conventions, fan publications, and so on, and by looking closely at the texts that fans produce around the media, Jenkins (1992) situates the fan experience within social networks rather than in isolated relation to a television show. Within "fan cultures," as he calls them, one's relationship to the show serves as a form of currency that enables participation in a fan community at least as rewarding as the show itself. Despite this social grounding, Jenkins focuses on how these communities function as organized institutions of interpretation. As Anderson (1996) describes it, this type of research characterizes the audience as "strategic," meaning that the emphasis is shifted from the autonomous individual to a collective, most often called an interpretive community. . . . It is the community that develops the strategies, provides the means for dissemination and instruction, and supervises particular performances of them. The individual in any strategic situation is a local and partial representation of the interpretive community." (p. 87)

Jenkins (1992) describes fandom as "an institution of theory and criticism, a semistructured space where competing interpretations and evaluations of common texts are proposed, debated, and negotiated and where readers speculate about the nature of the mass media and their own relationship to [them]" (p. 86). In fandom, Jenkins finds that fans appropriate the texts, engaging them in all the ways one would expect from previous analyses of media texts but also using the shows as the raw material for their own creative impulses. The detailed collaborative analysis of past episodes, produced by fans, becomes the fan culture's "meta-text" against which members evaluate the shows (Jenkins, 1992).

Applying this perspective to soaps, Harrington and Bielby (1995) explain that

the discourse created by daytime fans as they talk on the telephone, interact on computer bulletin boards, and write fan magazines forms a web of interaction that surrounds the viewing process and is read back into it. Connecting with other fans and sharing viewing experiences is vital to both the social construction of shared meanings and to the persistence of long-term viewing patterns. (p. 47)

Meta-texts are based on meanings that "resonate with the cultural needs of that particular talk community" (Fiske, 1987, p. 78). Although still allowing room for enjoyable debate and difference, an individual's reading of a show becomes shaped to conform to the collaborative reading (Jenkins, 1992). Thus, watching a show regularly is not the same as being a member of a fan community. Being a member of a fan community entails knowledge of the interpretive conventions and collaborative meta-text used to read the show (Jenkins, 1992).

There are many strengths to this research, not least among them the recognition that audience interpretations may differ from what media producers or academic textual analysts expect and that audience interpretations are situated in networks of other people. But Jensen and Pauly (1997) note that despite these strengths, "To consider the audience an interpretive community is still to locate people through texts rather than through the social processes by which texts influence and engage people in actual circumstances" (p. 158). As they see it, "To presume that we are best understood as readers of texts, rather than people who act, is to presume that we constantly perform interpretive acrobatics in relation to texts rather than in relation to other people" (p. 158).

Thus, even in work that explicitly locates fans within an audience community of other people, the focus is on the media text and the fan text generated in response,[8] not on the interpersonal connections through which the meta-text emerges. In the words of Nightingale (1996), "The fan/viewer remains atomised and alienated even if elaborated historically and sociologically" (p. 124). Although there might be communal readings, the interpersonal communities in which they emerge "remain to be revealed" (Anderson, 1996, p. 88). Anderson (1996) suggests that the promise of Radway's (1984) work to document the inner workings of an interpretive community fell short because she did not document audience interconnections. Indeed, Radway created the "community" she studied by bringing together women who bought their books from the same seller but who had not met prior to Radway's focus group interviews. According to Press (1996), in later work, Radway recognized that "ethnographic audience studies (including her own) have . . . been far too limited in their focus on subjects as audience rather than as fully articulated individuals embedded within their community" (p. 121). The present study of r.a.t.s. seeks to shed some light on the previously obscured interpersonal dimension of audience community.

One reason that audience research such as Radway's or Hobson's has been expected to speak for a community, or culture, stems from the label under which it has been read and sometimes written—*ethnography*. As recent critics have elaborated, this term is a misnomer when applied to most audience research (Nightingale, 1996; Press, 1996). As it has been developed within anthropology and sociology, ethnography involves explaining (or at least presenting a coherent narrative about) a culture or subculture. By contrast, the *ethnographic* audience work has little to say about "the ideal of the cultural whole" (Press, 1996, p. 116), substituting instead social conditions such as gender, class, and ethnicity.

When one conceptualizes culture or community as geographically bound (e.g., Samoans [Ochs, 1988]) or linguistically bound (e.g., living speakers of Maya [Hanks, 1996]), it is far simpler (although by no means simple) to imagine what the cultural whole might be. By contrast, audience communities are diffuse. Rather than national or linguistic cultures, audience communities (e.g., online communities) are one of many specialized communities in which people are members "simultaneously and over time" (Hanks, 1996, p. 221). All members of audience communities are members of other communities as well. Therefore, it has been both theoretically and empirically difficult to separate out the audience component of the community without relying heavily on the text. This is magnified by the fact that audiences rarely "represent and organize themselves as 'we, the audience,' and on the rare occasions when that happens, they are generally not taken very seriously" (Ang, 1991, p. 6). In short, even if one wanted to find a nicely bounded, self-defined audience community of interrelated members, it has not been easy. The Internet has changed that, in part by making audience communities more visible and in part by enabling their proliferation, a point that Harrington and Bielby (1995) make as well. This study of r.a.t.s. makes no claim to represent all soap fan communities, let alone all audience communities. It does, however, provide us with a sustained look into how the social dimensions take over from the textual ones as an audience becomes a community. This example of one audience community, a group that existed before I arrived and continued after I left, is meant as one turn in what deserves to be a long discussion about a realm too long relegated to asides.

As I have suggested, in addition to its inattention to the cultural whole, ethnographic audience research has fallen short methodologically. In fields such as anthropology and sociology, ethnographies traditionally have involved extensive fieldwork, the collection of multiple forms of data, and continual movement between data and theory peppered with a good deal of self-reflection. In contrast to these traditions, "the literature on audiences pales. . . . Our subject pools are small, our time in the field [is] too brief, our descriptions of the audience's lives [are] too scant" (Jensen & Pauly, 1997, p. 165). In place of extended participant observations and inobtrusive field notes, ethnographic media scholars have relied on brief visits and individual and focus group interviews (Moores, 1993). Press (1996) writes, "One increasingly feels that part of the impetus for the 'turn to ethnography' in communication is the theoreticians' search for an empirical method that is 'not too empirical' " (p. 118).

One of the unfortunate consequences of the heavy reliance on focus group interviews is that they allow us access only to the social relations that researchers have put together for research purposes (Liebes & Katz, 1989; Radway, 1984) rather than "social relations that connect individual subjects or the social occasions on which individuals express and defend their interpretations to others" (Jensen & Pauly, 1997, p. 165). Interviews also can lead audience members to reproduce stereotypical beliefs in place of their understandings of their own experience. After all, they are performing for researchers within a cultural context, and research participants have access to cultural scripts about what they should say just as researchers have access to schematic ideas about what they should ask. Furthermore, people are not aware enough of the nuances of their behavior to explain them. Indeed, people often are unaware of the practices that define their experience (Bourdieu, 1978). Interviews offer a wonderful source of insight into participant perspectives and are a form of discourse worthy of examination as such (Silverman, 1993; Tracy, 1997), but they should not be taken as complete or accurate explanations of practice. The problem of interpreting interview material is further complicated in many studies by cultural differences between the researchers and the researched (Briggs, 1986; Nightingale, 1996). In British cultural studies, most scholars are middle class academics, whereas most audiences are conceptualized (and studied) as working class housewives or elderly homebound populations. Assuming that the cultural referents in interview responses mean what they would mean if the interviewers were to say them is highly problematic:

> Not only may there be a gap between what is said and what is understood, but a reliance on what is said suggests an underlying definition of the historical subject as someone who is in possession of a "reality," a reality of which an account can be given. . . . In other words, it suggests both a shared culture and an awareness of one's own position within that culture. (Nightingale, 1996, p. 99)

Nightingale (1996) situates this as part of a broader failure of cultural studies work on audiences to demonstrate the ethnographic sensitivities about the researcher-participant relationship "which have come to signal enlightened practice—particularly sensitivity to negotiation, the sharing of research goals, and the presentation of research outcomes with research participants" (p. 115).

Many of the failures of this research to adequately explore audience communities as communities rather than as textual interpreters can be overcome with a version of ethnography that has a clear vision of the community in question and that uses multiple forms of data and an extensive period of fieldwork. The ethnography of r.a.t.s. offered here rests on a 3-year period of participant observation, supplemented by a return to the field several years later and nearly 33,000 naturally occurring messages. Nearly 100 lengthy qualitative survey responses, akin to face-to-face interviews, represent one form of data, but they serve as supplements to the posts written about the soap, posts that would have been written whether they were studied or not. By focusing on "the performance of audience" (Nightingale, 1996, p. 95) in naturally occurring Usenet posts, I seek to show some of what Press (1996) calls "the interplay between people's dimension 'as audience' and the meanings, rituals, practices, struggles, and structural roles and realities that make up the rest of their lives" (p. 113). When I tell the story of r.a.t.s. as an audience community, then, I am seeking to show how a collection of previously disconnected individuals took their shared interest in a pop culture text and transformed it into a rich and meaningful interpersonal social world.

Community as Practice

The ethnographic approach I use here is grounded in a set of related, if independent, theories that have been termed the *practice approach* (Hanks, 1996; Ortner, 1984). The practice approach solves a number of problems in the study of both online and audience communities by providing a detailed empirical way in which to examine such groups while focusing on their internal coherence. From the practice approach, any social grouping—in this case r.a.t.s.—should be understood as a community of practice. As Hanks (1996) explains,

> This way of defining community . . . shifts the ground of definition from either language or social structure per se to the engagement of actors in some project. A family or domestic group is a community of practice in this sense, as is a sports team, a work crew, a neighborhood organization, a church congregation, the crew of a ship, members of an agricultural cooperative, and members of an academic department. Because some endeavors last longer than others, communities so defined clearly have different durations and arise under different

circumstances. And because we all engage in multiple group endeavors at any time and throughout our social lives, we are members of
multiple communities. (p. 221)

At the center of the practice approach is the assumption that a community's structures are instantiated and recreated in habitual and recurrent
ways of acting or *practices*. When people engage in the ordinary activities that constitute their daily lives, they are participating "in an activity
system about which participants share understandings concerning
what they are doing and what that means in their lives and for their
communities" (Lave & Wenger, 1991, p. 98). In short, if one wants to
understand a community, then one should look to the ordinary activities
of its participants. This is a fairly minimalist definition of *community*,
without the warm and fuzzy connotations that many link to the term,
but it is a definition that provides a workable core. Without shared
engagement in a project, there can be no warmth and fuzziness.

Language activities have been given particular attention in practice
theory for their community-instantiating force. Although open to infinite variation, language practices are microcosms of the communities
in which they are used. They are socially organized and derive their
meanings from cultural systems (Bourdieu, 1990; Gaskins, Miller, &
Corsaro, 1992; Miller and Hoogstra, 1992; Ortner, 1984; Schieffelin &
Ochs, 1986). According to Ortner (1984), linguistic routines

> are predicated upon, and embody within themselves, the fundamental
> notions of temporal, spatial, and social ordering that underlie and
> organize the system as a whole. In enacting these routines, actors not
> only continue to be shaped by the underlying organizational princi-
> ples involved, but continually reendorse those principles in the world
> of public observation and discourse. (p. 154)

The social meanings invoked by language include situational purposes
or goals; situational structures or conditions; the interpersonal identities of the interlocutors; the frame and genre of events; and the beliefs,
values, norms, and mood of the interaction (Bakhtin, 1981, 1986; Hymes,
1986; O'Keefe, 1988; Schieffelin & Ochs, 1986).

Although it draws on multiple methods, the practice approach's
focus on language lends itself to the method of discourse analysis in

which naturally occurring interaction is examined closely. Social mean-ings are invoked in part through the actor's choice of linguistic options (Miller & Hoogstra, 1992, p. 85). Bakhtin (1981) offers an almost poetic perspective on the social meanings inherent in the choice of wording:

> All words have a "taste" of a profession, a genre, a tendency, a party, a particular work, a particular person, a generation, an age group, a day and hour. Each word tastes of the context and contexts in which it has lived its socially charged life; all words and forms are populated by intentions. Contextual overtones (generic, tendentious, individual-istic) are inevitable in the word. (p. 293)

Others have shown that language offers cues to context that enable people to create common interpretations (Gumperz, 1982; Schieffelin & Ochs, 1986). Meta-communicative *contextualization cues* include the choice of wording as well as prosody, paralinguistic signs, code choices, and so on (Gumperz, 1992). Although such cues might be "marginal or semantically insignificant," speakers rely on them to "contextualize what they say in order to signal implicit meaning" (Basso, 1992, p. 255). Actors do not simply act, they frame their actions. Such framing, or contextualizing, "is accomplished through the em-ployment of culturally conventionalized meta-communication" (Bauman, 1975, p. 295). "In empirical terms," Bauman (1975) continues, "this means that each speech community will make use of a structured set of distinctive communicative means from among its resources in culturally conventionalized and culture-specific ways" (p. 295). As actors use contextualization cues to invest their behavior with social meaning, they invest those resources—and the contexts of their use—with further meaning. This further codifies socially significant systems. Thus, analysis of community can be accomplished in part through close study of these small discourse features.

Although practice theories have largely been developed in the close examination of geographically grounded communities, there is nothing in the approach that precludes its application to other types of commu-nities. To the contrary, the focus on language practice is particularly well suited to the study of online communities in which language stands in place of the geography, institutions, and artifacts taken for granted in offline communities. Practice theory also is well suited to the examination of audience communities given that their defining quality is the joint endeavor of making sense of the media. When I view r.a.t.s. as a community of practice, then, my focus is on how the verbal (and, to a lesser extent, the nonverbal) communicative practices that take form in the group's messages can explain "the genesis, reproduction, and change of form and meaning of a given social/cultural whole" (Ortner, 1984, p. 149), in this case the community of r.a.t.s. The story of r.a.t.s. as a community of practice is that of how participants dynamically appropriate a wide range of resources drawn from the structure of Usenet and the soap opera text and combine them with other resources in unpredictable yet patterned ways, ultimately constructing a social space that feels like community.

Researching rec.arts.tv.soaps

This study, like most ethnographic work, has evolved as it has developed, and I have maintained a dialectical relationship with the data (Gaskins et al., 1992). I began with a set of research questions knowing that as I moved among observation, data analysis, and theory, I would end up taking paths I had not foreseen. One of my primary methods was participant observation. I began participating in r.a.t.s. in 1990, a year before I began to study it, and continued to participate actively through 1993 (at which time I began writing about it so much that I no longer had time to read it). My experience as what one r.a.t.s. participant called "a member in good standing" (at least at the time this research was conducted) lent me a certain degree of legitimacy in speaking for r.a.t.s., and my intuitions and understandings as a member guided this project at many stages. The r.a.t.s. newsgroup is written in English but has its own style and referents, and my participant status gave me the background and experience to interpret these social meanings. The group's trust in me also resulted in support for, and willingness to help with, this project; indeed, the group's enthusiasm when I announced and followed through on my research intentions was one of the main reasons I have continued with this work. As a participant, I sought to remain sensitive to how my status as a researcher could, at least hypothetically, have influenced patterns of interaction on r.a.t.s. I did my best to avoid influencing practice in any way that would differ from my participation before I began the study by refraining from expressing any evaluations of behavior in r.a.t.s. Although I told the group about my work as I was conducting it and have shared my writings with participants who are interested, I never raised its contents as a topic of discussion on r.a.t.s. I continued to interact as a member throughout my data collection, but I consciously avoided infusing the soap-related interactions with any explicit discussion of my analyses.

I also was aware that although my position within the group gave me greater access to social meanings and participants than I might have otherwise had, as a member I was no more able to articulate the community's inner workings than were other members. For this, I would need data. Thus, the initial problem I faced was how to collect the types of additional materials that would allow me to describe r.a.t.s. thoroughly and with a minimal amount of bias. As several practice theorists have pointed out, two potential problems with looking for cultural wholes in close analyses of language use are that it is easy to generate incorrect interpretations of detail and it is easy to select only cases that confirm researcher beliefs, creating a reflection of researcher assumptions rather than a valid (if necessarily incomplete) story of a community. Therefore, my ethnographic analysis supplements participant observation with other methods in an effort to enhance its cultural validity (Gaskins, Miller, & Corsaro, 1992; Schieffelin & Ochs, 1986). The two methods that ended up driving this research were discourse analysis of posts and online surveys. I collected posts to the group systematically over a 10-month period from February 22 through December 15, 1992. Although I tried to save all messages, at times some messages had expired and been removed from the system before I was able to save them. During that time span, I collected 32,308 messages. There were 35,235 messages in that time span; thus, I was able to save 92% of the total public discourse during those months. At the time when I stopped collection, the corpus constituted approximately 40% of the public discourse since the very first post to r.a.t.s. For this earlier phase of the study, I posted two sets of open-ended survey questions to the group, to which I received 51 responses. When I returned to the group in 1998 to see how the many changes in the Internet over the previous 5 years had affected r.a.t.s., I posted a third survey, which I also sent directly to several current and former participants (Appendix A), and 41 people responded. A "yearbook" compiled by 57 members of the group in 1991 served as a fourth form of documentary data. Finally, I collected statistical information about events and participants including how many people participated, how many messages there were, and other broader contextual information. Therefore, I remained open to the potential of data contradicting my expectations, a potential realized throughout the duration of this work.

Once data were collected, I immediately faced a second problem: I had way too much data. Although it was clear to me that analyzing so many messages closely was impossible, the best ways in which to narrow them down were not immediately apparent. The challenge was to narrow the data down in a way that retained the coherence both of the group and of the discussion. Because r.a.t.s. is subdivided internally by soap opera, and participants in each soap opera discussion often do not read one another's messages, r.a.t.s. really contains several groups. I sought to retain group coherence by focusing my analysis on only one soap opera, *All My Children*. As indicated earlier, the *AMC* participants generate the most traffic in the group; just over a quarter of the posts were about *AMC*. Through those posts, the *AMC* discussants had created what was possibly the friendliest and most cohesive subgroup in r.a.t.s., a point on which many *AMC* participants prided themselves. At the time I began this research, I had watched *AMC* more continuously than the others during the previous decade and had participated most actively in the *AMC* discussions on r.a.t.s. Finally, in part because I was an accepted member of the group and in part because they are among the friendliest and most involved participants in r.a.t.s., the *AMC* fans were particularly willing to respond to my surveys and were particularly enthusiastic about sharing their insights. Unfortunately, narrowing the data to one soap involved sacrificing the opportunity to explore differences among soap discussion groups on r.a.t.s. Participants from other subgroups provided important views in their questionnaire responses and other interactions with me, and I will draw on those as well in hopes of at least suggesting the diversity of this phenomenon.

More challenging than narrowing the soap opera (and hence the community) was to select practices for close examination that would demonstrate the range of the group's practices as well as how those practices are interrelated. A further dimension of this challenge was to find a way in which to select data that would be comprehensible to readers who were not participants themselves. In narrowing to specific practices, I was guided by the sense of the group I had gained in my time before becoming a researcher and by four qualities that emerged repeatedly as participants described r.a.t.s. in their survey responses.[9]

First, the talk was described as framed in different *genres* with different social meanings. Second, the interaction was described as filled with *diverse perspectives*, which was seen as one of the group's great appeals. Third, the talk almost always was described as *friendly*. Fourth, the interaction was seen as both *fun* and *funny*.

These insights led me to narrow the discourse data to the three primary analyses on which this book is built, each of which exemplifies at least one of these qualities. To make the discourse make sense to those who do not happen to remember everything that happened on *AMC* in 1992, I focused two of these analyses on the discussion of one story line in which a character named Carter Jones came to town and wreaked havoc with characters' lives. Unlike other ways of sampling, such as episodically or for predetermined time periods, this method retained the coherence of the messages for group participants while still representing a wide range of messages. I separated out all messages from the first rumors of the story line's inception until the final mention of its events, resulting in 524 messages. By retelling the story line in Chapter 1, I hope to give readers enough common ground with r.a.t.s. participants to make some sense of the messages I will quote. Again, the choice of a single story line is limiting as well in that any story line raises some issues and not others, but the sacrifice seemed balanced by the opportunity for coherence that this focus allowed.

Because each of these three analyses offered a different route into the same phenomena, I combine their findings throughout the chapters that follow. I offer here an overview of each of these three studies and the logic that motivated them. More detailed discussions of the methods and summary findings are available in the appendixes and in N. K. Baym (1993, 1995, 1996).

Genres of Post

I began with a systematic examination of how message subject lines were labeled in conventionalized ways. Just as the inclusion of "AMC" in the subject line can indicate topic and subgroup, other conventionalized markers are used to cue genre. The phenomenon of indicating message type with conventionalized subject line components is common across Usenet groups. Talk often is differentiated into an unmarked category and one or more marked categories. For example, rec.food.recipes distinguishes posted recipes from requests for recipes with the inclusion of "REQUEST:" or "RECIPE:" in the subject line. Erotic stories often are distinguished from discussion in sex-oriented groups with the inclusion of "STORY:" in the subject line. Nearly all groups have subject line-labeled "FAQ" (frequently asked questions) posts to explain group norms and to facilitate new users' entries into the group. This type of labeling practice is highly functional in that it enables readers to tailor their involvement. They can use these cues to ensure that vague subject lines do not lead them away from the types of posts that interest them. In the other extreme, they can use most common newsreaders to construct KILL files, which edit out posts with subject lines containing particular patterns. These conventionalizations allow people to make informed choices about what to read and what not to read and, hence, in which events to participate.

I focus on the explicit generic scheme that organizes r.a.t.s. posts. One of the most interesting things about the categorization of genres in r.a.t.s. is how few of the genres mentioned in surveys are explicitly labeled in subject lines. Survey responses frequently refer to opinions, predictions, story line suggestions, and other interpretive practices, yet these genres (which make up most of the posts) are not marked with explicit genre labels. This raises the obvious question of why some genres need to be labeled and others do not. Following Duranti (1988), I took this as a clue to look to the "dimensions and features underlying taxonomic categories" (Hymes, 1986, p. 49). By looking at those genres that are explicitly labeled in subject lines and comparing them to those that are not, I am able to make an argument about the particular dimensions of concern that shape the categorizations and markings of genre. I present a discussion of the specific methods I used to assess the genres in Appendix B. In this appendix, I also provide a description of each genre and a table summarizing post distribution by genre.

Strategies and Topics of Disagreement

The two other analyses provided different angles into the substance of the discourse, focusing on the discussion of the Carter Jones story line. The first practice I examined in this discussion was disagreement, an activity in which two of the qualities described as valuable by r.a.t.s. participants clash. As a comparison, I also examined the agreements. For reasons that I also will discuss in Chapter 1, diverse perspectives are highly valued. This can be seen in comments such as "It's fascinating to see all the different points of view on such a range of topics" (Jamie, 1993 survey). The fondness for diversity also shows in the descriptions of "successful" posts as those that "are either people's own views on what happened on a soap opera or new plot ideas" (Kelly, 1991 survey). One would think that their novelty would make disagreements desirable.

However, the third quality of r.a.t.s. interaction that emerged in respondents' descriptions of r.a.t.s. was its "friendliness." Friendliness, as described, exists on two levels. First, friendliness is associated with the courteousness or, more precisely, lack of rudeness of the interaction. In this sense, it means that there is little flaming relative to other Usenet groups. This location of friendliness sometimes is described in terms of the politeness features of the discourse. The r.a.t.s. newsgroup also is described as "friendly" in a more abstract, relational sense. Some participants describe the group as "a group of friends." Some of those participants not only view the group as a large collection of friends but also form distinct friendships with particular others in the group. Such friendships may extend beyond r.a.t.s. into e-mail and face-to-face communication. For some of the participants, r.a.t.s. comes to provide a source of genuine friendship with others. The group becomes a way for those people to perpetuate and develop those friendships. Like many others, Lynn, a frequent poster in the *DOOL* discussion, indicates that, for her, r.a.t.s. has gone beyond its role as "a place for information and updates" and has become "more importantly, a place where I keep in touch with friends and have fun during the stressful work day" (1993 survey).

If the preference for diversity would seem to make disagreement desirable, then the preference for friendliness would seem to do the opposite. Expressing a diversity of perspectives on a soap opera often is nonproblematic because soaps are designed to be open to multiple interpretations (as I will discuss in Chapter 1). People likely will notice different things and make different inferences that are entirely compatible. In these cases, diversity can be achieved without disagreement, and the social order is not threatened. At other times, different interpretations are not compatible, and people are likely to disagree with one another. It is in the voicing of these disagreements that the tension between diversity and friendliness is the greatest. In other words, the practice with the most potential to challenge friendly unity is encouraged because it continues the interpretive process. Because disagreements raise competing goals for participants—interpretive diversity and social unity, goals at the heart of r.a.t.s.—I expected these practices to exaggerate the types of communicative mechanisms used to create the social environment prized in the group in all of the discussions. I examined this by developing a detailed coding scheme of message features.

These disagreements (and agreements) also offered an opportunity to see what was important to the participants about the soap in a way that previous research had not allowed. After all, one would have to feel relatively strongly about a subject to bother agreeing or disagreeing, especially given the potential fallout each practice entails. Therefore, I also created a coding scheme for the topics of these posts. The coding schemes for message features, topics, and tables summarizing the distribution of topics in agreements and disagreements are in Appendix C.

Humor

Having fun was the fourth and final quality mentioned recurrently throughout the participant questionnaire responses. The general function of the group often is defined in terms of pleasure rather than knowledge. Angela, a 30-year-old technical writer, compares what she seeks in r.a.t.s. to what she seeks in the other newsgroups she reads:

> In general, I usually read news to get (or share with other folks) information about certain topics. Not all of that information is job related, but it's still important (some good examples of the informative groups that I read—alt.privacy, misc.consumers.house, misc.kids, news.announce.important, sci.med, comp.sys.ibm.pc.*, comp.text.frame). The r.a.t.s. group is more just "for fun" than to get "useful" information, but I still consider it just as important! (1991 survey)

As Zoey, a 23-year-old undergraduate student, puts it, "The other rec groups may have a more intellectual (sometimes) quality of response, but for pure enjoyment, you can't beat r.a.t.s." (1991 survey).

The primary "fun" quality of the communication itself often is identified as humor. Soap operas tend to bring to mind images of characters wrapped in constant melodrama, crisis, and emotional torment. Except for the laugh with which they often are dismissed, soap operas rarely are taken to evoke humor, yet r.a.t.s. interaction is described repeatedly as "funny." When I asked what makes a poster successful, I often received answers along the lines of "Well, a good sense of humor, definitely. I love the posts from people who are funny!" (Kelly, 1991 survey). Another woman says she reads r.a.t.s. because "the people posting here are hilarious" (Samantha, 1993 survey). But a good sense of humor is not the only thing that can make a post fun. People also laud posts that are "creative" and "imaginative." "I believe funny and creative posts are the most fun," says the most prolific poster succinctly (Anne, 1991 survey).

The final analysis on which my examination of r.a.t.s. relies is of the humor in the Carter Jones story line. Analysts have argued that conversational humor is profoundly social; humor is embedded in shared knowledge, shared codes, and shared emotional significance that provide its meanings and determine its appropriateness (Chiaro, 1992; Oring, 1992; Palmer, 1994). Most theories of humor also argue that it arises out of problematic and irreconcilable juxtapositions (Mulkay, 1988; Oring, 1992). Thus, at the same time that humor offered me a way in which to examine the claim (and experience) that r.a.t.s. was fun, it also offered a way in which to examine the meanings that were particularly problematic in r.a.t.s. Humor also is an excellent way in which to view the variation within r.a.t.s. practices. The analyses of genres and disagreements show patterns across posters, but what is funny almost always is in some way original. Although I offer some descriptions of humor in the data corpus as a whole, I concentrate the discussion of humor on the close examination of a handful of posts in the belief that close analyses can reveal significant phenomena lost in broader data sweeps.

Stay Tuned for the Rest of This Book

Central to my argument in this book is that the stories of r.a.t.s. as an audience community and as an online community both are stories of a community of practice. Both types of community arise and are maintained through the ongoing practices of their members. The first three chapters focus on r.a.t.s. as an audience community, and the final three chapters focus on r.a.t.s. as an online community. Chapter 1 provides what might be considered an introduction to the characters and setting of the r.a.t.s. story by introducing the participants and exploring the nature of the text that motivates their engagement. Because I write from the assumption that many readers are not soap fans, this first chapter examines the stereotype of soap opera viewers, and fans more generally, as mentally and socially deficient, a stereotype that forms a crucial backdrop to practice in r.a.t.s. I compare this stereotype to what is known about soap viewer demographics and the participants in r.a.t.s. The chapter also draws on the extensive research on soap operas to explain the genre, why it might lend itself to misreadings of it and its fans, and what sensible fans might find appealing in the soaps. Chapters 2 and 3 provide what might be considered the events of the audience story by looking at what happens when these fans turn soap watching into a collaborative activity. Chapter 2 presents analyses of the labeled and unlabeled genres of r.a.t.s. posts and the subjects of agreements and disagreements so as to empirically document the complex range of social and genre-specific issues and competencies that "talking about soaps" involves. Whereas this chapter examines how participants use these issues and competencies creatively to work with the soap opera text and make it more enjoyable, Chapter 3 elaborates both how very critical these fans are and how they turn this criticism to pleasure through humor, creating a group identity in the process. Together, these chapters begin to reveal the important interpersonal dimensions of soap opera interpretation and audience community.

The remaining three chapters focus on the interpersonal action in the group, turning from how these fans relate to the show to how they relate to one another. The story here takes place in a soap opera discussion group, but the types of processes discussed are at play in any online group that develops into a community. Chapter 4 examines how participants create a particular type of social atmosphere in the way they conduct interpersonal relationships. I examine closely the ethic of friendliness that pervades the forum and the linguistic means through which this relational atmosphere is continually constructed. The adherence to this ethic of friendliness exemplifies the process of creating and maintaining social norms for behavior in online groups. Chapter 5 looks at the emergence of individualized identities online, showing how identities develop out of specific types of practices and how those practices are shaped by the context of the group and its (in this case soap-related) needs. Before concluding, Chapter 6 provides the epilogue, a return to r.a.t.s. 5 years later in which I address the group's struggles and triumphs in maintaining a sense of community in the face of the Internet's enormous growth.

Notes

1. Less surprisingly, many of the first "Netheads" were *Star Trek* fans.

2. There are other soap opera discussion forums on the Internet. For example, the ABC television network and *Soap Opera Digest* have message boards on their Web sites, America Online has soap opera message boards and chat rooms, and many fans run their own soap discussion forums on Internet relay chat and other publicly accessible sites.

3. I also will speak of r.a.t.s. in the present tense, although the time period discussed is primarily 1992-1993.

4. Although I use the category of "lurker" to denote people who never post, people who post only very rarely might consider themselves to be lurkers as well rather than posters.

5. These numbers are not exact given that messages might not have been explicitly marked with an acronym, one message might have been marked with multiple acronyms, or variations on the acronyms might have gone undetected by the search script. Also, single participants might post from more than one account, thus leading them to appear as more than one poster, whereas others might have similar user identifications in their from lines that cause them to be counted as only one person. But these circumstances are unusual, and the numbers presented here are reliable approximations. It is interesting to note that these numbers are quite different from the Nielsen ratings of the daytime soap operas in 1993. *The Young and the Restless* was consistently first, *AMC* was second, and *DOOL* hovered near eighth. *The Bold and the Beautiful* and *One Life to Live* often tied for fourth.

6. Throughout this book, a first name plus a survey year indicates a quotation from a survey response in that year. Names have been changed but kept consistent so that the reader can tell when the same person is being quoted repeatedly. Pseudonyms have been selected to preserve gender information.

7. The strengths and shortcomings of these ethnographic studies of the audience are thoroughly reviewed in Nightingale (1996) and Moores (1993).

8. Harrington and Bielby (1995) are an exception, although they locate fans primarily in relationship to the media producers and celebrities.

9. I also was guided by the excellent advice of Peggy Miller.

1

The Soap Opera and Its Audience: TV for the Less Intelligent?

The people I encounter in daily life—colleagues, students, neighbors, babysitters—often find it hard to believe that I watch soaps. As one of my students recently put it, "I had to change my stereotype of soap opera fans because my professor is a soap opera fan and she has a Ph.D." Without debating the relationship between a Ph.D. and intelligence, her comment and those of the others indicate a pervasive cultural stereotype that soap operas are vapid and so too are their fans. That soap operas merit a stereotype at all indicates how omnipresent in cultural life they have become. Even those who do not watch them know something about them (although usually less than they think).

One reason for this is simply that soaps have been around longer than have most television genres. Depending on how far one is willing to stretch the defining boundaries of the genre, daily broadcast serials made their debut on Chicago radio sometime during the late 1920s or early 1930s (Edmundson & Rounds, 1973). By the late 1930s, the day-time serial was fully defined (Macdonald, 1979). Soap operas quickly became and have remained a beloved genre, drawing millions of view-ers each day. Macdonald (1979) recounts Summer's findings on the growth of the daytime serial during the 1930s: "In 1931 the number of 'women's serial drama' programs was [3], while in 1934 it was [10], in 1936 it was [31], and in 1939 it was [61]" (p. 240). By 1942, radio soap operas had 20 million listeners (Herzog, 1944). During the 1950s, soaps were one of the few genres to make the leap to television successfully (Macdonald, 1979). Although their viewership has waned in recent years, soap operas remained popular into the 1990s.

The ubiquity of soaps might explain the presence of a stereotype but does not in itself explain the negative content of that stereotype. This post to rec.arts.tv.soaps (r.a.t.s.), which Usenet participants will recog-nize as *flame bait*, almost parodies the popular conception of soaps and their fans:

```
Soap operas are for fat old house wives who have
nothing better to do with the time they have then
sit around in curlers, eating bon bons, and getting
fatter. Then they watch these show and it just
shows them how pathetic their lives really are.
(October 5, 1991)[1]
```

There is a pervasive sense that soap fans are too close to their shows and have lost the ability to separate them from what is real and, hence, what is important.

There are several forces at play in this perception of soap fans. One of the most common probably is the stories that all soap stars tell, often in the media, about being mistaken for their characters. Some have been accosted in public for their characters' behavior, been sent baby gifts when their characters had babies, been sent flowers when their on-screen spouses died, and so on. That these things do happen is undebat-able; what can be questioned is whether these anecdotes receive so much airplay because they are representative or because they make better stories than do the many fans who are clear on the actor-character distinction and neither write to nor harangue stars in public. After all, if I recognized a soap star in a restaurant but chose not to approach him or her, the star never would know that I was a fan, let alone tell a story about me. As Blumenthal (1997) puts it, we do not know whether most soap fans "engage in such extreme behavior . . . but given the millions of viewers soap operas enjoy, common sense dictates that it's unlikely" (p. 102). Indeed, in Harrington and Bielby's (1995) interviews, soap actors estimated the percentage of fan mail they received that fit the lunatic image as ranging from 1% to 30%, leaving at least 70% of the fan mail writers sane. When one adds in the many—probably the majority—who do not write at all, one has to assume that the over-whelming majority of soap fans have at least as firm a grasp of reality as does anyone else.

The negative perception of soap opera viewers also is grounded in the division between high-taste and low-taste culture that creates a value-laden distinction between aficionados (e.g., of opera) and fans (e.g., of soap operas) (Jensen, 1992). Whereas the former savor *good texts* that promote intellectual and democratic ideals, the latter wallow in *bad texts* that subvert these ideals (Jensen & Pauly, 1997). Jenkins (1992) draws on Bourdieu to argue that the sense of high and low taste seems like the natural order only because we have been so well socialized. Rather than absolute differences, the promotion of some tastes rather than others is deeply political, tied to a cultural hierarchy that keeps high tastes for the elite and low tastes for the masses. The image of the fan who revels in low-taste culture rather than displaying appropriate shame can thus be seen not as a reflection of the fans but as a "projection of anxieties about the violation of dominant cultural hierarchies" (p. 17).

Whereas high-taste culture is seen as promoting rationality, low-taste culture is taken to promote emotionality (Jensen, 1992), tying into a "deep suspicion" that these masses cannot think or act rationally on their own. Fans are seen as guided by an inappropriate emotionality that operates separately from (and overrules) their cognition (Jensen, 1992). As Jenkins (1992) suggests, this seems dangerous:

> Whether viewed as a religious fanatic, a psychopathic killer, a neurotic fantasist, or a lust-crazed groupie, the fan remains a "fanatic," or false worshipper, whose interests are fundamentally alien to the realm of "normal" cultural experience and whose mentality is dangerously out of touch with reality. (p. 15)

However, as Jensen (1992) articulates, this concern about fans stems from assumptions that affect all of us:

> What is assumed to be true of fans—that they are potentially deviant, as loners or as members of a mob—can be connected with deeper and

more diffuse assumptions about modern life. Each fan type mobilizes related assumptions about modern individuals: The obsessed loner invokes the image of the alienated, atomized "mass man"; the frenzied crowd member invokes the image of the vulnerable, irrational victim of mass persuasion. (p. 14)

In other words, people's fears about fandom stem from their own fears about losing community in modern life rather than from accurate descriptions of fan involvement. It surely is not a coincidence that these same issues are at play in the stereotype of people who spend a lot of time online as socially incompetent loners.

Even among low-culture forms, soap operas are singled out for particularly patronizing treatment. As Harrington and Bielby (1995) note, being a soap fan is "about as low as one can sink on cultural taste hierarchies" (p. 6). This heightened stigmatization is attributable largely to the fact that soaps are a women's genre that focuses on emotion. Although the stigma might masquerade as gender neutral, soaps involve "gendered people interacting with a gendered image" (Blumenthal, 1997, p. 47). Blumenthal (1997) might add that the gendered image in this case is one of the few produced primarily by women. Within the television industry, soap operas always have been and remain "a pink ghetto" (Coopers, quoted in Susman, 1997, p. 14). Asked why the network daytime television offices are the only ones staffed primarily by women, Dona Coopers, senior vice president for daytime programming at ABC, suggests that it is because "women are more comfortable with emotions, with having desires" (quoted in Susman, 1997, p. 14). Her comment demonstrates an awareness that soap operas are defined by their connections to women and emotion and that their stigmatization is a direct consequence.

It has been fashionable to deride women's fiction for centuries. Radway's (1984) analysis of romance novels and their female readers offers one contemporary example. N. Baym (1995) describes the early 19th-century American attitude toward women's novels:

> Critics saw novels as productive of social passivity, withdrawal, and global discontent. . . . Saturating women's interior worlds with fantasy, novels ruptured their connections with, loyalty to, interest in, and usefulness for the everyday republican world. . . . Not only was the reading of novels an idle activity, the content of novels saturated women's imagination with depictions of frivolous people. Novels

were thus associated with idleness, waste, and—dread word in the republican lexicon—luxury. (p. 17)

Almira Hart Phelps, in her 1833 book *The Female Student*, exemplifies this take on women's fiction, posing questions for her young readers that are not so different from those that contemporary soap viewers sometimes are called on to answer:

> I would appeal to the experience of every female who has indulged herself much in this kind of reading, whether, after the excitement of feeling occasioned by the perusal of some fascinating novel, she has returned to the realities of life with a spirit calmed and prepared to meet its realities with fortitude and resignation or whether she has not at such times experienced a distaste, almost amounting to disgust, for the homely beings with whom reality surrounded her and for the everyday scenes of life. And has it not required a strong and painful effort to regain that mental equilibrium so necessary for prudent conduct and amiable deportment? (Phelps, 1826/1833, p. 9, cited in N. Baym, 1995, p. 18)

As Blumenthal (1997) summarizes, the devaluation of soaps "takes place in a larger, intranational, and cross-national milieu in which women's general and representational cultures are actively subordinated" (p. 87). If there is general distrust of the masses' ability to maintain rationality in the face of popular culture, then it is considerably exaggerated when it comes to the "ability of women to control their indulgence in representational culture" (p. 108).

The image of the female fiction victim is especially easy to apply to soap viewers because they are unusually involved with their shows. Kielwasser and Wolf (1989) write, "What continues to set soap opera apart from other popular television genres is the intense and lasting loyalty of its fans" (p. 111). Many soap viewers begin watching as children with their mothers and continue watching throughout their lives (Blumenthal, 1997). I am 2 years younger than *General Hospital*; as of this writing, I have followed it for 18 years—more than half my life. I have known some of its characters longer than anyone I see daily. Observers from all camps have noted the distinctive viewer loyalty (Cantor & Pingree, 1983; Edmundson & Rounds, 1973; Rubin & Perse, 1987), describing fans as *addicted*,[2] unusually involved in the shows, and among the most active of television viewers. More so than most media, soaps are integrated into the rest of life through discussions, soap periodicals, and the like (Blumenthal, 1997).

Soap industry professionals, especially the writers, are well aware of how much time their viewers devote to the messages they produce. In this regard, it is striking to note how seriously they strive to create a moral text that will educate and enlighten as it entertains their audiences. Agnes Nixon, creator of *Search for Tomorrow*; cocreator of *As the World Turns*, *One Life to Live*, and *All My Children* (*AMC*); and head writer of *Guiding Light*, *Another World*, and *AMC*, acknowledged this sense of responsibility nearly 30 years ago:

> The simple fact is that each of the serials on the air is watched by an average of from [3] to [8] million viewers per day—men, women, and children. And when one multiplies that number by [5] days a week, [52] weeks a year, one must be struck by the power of this form of entertainment and the force it can have in our society. (p. 62)

Coopers elaborates:

> Agnes Nixon has wonderful stories about people who've had the courage to have abortions after being raped because they'd seen something on a soap. Even when you're not intending to get on your soapbox and talk, you never know who needs to listen and who needs to hear that message. (quoted in Susman, 1997, p. 14)

Soaps do deserve credit for taking on difficult issues before other popular media. For example, they introduced the Pap smear to the general public during the 1940s, introduced AIDS to (heterosexual) characters who the audience loved during the 1980s, and were concerning themselves with the humanity of lesbians 20 years before Ellen DeGeneres came out on prime time.

Much to the chagrin of those in the soap industry, soap operas, their viewers, and their actors have been actively belittled not just by the outside world but also by their own. "The simple truth," says Coopers, "is that within the network hierarchy, prime time feels about daytime the way the outside world feels about daytime" (quoted in Susman, 1997, p. 14). Derision by the media is a tradition going back to the earliest days of the genre. It was the trade magazines that renamed serials *washboard weepers*, *sudsers*, and *soap operas* because of their melodramatic flair and, often, sponsorship from soap manufacturers

(Macdonald, 1979). For various reasons, the networks present soap operas in prime time and promotional clips as featuring "hunks" in sexual situations with women. Clips such as these obscure the deep emotions in which soap sex is contextualized and exaggerate the amount of attention that soaps focus on sex. Indeed, these clips sometimes are filmed solely for advertising, with the sexual events they depict not even occurring on the shows (Susman, 1997). Sex is used as a lure for new viewers at the expense of the genre and the existing viewers. Margot Wain, CBS's west coast director of daytime programming, laments, "I think the people who write about it and talk about it the most are the people who don't watch the shows and who don't know what they're about" (quoted in Susman, 1997, p. 13).

Together, these many forces provide a deep unspoken foundation of historical cultural assumptions and contemporary representations that delegitimize soap operas and their viewers. In a nutshell, soap operas' orientation toward emotion makes them bad, possibly even dangerous. Viewers' gender and loyal engagement with soaps demonstrates vulnerability. We watch because we are unable to satisfy the emotional needs in our real lives. We turn to soap operas to escape our own despair by dwelling in other people's problems. Obviously, this is not how soap opera viewers understand themselves, but we generally are not granted, nor do we seek, the spaces to articulate our point of view in scholarship or the mainstream media. One reason is an assumption on the part of many theorists that the audience is too unsophisticated to have anything interesting to say (Blumenthal, 1997; Jensen & Pauly, 1997). I will return to such theorists later in this chapter. A more practical reason is that soap viewers are well aware of soaps' stigmatization and choose to remain in the "soap closet" rather than battling the misperception (Blumenthal, 1997; Harrington & Bielby, 1995). Even at home in the most intimate relationships, women find opposition to watching soaps from husbands (whose distaste for soaps seems to be inversely related to the amount of time they have actually watched with their wives). There are no public spaces where soap fans can assume that their habit will not be seen as a flaw.

The r.a.t.s. Newsgroup as an Alternative

For participants in r.a.t.s., this stigmatization is part of daily life. Although not its only function, the accepting refuge of r.a.t.s. is one of the newsgroup's main appeals. For example, in my survey responses,

Helen, an insurance auditor, registered nurse, lifelong soap viewer, and enthusiastic participant in r.a.t.s., describes her colleagues: "Most professionals I know won't admit to watching or think they are TV for the less intelligent" (Helen, 1991 survey). Another respondent, Adele, explains that she "used to be a bit embarrassed by the fact that here I am, a professional woman [in a male-dominated field], and I go home and watch soap operas at night" (Adele, 1993 survey).

The next two chapters will discuss how soap operas are valued (even as they are criticized) and how viewers are assumed to be rational as well as emotional in r.a.t.s. For the most part, the construction of these r.a.t.s. values is implicit. Rather than decrying the negative stereotype, it is simply ignored as fans go about the business of enjoying the genre. However, the post quoted earlier in this chapter, in which r.a.t.s. participants were characterized as fat, pathetic housewives eating bon-bons, provided a rare chance to see participants' responses to this stereotype made explicit. The discussion, of which I provide several excerpts, reveals the ways in which soap viewers resist the stereotype.

Although some people left unchallenged the assertion that there are housewives like this, several people explicitly rejected the vision of housewives entailed in the soap viewer stereotype, thus undermining its foundations:

```
I vividly remember hearing this stereotype of a
housewife over and over again when growing up.
I credit it with partial responsibility for
bringing on the women's movement. I know that
as a very young girl, I vowed *I* was never going
to be like that (even though I didn't know any
housewives who either sat around in curlers
OR ate bon bons—does anyone eat bon bons anymore?).
(October 8, 1991)
```

Others added that not only was this an inaccurate and disrespectful portrayal of housewives, it also was an inaccurate portrayal of the demographics of soap opera viewers:

```
It is interesting to me that you are taking
several stereotypes as fact. Clearly, you
a) have a warped sense of what homemakers have
to do to keep house—my mother kills herself
```

```
running her household and sits down only to eat
lunch; & b) are ignorant of the demographics
of soap opera watchers on this group and in
general. (October 8, 1991)
```

This poster is right that soap opera viewers are widely distributed demographically. According to a study of the soap audience by Mediamark Research Inc. (MRI) cited in *Soap Opera Weekly* (Liccardo, 1996), 74% of soap viewers are women, meaning that more than a quarter of them (26%) are men. Liccardo (1996) goes on to compare MRI's demographics to those of the American population. According to these data, soap opera viewers on average are somewhat less educated, less affluent, and less employed than the general population. I suspect that these demographic disparities are somewhat skewed by soap-watching college students who appear as low-income and unemployed viewers, although they are not likely to remain so. However, even if one accepts these figures, a sizable percentage of soap opera viewers have been to college (34% vs. 45% of the general population), have household incomes above $30,000 (47% vs. 59%), and work full- or part-time (47% vs. 66%).

Most responded to the affront by emphasizing how far from the stereotype they themselves were:

```
Hmmm...not a very accurate desription of me....
I'm a twenty something male engineer...and most
of the people I know who post here, at least about
Days, are engineers, programmers and the like.
(October 7, 1991)
```

```
What do I know? I've only got a summa cum laude
BA degree, an MS in chemistry, and in a few more
than a few more months, a PhD in X-ray
crystallography (that's structural bio-physical
chemistry). You say you are well read, Mark? Let's
discuss Sartre, Kuhn, Locke, Tolstoy, quantum vs.
classical mechanics, cloning, new advances in
immunosuppression and drug design, Montessori,
James (Henry or William), Kierkegaard, Friedman,
Piaget, classical or modern theatre, the pros and
cons of recycling, the deterioration of the ozone
layer, global warming, James Bay, the Alaskan
```

```
wilderness crisis, hiking/climbing/camping,
cycling, gourmet cooking, fitness and nutrition,
or any other topic in which you may feel adept.
Feel free to reply in French, German, or Spanish.
Chinese or Japanese, I admit, will take me a
little longer to handle. (October 10, 1991)
```

Soap viewers in r.a.t.s. also took ownership of the stereotype rather than rejecting it fully, recasting it in a celebratory way:

```
I'm so young, beautiful, thin, and successful
(electrical engineer) that you would have to
crawl over a line of men 100 deep to get near
my bon bons. (October 8, 1991)
```

```
Hooray! Hoot! ALL POWER to those fat housewives who
get to eat bon bons and watch soaps all day!!!!!
Ladies, how DID you do it?!!!!! Please, clue in
those of us who are still WORKING for a living,
don't have the time to watch in real-time, who
aren't married and certainly don't hav the luxury
of bon bons! (October 6, 1991)
```

Throughout this thread of conversation, as r.a.t.s. participants rejected the soap opera stereotype, they interactively constructed an implicit, and sometimes explicit, understanding of r.a.t.s. participants, functions, and social atmosphere. In comments such as these, this process of defining r.a.t.s. and its participants occurred explicitly:

```
we KNOW we are all intelligent, witty, wonderful
people. WE do not need to allow a simple minded one
dimensional person the opportunity to bother us.
(October 8, 1991)
```

```
People here on the net are good people who use the
net and soaps to escape the daily humdrum of life,
They are witty, intelligent persons (otherwise
would they even know how to use a computer, not to
mention using a news program) who would like to
share their opinions, post updates and get to meet
```

```
others who share the same regard for these shows.
(October 13, 1991)

I can't tell you how hard I have laughed at
your responses to this guy....Not only have I
discovered that this is ONE FUN GROUP OF PEOPLE,
but a witty one as well. Cheers to all of you!
(October 11, 1991)
```

In sum, in this rare and explicit discussion, fans argued against the stereotype as an inaccurate construal of housewives, of the soap audience, and of themselves. When not idealizing and appropriating the stereotype in an almost celebratory way, they substituted a positive self and group definition that emphasized wit and intelligence.

For many in r.a.t.s., then, among the appeals of the newsgroup are its offer of refuge from the stereotype and provision of strong evidence that, as Helen puts it, there "are other intelligent people out there who watch soaps" (1991 survey). Suzanne, who wrote a master's thesis on soap operas, summarizes this supportive function of r.a.t.s.:

> For one thing, it's refreshing to find a place where adult, professional, intelligent people admit to liking and even becoming emotionally involved in soap operas. As a woman with an advanced degree and a thinking, rational mind, I have always been insulted by the stereotype of soap viewers as passive, overly emotional housewives who have nothing better to do with their time. I've always known that this was not the case, and doing my own project on soaps last year gave me the evidence to back up my belief, but it's still considered (especially among the PC [politically correct] crowds that I hang out in) somehow wrong to like them, and therefore, it's an embarrassing admission to make. But not on r.a.t.s.! (1993 survey)

Blumenthal (1997) argues that watching soaps is a "feminist praxis," even if the women who watch them do not consider themselves to be practicing feminism. By choosing to make time for their own relaxation and enjoying emotions despite "a gendered social context in which women's culture is defined as inferior," women empower themselves (p. 97). In r.a.t.s., fans create an ongoing social space in which the soaps and their fans are legitimized and their pleasures are enhanced rather than shamed. Although it is not a point on which the participants focus, and not one on which I will dwell, Blumenthal is right that this must be understood as deeply gendered. As they legitimize themselves and soaps, women and men in r.a.t.s. are legitimizing the emotional concerns traditionally associated with women.

Then Who Is the Soap Opera Audience?

If the stereotype is not an accurate depiction of the soap opera audience, then just who is the soap opera audience? The answer offered by Ang (1991) is that the " 'television audience' only exists as an imaginary entity, an abstraction constructed from the vantage points of institutions, in the interest of the institutions" (p. 2). The audience categories used in audience studies, such as A. C. Nielsen's highly desirable "working women ages 18 to 49 years" category, have nothing to do with audience practices or experiences but rather are strategic groupings designed by marketers (Anderson, 1996). Ang (1991) characterizes researchers' "search for totalizing accounts of 'the audience' " as "desperate" (p. x):

> Research projects have consistently proceeded by implicitly singling out the television audience as a separate domain, treating it as an aggregate of individuals whose characteristics can then presumably be operationalized, examined, categorized, and accumulated into an ever more complex picture. (p. 11)

The messier reality is that there are "infinite, contradictory, dispersed, and dynamic practices and experiences of television audience-hood enacted by people in their everyday lives" (p. 13). As such, explanations of audience are "always local and partial" (Anderson, 1996, p. 79). The soap opera audience is a diffuse phenomenon, a performance rather than a social category (Nightingale, 1996).

Even within the self-constituting soap opera audience of r.a.t.s., there is a good deal of diversity.[3] A quick look at the demographics of r.a.t.s. (as best as I have been able to construct) shows that its participants disproportionately represent the high end of the American socioeconomic spectrum but that there is a wide variety of careers represented. Drawing on r.a.t.s. participants' descriptions of themselves and on a "yearbook" put together by r.a.t.s. fans of *AMC*, I was able to ascertain the careers of 59 participants. If these are representative of the

TABLE 1.1   Careers of rec.arts.tv.soaps Participants (*N* = 59)

Career	Number and Percentage
Computer professional	
Software engineer	9 (15)
Consultant	3 (5)
Other	11 (19)
Student	
Graduate	11 (19)
Undergraduate	8 (14)
Other professional	
Technical writer	3 (5)
Secretary	3 (5)
Librarian	3 (5)
Scientist	3 (5)
Other	4 (7)
Homemaker	1 (2)

NOTE: Percentages are in parentheses. Percentages do not add to 100 due to rounding.

whole, then nearly half of r.a.t.s. participants are computer professionals who work primarily as software programmers but also as consultants, testers, managers, trainers, and graphic designers, among other specialties. Students, both undergraduate and graduate, form the next largest contingent. Noncomputing professionals include scientists (working for both private and governmental laboratories), librarians, secretaries, nurses, high school teachers, and public relations and marketing professionals. There was only one homemaker who responded. Table 1.1 summarizes the careers of the participants.

Although participants describe the group as being "worldwide," the overwhelming majority of participants, based on the 67 whose locations I was able to assess, live in the United States. Nearly a third of them live in California, which is not surprising given the presence of so many computer-oriented businesses online in that state. The others span 21 states, and 1 lives in Canada. People have posted from Belgium, Germany, England, and New Zealand, but those who do not live in

North America, particularly the United States, are in a minuscule minority.

As one would expect, r.a.t.s. participants are primarily women. Judging from the names in the headers of one month's worth of r.a.t.s. posts, of the 492 people who contributed, 60% had female names, 20% had male names, and another 20% had addresses that left their genders ambiguous.[4] If one assumes a proportionate split among the ambiguous population, then r.a.t.s. is approximately 72% female and 28% male, nearly exactly the gender balance of soap viewers found by MRI. This gender balance makes r.a.t.s. unusual given women's underrepresentation online during the early 1990s (Kramarae & Taylor, 1993). However, r.a.t.s. participants often remark on how many men there are given the topic.[5]

Understanding the Soap Opera Genre

R.a.t.s. is socially constructed as a space where intelligent, friendly people discuss a genre that is worthy of their sustained attention. If we are to take this seriously, as I hope I have convinced you to do by now, then we need to begin with an understanding of the soap genre and the types of involvement it promotes. If the appeal of soaps cannot be attributed to (shortcomings of) its audience, then it only makes sense to take a close look at the genre itself. The generic elements of soaps influence the interests, activities, organization, and pleasures of fans (Harrington & Bielby, 1995). To elaborate the genre, I turn to its writers, historians, and scholarly analysts. Soaps' early inventors saw themselves as storytellers, offering listeners tales based on common American experience with which they could identify (Macdonald, 1979). Irna Phillips, a writer and former teacher of storytelling,[6] often is acknowledged as the creator of the genre, especially within the soap opera industry. She credited the success of her shows to her devotion to reality and careful understanding of the women who comprised her audience (Edmundson & Rounds, 1973; Macdonald, 1979). Phillips held that the serial form's success was related to how it parallels life: "The serial drama is not 'such stuff as dreams are made of.' It is as fundamental as life itself. Our day-by-day existence is a serial drama" (quoted in Macdonald, 1979, p. 232).

Elaine Carrington was another independent writer who became one of the most successful and influential soap opera innovators. Carrington, who reportedly dictated all of her scripts in her bathrobe while chain smoking and reclining on her couch or bed (Edmundson & Rounds, 1973; Macdonald, 1979), also saw her serials' appeal as lying in their relevance to the lives of her listeners: "If they aren't a hifalutin' form of art, they frequently contain profound wisdom expressed in universal terms" (quoted in Macdonald, 1979, p. 253).

Frank and Anne Hummert, the other two people credited with solidifying the genre during the 1930s, did not write their scripts. Instead, they created multiple-author production lines that transformed their ideas and direction for more than a dozen serials into dialogue. This factory-style soap production now characterizes all soap operas.[7] In 1936, the Hummerts' organization produced 100 scripts a week. The Hummerts recognized the diversity of their audience and saw the key to their success as their ability to reflect "the everyday doings of plain, everyday people" and to create "stories that can be understood on Park Avenue and on the prairie" (Frank Hummert, quoted in Macdonald, 1979, p. 250).

Nixon was hired and trained by Phillips.[8] Like her mentor, Nixon (1970) argues for parallels between serials and life: "The serial form imitates life in that, for its characters, the curtain rises with birth and does not ring down until death" (p. 63). She summarizes soap operas' success as follows:

> For a serial to be successful, it must tell a compelling story concerned with interesting [and] believable characters. Characters with whom the audience can personally identify or emotionally empathize. The ingredients are the same [as those] required for any good dramatic fare but with one basic difference: that the continuing form allows a fuller development of characterization while permitting the audience to become more and more involved with the story and its people. (p. 63)

The most important ingredient in any soap opera is the characters, of whom there are at least two dozen. Soap writer Jean Rouverol writes,

> Whatever else a show may offer, it must contain people we *love*, people whose joys and tribulations we can share. It must also provide us with people we love to hate, people who offer a continuous threat to the welfare or happiness of those we are fond of. And though the need for suspense is always a given, there can be no real suspense if we don't care about the people we're watching. Above all, we need to *care*. (Rouverol, 1984, p. 36)

Photo 1.1. The Debonair But Dangerous Villain, Carter Jones
SOURCE: ©1998 (Ann Limongello/ABC Inc.) Used by permission.

Looking at one of the story lines that received the most messages
on r.a.t.s. during the 10 months I sampled helps to ground this discussion. This story line on *AMC* concerned Carter Jones, a villain who came
to town to seek revenge against his ex-wife. In later chapters, I will
examine the discussion of this story line in r.a.t.s.; the retelling should
provide enough expertise to catch the gist of those online discussions
as well. The Carter story line, which did not involve many of the soap's
characters, did have 12 different characters in fairly major roles, although the extent to which the audience cared about them was debatable (and, as we will see in subsequent chapters, was debated on r.a.t.s.).
Here are the major players:

   Carter Jones (Photo 1.1): This was a new character and former lawyer
      who had just been released from jail, where he had served time
      for beating his then wife, Maggie Jones, to the point where she
      was hospitalized with serious injuries.
   Galen Henderson (Photo 1.2): a.k.a. Maggie Jones, Carter's ex-wife,
      who had switched identities and moved to Pine Valley so that
      Carter could never find her. In Pine Valley, she was the assistant
      district attorney. Carter appeared in Pine Valley just as she had

Photo 1.2. Galen Henderson (left) and the First Natalie Dillon (Kate Collins, right)

SOURCE: ©1998 (Ann Limongello/ABC Inc.) Used by permission.

decided to run for district attorney. The character of Galen had been on *AMC* for less than a year when this story line began.

Natalie Dillon: This was an independently wealthy foundation administrator married to Trevor, mother of Timmy and baby Amanda. At the beginning of this story, she was portrayed by Kate Collins, the actress who originated the role and had played her for 7 years (Photos 1.2 and 1.3). She had been a fully developed character. Midway through the story line, the role was taken over by Melody Anderson (Photo 1.4), a move that always threatens the character's consistency and fans' attachment.

Trevor Dillon (Photo 1.3): This was a former mercenary turned member of the Pine Valley Police Department, husband of Natalie, stepfather of Timmy, father of Amanda, and friend of Galen's. Trevor was an established fan favorite and was one of only four of these characters still on the show in 1998.

Timmy Hunter (Photo 1.3): This was Natalie's son, Trevor's stepson, and Jeremy's considerably younger half-brother. The owner of a sheepdog named Harold, Timmy is well liked on r.a.t.s. and remained on the show until 1999.

Photo 1.3. The Dillon Family: Trevor, Natalie, and Timmy
SOURCE: ©1998 (Ann Limongello/ABC Inc.) Used by permission.

Photo 1.4. The Second Natalie Dillon (Melody Anderson) or, as Participants Called Her on rec.arts.tv.soaps, "Not"

SOURCE: ©1998 (Capital Cities/ABC Inc.) Used by permission.

Stephen Hammill: This was a doctor at Pine Valley Hospital who recently had become involved with Galen. He also had been on the show for only a relatively short time.

Brooke English: This was the editor of a successful magazine called *Tempo.* At the time, Brooke had been on the show for 17 years and was, as she remains, a core character.

Jeremy Hunter: This was one of Trevor's closest friends, Natalie's former lover and former stepson, and Timmy's half-brother. He had been on for many years and, like Trevor and Brooke, was an established and fleshed-out character. He was an ex-mercenary turned monk, turned painter and gallery owner who had occasional psychic visions known in r.a.t.s. as "Jerivision." At the end of this story line, he moved (in character) to the soap opera *Loving,* where he was made dean of humanities at the local college and eventually was murdered.

Mimi Reed: This was another member of the Pine Valley Police Department. Mimi, like Galen, was a relatively new character.

Derek Frye: This was another member of the Pine Valley Police Department. Derek had been on the show somewhat longer than had Mimi or Galen, but his character, as one of the show's few African Americans, had been relatively marginalized, although he remained on the cast.

Charlie Brent: This was a character who had just returned from a busy career elsewhere as a model and was looking for focus in his life. At this time, Charlie was being portrayed by the third actor. This one was considerably older than either of the previous actors. Thus, even though he was an old character, he, like the recast Natalie, was in many ways a new character.

Dinah Lee: This was a character from the ABC soap opera *Loving* who came from the same town as Carter and who went to Pine Valley to escape her problems back home (and to boost the ratings of her home show).

During the early days of radio serials, characters were supposed to be average to facilitate identification and, thus, caring (Edmundson & Rounds, 1973; Macdonald, 1979). Although characters often are exaggerated in soaps, they remain overwhelmingly White, middle class, mainstream Americans, people who viewers might know in real life. Of the characters in the Carter Jones story line, the African Americans

Derek and Mimi were the only non-Whites, and like all the others (except the child Timmy and his independently wealthy mother, Natalie), they were middle class professionals. As Rouverol (1984) indicates, soap characters include both heroes and villains. In this case, Carter was a villain, and who (if anyone) served as the hero became debatable (on r.a.t.s., Timmy seemed to get the most votes).

The ability of the female fan to identify with soap characters is enhanced by the fact that, unlike most fiction, the central protagonists of soap operas usually are women. Although all soap opera women originally were housewives, they appeared as capable professionals as early as the 1940s (Macdonald, 1979) and are now frequently portrayed as competent career women. The women in this story line include a lawyer, a police officer, a foundation administrator, and a magazine editor. Dinah Lee, the only woman with no apparent job, was a single apartment dweller. These women, like all soap characters, experience a range of emotions that all women are deemed to share (Blumenthal, 1997; Geraghty, 1991). Characters become "emotional representatives," taking fans through a wide variety of familiar feelings (Geraghty, 1991). Although Carter motivated the story line, it was his stalking of the knowable Galen, Natalie, and Dinah Lee that provided the possibility of identification.

Indeed, soap operas glorify and exaggerate emotions. Like the network personnel quoted earlier, all of the soap writers I have discussed understand the stories they produce to be first and foremost about emotional experiences in intimate relationships, experiences that all of us are taken to feel. From the other side of the text, Livingstone (1989), drawing on research by Allen, Hobson, and Seiter, suggests that soaps revolve around "cultural and social issues of fundamental concern to people such as kinship relations, reproduction, gender, the role of the community, and so forth" (p. 29). "Soaps' main effects," write Harrington and Bielby (1995), "are to evoke emotions and to glorify and exaggerate the emotional meaning of everyday life" (p. 45). I think of soaps as akin to funhouse mirrors, reflecting reality, but in a way that exaggerates some (emotional) aspects while minimizing others (e.g., work). The real story in soaps always is the "building up and maintenance of [personal] relationships" (Geraghty, 1991, p. 117).

Many of the emotions that soap operas engage are negative. Rouverol (1984) insists that soaps are about conflict and that the potential for conflict should fill every scene. She writes, "*There is conflict inherent in every human situation,* and it is the head writer's task to recognize it and make use of it. *Without conflict, there is no drama"* (p. 47, italics in original). Kilguss (1977), in her psychological content analysis, argues that the primary themes in soaps are incest, suspicion, distrust, victimization, dependency, joylessness, fear, and loneliness—a veritable laundry list of relational conflicts. "Given that women must often suppress their feelings in reality," writes Blumenthal (1997), "it is not surprising that they will gravitate toward an entertainment medium that expresses the importance of plumbing one's emotions" (p. 56).

Unless it is seen as a neuroticizing force (e.g., Modleski, 1984), women's emotional engagement with soaps usually is taken to be cathartic. Seiter, Borchers, Kreutzner, and Warth's (1989) respondents, for example, discuss the pleasure of working out aggressions through soap opera viewing. Hobson's (1982, 1989) and Ang's (1985) respondents also describe using soaps to "have a good cry" or otherwise let loose emotionally. Participants in r.a.t.s. certainly describe soap viewing as a form of emotional release. In short, soaps "attempt to elicit as many and as complex emotions from viewers as possible" (Blumenthal, 1997, p. 53), and viewers enjoy the opportunity to engage wholeheartedly in exploring these emotions. Although Blumenthal (1997) is exactly right when she argues that "women watch soap operas to explore emotional reality" (p. 55), most research has neglected the importance of comedy in soaps. Rouverol (1984) implores the would-be writers she addresses to remember the importance of comedy, whereas columnists and industry professionals lament the lessening presence of comedy in soaps. As we will see in the r.a.t.s. discussion, the soap often is taken as comedic even when it is intended quite seriously, considerably complicating the indulgence in emotion that soaps encourage.

Emotion is brought out by showing characters in a wide range of familial and nonfamilial relationships including the often ignored relationship of friendship. Much of the dialogue on soap operas is between female friends (Geraghty, 1991), and men such as Jeremy and Trevor often were seen together ruminating over their personal lives. Even external power relationships, such as those between bosses and employees or those between business competitors, always are translated into personal relationships (Geraghty, 1991). Derek and Mimi's story was a romance, not a police story, and Trevor's relationship with them was more as a friend than as a colleague. Another *AMC* story, the 1992 drama of whether or not Erica Kane would lose control of the cosmetics company that had become her life's work, unwound as a warped romantic triangle among Erica, her despised husband, and the married man attempting a corporate takeover, all three of whom wound up on the board of directors. These close relationships allow the characters to be richly interconnected in complex (and downright incestuous) communities. Natalie, for example, had been married to Jeremy's father (who also was Timmy's father) and Jeremy (among others) before marrying Trevor. Jeremy and Timmy were half-siblings, and Jeremy and Trevor got to know each other when they were mercenaries. Trevor worked with Derek, Mimi, and Galen. Derek and Mimi were a couple. Galen dated Stephen, who worked at the hospital where Natalie had been a nurse. And so on . . .

The main thing that soap characters do is talk. Most all events in soap operas "serve as occasions for characters to get together and have prolonged, involved, intensely emotional discussions with each other" (Modleski, 1983, p. 68). This focus on conversation leads Modleski (1983) and others to suggest that on soap operas, "action is less important than reaction and interaction" (p. 83). However, as Blumenthal (1997) notes, to say that dialogue is not action is to take a masculine perspective: "As a woman, I see plenty of action on soap operas, but it is emotionally and not physically centered" (p. 78). Much of the action also is supplied by the viewer in the interpretive process. Although a scene might show only one or two characters, regular viewers see it in the context of the community in which those characters dwell. Most actions and utterances carry implications that ripple throughout the community (Allen, 1985). What is *not* said in these dialogues often is more important than what *is* said (Rouverol, 1984). Knowledge of the characters' extensive histories and places in the soap community allows viewers to bring much more to bear on reading each scene than is possible for outsiders (Geraghty, 1991).

The soap opera community is located on sets at a soundstage. These sets serve as a "familiar geography" that provides a sense of how its spaces are related to one another and allows the audience to know them intimately (Geraghty, 1991). With some exceptions, such as *The Bold and the Beautiful* (which is set in Los Angeles), soaps always take place in middle- or small-sized fictional towns. *AMC* is set in Pine Valley, a fictional town in Pennsylvania that seems to be located near Philadelphia, although its precise location remains conveniently ambiguous. Soap sets usually are the interiors of homes, offices, hospitals, and restaurants. *AMC* sets include an upscale and a downscale restaurant, many living rooms, a few bedrooms and nurseries, a hospital, a police station, a seedy hotel room, and a variety of professional offices. The Carter Jones story line featured a houseboat.[9] Sets, and the towns they are taken to represent, come to have their own histories. The history of this narrative space creates some minimal homogeneity among disparate characters and gives a sense of their unified experience (Geraghty, 1991). It also creates the illusion that the town exists even when the cameras are not present to display it. The familiarity of the settings and the consistency of the camera shots through which the audience sees them also function to focus attention on characters and their dialogue (Brunsdon, 1983).

The soap opera also is distinguished by the many ways in which it violates the narrative genre. Many of these features are directly connected to the enormous temporal expanse in which to develop a story that the serial form offers. Consider, for example, the many twists and turns in the Carter Jones story line told over 4 months.

It began when Carter saw a picture of Galen in the newspaper and headed to Pine Valley to seek revenge. In Pine Valley, he got Brooke English, the editor of *Tempo*, to give him a job as a researcher and began to taunt Galen with phone calls. A terrified Galen was immediately surrounded by her new lover, Stephen, and police officers Trevor, Derek, and Mimi, who began working voluntary overtime to protect her. Carter proved to be too smart for the law, and police officials were consistently unable to pin any offenses on him. He used his legal knowledge to keep the police on a short leash while insinuating himself deeper into Galen's life.

When, after weeks, Carter finally confronted Galen face-to-face, Trevor enlisted Jeremy, and the two began a campaign to scare Carter away from Galen by portraying themselves as violent and unpredictable former mercenaries (drawing on the show's deep history). Stephen responded by physically threatening Carter but was forced to back off when Carter put on a neck brace and threatened to take Stephen to court for assault unless Galen begged him not to do so. Meanwhile, Charlie, inspired to become a detective, moved into the seedy Pine Cone Motel in which Carter was living and tried to ingratiate himself with Carter and gain his confidence.

Carter, annoyed with Trevor for his interference, set fire to the house that Trevor and Natalie were renovating, knowing that Trevor was inside. Natalie also was caught in the fire and was blinded when a paint can exploded and sent countless shards into her eyes. She was hospital-ized with bandages over her eyes for weeks, during which time the new actress assumed the role. Carter, seeming to feel some remorse for harming her, invented the persona of "Kyle," a hospital orderly, and began to visit Natalie in her hospital room. The two struck up a friend-ship in which she divulged lots of information about Galen. Trevor, believing himself responsible for the fire, was wracked with guilt, and tensions (fed by "Kyle") developed between him and Natalie.

One night, Carter brought home a prostitute, who saw a photo of Galen and implied that Carter had feelings for her. Carter responded by beating the prostitute senseless. When she went to the hospital, Galen and her self-appointed squad of protectors tried desperately to con-vince the woman to file charges against Carter. Carter snuck into her room and terrified her out of filing. The prostitute left town, leaving Trevor and the other protectors increasingly frustrated.

Carter volunteered to work on Galen's campaign for district attor-ney and set about trying to sabotage it by canceling her press confer-ences. Galen, becoming increasingly concerned, bought a gun to protect herself. Natalie told "Kyle" that Galen had been romantically interested in Trevor before he and Natalie had reconciled. Because by now Carter had fallen in love with Natalie, he began plotting to murder Trevor and to frame Galen. He purchased a gun identical to Galen's and switched them. Around this time, Charlie deduced that Carter had a new love interest at the hospital, and Galen and her protectors tried to identify her. Carter fantasized about Natalie rejecting Trevor and falling in love with Carter.

At this point, Dinah Lee, a character from a soap opera with far lower ratings than *AMC* (which has since been canceled), came to stay in Pine Valley. By extraordinary coincidence, Carter was from her small town, where he was a hero to all. Against all warnings, and despite Jeremy's psychic visions of her in danger, Dinah Lee decided to befriend Carter. Working on his murder plan, Carter used the *Tempo* facilities to develop potentially incriminating photographs of Galen hugging Trevor. Brooke caught him in the act and fired him.

On the night Carter's plan was set to take place, he lured Trevor to Galen's apartment. But Dinah Lee unwittingly interrupted, and the plan was foiled. Furious with Dinah Lee, Carter later beat her viciously. Hospitalized, the protectors rushed to her bedside to convince her to file charges against Carter. Despite Carter's repeated visits to convince her that she deserved the beating, she finally agreed to press charges and returned home (i.e., to the other soap opera). Shortly thereafter, Derek figured out that Carter, not Trevor, had actually set the house fire. Everything seemed set for Carter's arrest.

However, before the police could arrest Carter, "Kyle" lured Natalie from her hospital bed under the pretense of going out for ice cream. They began to drive away and did not stop. Along the way, he began to whistle Debussy's *Reverie,* which Trevor had told Natalie that Carter used to whistle as he beat Galen. Natalie felt his face and, from the stubble, realized that "Kyle" was actually Carter. She was unable to escape, and he took her to a houseboat. Trevor and Jeremy eventually rescued her, but not before Carter beat her as well.

Carter escaped and moved to the soap opera *Loving* to get even with Dinah Lee. On *Loving,* but not on *AMC,* Trevor and Jeremy finally apprehended Carter as he was about to strangle Dinah Lee. They brought him back to Pine Valley (and *AMC*). In the Pine Valley jail, Carter further prolonged his malevolence by pretending to be catatonic so as to avoid trial. Both Galen and Natalie visited him to try to break his act, but neither succeeded. He eventually was moved to Pine Valley Hospital for evaluation. Galen convinced the team of psychiatrists to allow her to be present during their examination. When she told the psychiatrists that Carter was an incompetent lover, he leaped up and threatened to kill her, destroying his catatonic facade.

In the story line's concluding scene, Natalie and Carter had a long discussion in Galen's presence in which he admitted that what he did to all of them was wrong and that he had a problem with women. He told Natalie that there was a "Kyle" inside of him somewhere. Galen and Natalie hugged and Carter never was seen again.

One characteristic of this story line, like those in all soap operas, is that it appeared to be nonauthored (Allen, 1983). Unlike most narratives, soaps create worlds that seem to have independent existences, as if the hour of the show were a window rather than a text. In fact, although they have head writers, soaps do not have single authors to whom one can attribute ownership of the stories. Soaps are produced by writing teams rather than by individual authors, and few (if any) writers ever remain with a show throughout its entire lifetime. This sense of authorlessness is textually enhanced by the fact that the narratives are constructed so that viewers have access to everyone's perspective rather than viewing all from one narrator perspective (Ang, 1989;

Geraghty, 1991; Modleski, 1984). In Carter's story line, the audience is given the potential to see things from the points of view of most every character involved.

The sense of *nonauthoredness* is further enhanced by the overwhelming size of the soap opera text, which "can be specified only as the sum of all its episodes broadcast since it began" (Allen, 1983, p. 98). The script for each episode is likely to be around 70 pages (Rouverol, 1984). The Carter Jones story line was told over 4 months, which is quite a long time compared to other narrative forms, but the presence of characters who had been on the show years prior to Carter's arrival gave it an even deeper history. Indeed, r.a.t.s. fans who criticized Brooke's behavior drew on events over a decade earlier to support their arguments. Because soap opera texts are so big, it is impossible for viewers, and even for writers, to know the entire stories (Seiter et al., 1989). A soap opera such as *AMC* has broadcast well over 5,000 hours of episodes from more than 350,000 pages of scripts in its decades on the air. (Compare this to the approximately 4,000 pages of Richardson's notoriously long 18th-century novel, *Clarissa*.) It would take nearly 30 weeks of constant viewing to watch it all, and in that time, 150 new hours would have been produced. This expansive text allows for the deep development of characters and their relationships that I have discussed.

This huge text also is temporally unique in that it is broadcast 5 days a week, every week, every year. The story never can end. There never is even a sense that resolution is possible or imminent (Geraghty, 1991). Soaps have an "absolute resistance" to the final resolutions that often are taken to be a defining characteristic of narratives (Allen, 1985). Even as Galen and Natalie hugged in the final scene of this *AMC* story line, viewers knew that new troubles would find them soon; indeed, within a few months, Natalie had died in a car accident.[10] Soap operas also use their luxury of time to pursue a plurality of story lines simultaneously. Characters with central roles in one story line might well be playing minor roles in others. Rouverol (1984) discusses a writers' *story meeting*:

> And everyone at the meeting has come up with ways to interweave the various stories because—as our newcomer soon learns—stories cannot run parallel only, they must carom against each other like billiard balls. What happens to Characters A and B, he learns, must have an impact on Characters C and D and a catastrophic effect on [Characters] E and F. The ripple effect even touches Characters G and

H. For a [1-] hour show, [8] to [10] story lines are needed—all inter-
woven. Each story line must be designed for growth; each must
contain contradiction and conflict and must promise suspense. Again
and again, each story line must resonate against the others. (p. 30)

The variety of stories ensures that at the end of every episode, most are
unresolved (Allen, 1985; Brunsdon, 1983). When single story lines are
resolved, secondary plots move into the central position. Because of
this, soap operas feature hundreds of plots over the years.

Soap operas also resist local resolutions, ending each episode with
a cliff-hanger and saving the biggest cliff-hangers for Fridays. Showing
these moments of maximal suspense just before temporal gaps in viewing encourages fans to use this time to think through and sometimes
discuss possible outcomes and interpretations (Allen, 1985; Ang, 1985;
Brunsdon, 1989; Geraghty, 1991; Nochimson, 1992).[11] Soap suspense is
generated by the continual disruptions that generate personal conflicts
and emotional entanglements for soap characters (Brunsdon, 1983;
Geraghty, 1991; Hobson, 1989). The more emotionally entangled the
characters, the more emotionally entangled the viewers. "When issues
are murky," writes Blumenthal (1997), "the audience has a harder time
deciding who is right and who is wrong and what an appropriate
punishment would be" (p. 56). As a result, there is more to consider
between shows.

Finally, soap operas are distinctive in that they skew the narrative
form through what Allen (1983, 1985), drawing on Eco, calls *overcoding*.
This means that soap operas carry far more signifying possibilities than
are necessary just to move the narrative forward. We are encouraged to
imagine many more ways in which the story could go than the route it
eventually will follow. Geraghty (1991) indicates that some of the technical ways in which this is accomplished include

the close-ups of faces, of important objects, the deliberate movement
of a character across a room, the lingering of the camera on a face at
the end of the scene, the exchange of meaningful glances—work to
make every gesture and action seem highly coded and significant,
marking out emotional relationships and enabling the audience to
understand the significance of every action. (p. 30)

Because soap operas are overcoded, the audience must generate its own
satisfactory explanations of what the narrative does not (Allen, 1985;

Geraghty, 1991; Livingstone, 1989). Rather than telling the audience how to feel, soaps allow for and encourage multiple interpretations, a fact that cannot be underestimated in explaining their appeal. As Livingstone (1990) examined in her insightful audience research, "A number of normative alternatives may be encoded in a text, so that different viewers may select different readings and yet remain within a dominant framework" (p. 83). Soap opera texts might suggest preferred readings, but they become meaningful through "the imposition of the individual's frame of reference upon the world of the text" (Allen, 1985, p. 89). Whereas the text might provide determinate conditions for its interpretation (Morley, 1989), the encounters between viewers and text are overdetermined (Ang, 1985). Furthermore, as Jenkins (1992) argues, the texts' provision of coded instructions for preferred readings do not necessarily subdue and overpower the readers. Viewers may build readings that resist the possibilities to which the text seems to limit them. Thus, there always are more possible readings than can be predicted from the text.

Viewers' interpretive processes rely on several factors. The emotional and social framework that we use to make sense of the shows is what Allen (1983) calls an *ideological code,* a common frame of experience that allows us to evaluate the stories. Allen elaborates three additional codes that expert soap viewers use. *Video-cinematic codes* decipher the logic behind the filming. If the camera movement is changed, for example, then a competent soap viewer will understand that this signals something important. *Generic codes* of the soap opera form include the use of time, space, style of acting, and multiple intersecting narratives. *Intertextual codes* are those that draw on other genres and texts, as when soap operas have mysteries or, as in the case of the Carter Jones story line, echo popular films (e.g., *Cape Fear*) and television shows (e.g., *Knots Landing*). Brunsdon (1983) proposes a similar framework, arguing that soap opera watchers need knowledge of the genre, the specific program, and "cultural knowledge of the socially acceptable codes and conventions for the conduct of personal life" (p. 80; see also Brunsdon, 1989).

To use all these codes, viewers watch soap operas in close and distant ways simultaneously. In close readings, viewers operate within the story's terms, accepting the characters and settings as real and suspending disbelief. At the same time, to use video-cinematic and generic codes, viewers must step outside the story world to view it as a constructed fiction. As I will elaborate in Chapter 3, distant viewing frequently generates viewer criticisms; competent viewers continually assess the shows' ideological messages, story construction, and (above all) realism, often finding them wanting (Ang, 1985; Hobson, 1989; Liebes & Katz, 1989; Seiter et al., 1989). Viewers also critique their own involvement, contemplating the contradictory pulls toward pleasure and cynicism (Ang, 1985; Brown, 1994; Liebes & Katz, 1989). Despite stereotypes, viewers are quite able to judge and to consciously resist the *message* of the text (Ang, 1985; Geraghty, 1991; Seiter et al., 1989).

Dismissing the Soaps, Take 2: Misreading the Genre or Its Viewers

Let us return again to the stereotype of soaps and their viewers as what one comedian called "thinking impaired," bringing this better under-standing of the soap opera text to bear. One source of the stereotype surely is the fact that most people who do not watch soap operas regularly see them in small doses, perhaps seeing only occasional scenes. What these viewers see is quite different from what regular viewers see; it is not hard to see why soaps would appear so absurd and their viewers so limited from this perspective. Any soap scene usually features two or three beautiful people having an intense conversation about their relationships or something that appears to be either too trivial to warrant such focus or too emotionally overwrought to be realistic. The camera lingers on their faces in a way that often seems hokey (even to fans), the sets are cheap, and the camera work is simplistic (compared to film or prime-time programs). Compared to an episodic show, there is very little happening. "How can this possibly interest people enough that they would watch 5 hours a week?" would seem to be an entirely appropriate question. Such people can be for-given for failing to recognize how much of the action they are unable to see.

Less forgivable are the textual analysts who have studied the genre closely yet have mistaken the audience that the text seems to imply for real viewers. Although scholars who have looked to the audience have recognized the distinction between "subject positions that a text con-structs" and the actual viewers who "may or may not take up those positions" (Brunsdon, 1983, p. 76), many theoretical and content-analytic textual analysts have not. By asserting what they take to be the "true" meanings of the shows, textual analysts often take themselves to have asserted something about the audience. Kilguss (1977), for example, concluded from her analysis of the themes of soap operas mentioned earlier that soaps reflect the female audience's strong dependency and rescue fantasies. "While not all viewers may be so naive," she writes, "the programs may also represent the primitive wishes of more sophisticated viewers" (p. 528). With only psychiatric inpatients as her sample viewers, Kilguss assumed that her analysis of the text reflected subconscious fantasies of all viewers. Arnheim (1944), similarly, took his reading of settings and characters to be a representation of the world the way the viewers would like it to be.

Although dated, Arnheim's (1944) work provides a wonderful example of just how patronizing "scholarly" deductions made about viewers from soap texts can be. He takes the mid-sized town setting, for example, to demonstrate that listeners prefer settings that reproduce their own rather than those that permit "access to the higher sphere of metropolitan life" (p. 38). Whereas he takes the early predominance of housewife characters to mirror their presence in the audience, he conveniently attributes the overabundance of professionals to the audience's aspiration to those positions. Arnheim attributes the absence of the truly rich in the early serials to the listeners' resentment of those who held such high positions.

Arnheim (1944) is at his worst, however, in his psychological analysis of the audience. He argues that soaps satisfy psychological needs "the easy way." They "evoke the satisfaction of being good oneself while others, unfortunately, are bad. Instead of opening the road toward humble self-knowledge, they nourish the cheap pleasure of self-complacency" while inviting "neither self-knowledge nor self-criticism." His analysis reaches its conclusion in what he calls his *psychological formula:*

> Our *psychological formula* could then be stated in about the following terms. Radio serials attract the listener by offering her a portrait of her own shortcomings, which lead to constant trouble, and of her inability to help herself. In spite of the unpleasantness of this picture, resonance can be enjoyed because identification is drawn away from it and transferred to an ideal type of the perfect, efficient woman who possesses power and prestige and who has to suffer not by her own fault but by the fault of others. This enables the listener to view (and to criticize) her own personal shortcomings, which lead to trouble, as

occurring in "other," less perfect creatures. Still, these shortcomings, being her own after all, are presented as springing from mere weakness of character; reform is possible and often achieved. No such tolerance is needed for the outside causes of the listener's suffering. Her resentment against them is confirmed and nourished by the introduction of the villain type, who personifies and assumes responsibility for any detrimental effects of nonpersonal forces (in whose immunity the listener is interested) such as the institutions of society. (pp. 60-61, italics in original)

Although seemingly more sympathetic to viewers because of their explicitly feminist stances, the works of Kilguss (1977) and Modleski (1983) perpetuate this image of the psychologically vulnerable viewer. Modleski, for example, argues that by showing so many characters' perspectives, soap operas "activate the gaze of the mother—but in order to provoke anxiety (an anxiety never allayed by narrative closure) about the welfare of others" (p. 70). Modleski adds, "In other words, both high art critics and politically oriented critics, though motivated by different concerns, unite in condemning daytime television for distracting the housewife from her real situation" (p. 74). Blumenthal (1997) locates the feminist mistrust of soaps in a concern that "women's identification with the feminine is a source of subordination" (p. 68). Because soap operas are about relationships and feelings, "the feminist movement has traditionally framed women's love of the soaps as a problem" (p. 68). This sort of critique implies profound doubt that women can manage their own experiences. These privileged academic readers, and they alone, are "in a position to decide what types of shows benefit women" (p. 81). "The arrogance lies in the belief that, unlike other people, certain theorists have located and articulated what is real and what matters, not just about their own lives but about everyone else's" (Jensen & Pauly, 1997, p. 160).

Soap opera viewers are neither texts to be read by researchers nor little, lost, emotional lambs to be shepherded to safety by critics. We are no different from anyone else, or at least we are as different from each other as we are from anyone else. Soap fans are thinking individuals, quite capable of making their own entertainment choices and evaluating their worth to culture and to themselves. Certainly, soap operas are not great art. Certainly, people sometimes are mindless when they watch soaps, and some people probably have an unhealthy absorption in the drama. But mindlessness and overengagement are potential drawbacks of most human activities, even those held in high cultural esteem. For many soap viewers, the joys of watching come not from the mindlessness but rather from the types of active engagement it entails, as viewers immerse themselves in an emotional world without real consequences, interpreting a world of story possibilities. There often is an element of escapism, but soap viewing is not inherently mentally passive.

As I will develop in the next two chapters, the joys of soap viewing need not be solitary; as soap viewers discuss soaps with one another, they become social. Soap operas offer people the chance to create relationships in which they can explore emotional reality together. Talking about the emotional dilemmas of soap characters "reinforces women's interest in relationships without enmeshing us in them, for it produces a location from which we can stand outside and analyze others' connections with each other without becoming implicated in the consequences" (Blumenthal, 1997, p. 105). The remaining chapters examine this social process of soap opera engagement in r.a.t.s. Throughout, we will see that the nature of the soap text and the types of involvement it encourages are very active social forces shaping practice in this audience community.

Notes

1. As with all posts quoted in this book, I have not corrected this one for spelling or grammatical errors. I have changed names, however, keeping gender consistent. Changing names was not a simple decision given that the posters, many of whom are quite clever writers, deserve authorship credit. However, they did not see themselves as research participants when they posted, so I have followed the research tradition of using pseudonyms.

2. Harrington and Bielby (1995) provide a discussion of psychological definitions of addiction and its inapplicability to soap viewing in any literal sense.

3. Harrington and Bielby (1995) suggest several ways in which soap viewers can be differentiated from each other including what they orient to in the show, which shows they watch, whether or not they have access to the actors, whether their interest is in the genre or a particular show, and whether or not they self-identify as fans.

4. There is no way in which to know for certain that the genders indicated in "from" lines are accurate reflections of the genders of the senders.

5. It is interesting to note that the percentage of men on r.a.t.s. seems to parallel that of the offline soap audience, yet women experience r.a.t.s. as having a greater percentage of men than do offline social circles. This suggests that the social pressures to hide one's soap involvement are greater for men. Indeed, as Blumenthal (1997) discusses and as r.a.t.s. participants describe, men often hide their soap involvement as humoring their wives' habit, a ruse that seems to fool few wives.

6. Phillips also is one of the few female University of Illinois alumni whose pictures hang in the student union's hall of famous alumni.

7. Particularly good descriptions of the production of soap operas can be seen in Rouverol's (1984) book on writing soaps and in Hobson's (1982) book on *Crossroads*.

8. William Bell, creator and head writer of *The Young and the Restless* (the most popular soap opera), also was one of Phillips's protégés.

9. For reasons of limited production space and finances, all of these spaces are represented rather than presented (Newcomb, 1974). Spaces generally are signified through one or two sets, none of which actually has four walls or a ceiling. Sets often are characterized by what Geraghty (1991) calls the "light entertainment aesthetic," which values color and shape. This aesthetic treats the settings with style excessive to the narrative. Although this is more true of the prime-time soaps of which she writes, continual supplies of fresh-cut flowers and endless elegant wardrobes are examples of how the light aesthetic colors daytime settings as well.

10. Given the elimination of closure, time becomes the basis for organizing the narratives (Geraghty, 1991). The enhanced role of dialogue that I have discussed stems from this quality. The temporal ramifications for structure also are seen in the multiple time flows (Brunsdon, 1983). Often, sequential scenes will depict characters in different locations at the same point in time. Some episodes will span a full day and night in the storyworld, whereas sometimes it takes a full week of episodes to cover a single day. However, single episodes rarely will show a time period longer than 24 hours (Rouverol, 1984).

11. Hayward (1997) traces historically how the structure of serial fiction has encouraged fans to interpret the text collaboratively from the novels of Charles Dickens through to soap operas.

2

Interpreting and Comparing Perspectives in the Audience Community

---

Take a typical scene on a soap opera. The setting is a lobby outside a courtroom where a kidnapping trial is in progress on *Port Charles*. Lucy paces nervously. When Karen enters the lobby from the courtroom, Lucy asks how the trial is going. Karen tears into her for letting Scott (the man on trial) believe that Lucy was his friend and then testifying against him. Demanding that Lucy never speak to her again, Karen storms off. What even short-term viewers know is that Lucy has only pretended to betray Scott to get information that might clear him. For the plan to work, it must be kept secret from everyone in town. The audience is left to wonder about the consequences that this will have for Lucy's relationships with the others in town as the charade continues. We can contemplate the plan's success and resolution or possible ways in which it could fail. If we have known Lucy since the character debuted as a dowdy librarian (who was secretly a sexy villainess) on *General Hospital* in 1986, then we can empathize with the pain this more benevolent and mature Lucy feels as she loses what little respect she has gained. We also can imagine her guilty thrill at enjoying this rare recent chance to scheme. The more we know about the show, the more we know about the characters, the more we see on the television screen when we watch our soaps. The story taking place on the screen is designed to stimulate multiple interpretations, and the pleasure of creating those interpretations is the main appeal of soaps.

It is no surprise, then, that when we turn to one another and talk about our soaps, the primary thing that we do is interpret them. When I asked people in rec.arts.tv.soaps (r.a.t.s.) to describe the newsgroup, they said that they share *opinions, predictions, plot ideas, parodies,* and other varieties of interpretation. The soap text relies on the interpretive practices of the audience to realize its potential (Allen, 1985; Geraghty, 1991). Soap operas encourage viewers to draw on different types of knowledge to interpret including knowledge of the shows' histories, knowledge of the genre's conventions, and personal knowledge of the social and emotional world. The apparent lack of authorship, and hence authorial intent, particularly encourages people to refer to their own experiences for meaning (Allen, 1983). When one brings a wide group of people together, as is the case in r.a.t.s., one gets a variety of information about the show and a range of worldviews. The access to this range of perspectives greatly enhances the pleasures of interpretation that the soap text offers. This chapter examines the audience practices that respond to these textual qualities and considers how making these practices collaborative changes what can be done with the soap text. I draw, in particular, on the analyses of post genre and agreements/ disagreements summarized in Appendixes B and C. In illustrating these phenomena, I draw on messages from the entire Carter Jones discussion (see Chapter 1). There are at least three types of evidence for the dominance of interpretation in r.a.t.s. besides textual analysis of the soap opera genre. First, and most obvious, the majority of posts are interpretive. Second, interpretive practices are unmarked in r.a.t.s., whereas noninterpretive posts are labeled in their subject lines. Third, interpretation often spills over into the marked genres despite their ostensibly noninterpretive focus.

Interpretation is the most commonly mentioned type of activity in survey responses, yet these labels rarely (if ever) appeared in the subject lines of the group's messages. Without a conventionalized label, in other words, a post is simply assumed to be interpretive. Indeed, the six genres that are labeled share the quality of being noninterpretive. They are social (*tangents* and *unlurkings*) or informative (*updates, spoilers, sightings,* and *trivia*). Only 16% of the total posts were in these named genres, and each named genre produced interpretive responses. Thus, 84% of the messages are interpretive.[1] Because the two social genres do not address the soap, I will postpone my discussion of them until Chapter 4. Here, I consider the unmarked and informative genres, both of which serve interpretation, the former directly and the latter indirectly.

Interpretive Practices

Personalization

One core practice in interpreting the soap is personalization, whereby viewers make the shows personally meaningful. They do this by putting themselves in the drama and identifying with its situations and characters. They also bring the drama into their own lives, making sense of the story in terms of the norms by which they make sense of their own experiences. This referencing from the world of the drama to the lives of viewers is the overriding way in which viewers relate to soaps (Hobson, 1989). If I watch a soap alone, the soap world is understood by reference to my own experience. In r.a.t.s., collaborative interpretation facilitates a sharing of personal experience, providing the opportunity to explore the story from others' vantage points. As Lauren, a 27-year-old Harvard pre-med student, describes it:

> Well, we start out with our discussions of the soap itself. But I find that people get very personally involved. . . . By personally involved, I mean that the watcher of a soap becomes almost a "virtual" character. Every viewer projects [his or her] own experiences onto what is happening on the soap, so everyone interprets the story lines a little differently. (1991 survey)

Because interpretation involves personalizations, people sharing interpretations inevitably share their worldviews and, more or less explicitly, share themselves.

As I discussed in Chapter 1, the drama invites viewer personalization in many ways including its wide range of characters with accessible perspectives and its focus on realistic emotional and relational themes.

When people discuss soaps, much of what they discuss are feelings, relationships, and the cultural norms and standards in which they are embedded. Several analyses of soaps and their fans have suggested that this chance to discuss feelings and relationships is what motivates soap discussion (Brown & Barwick, 1986; Harrington & Bielby, 1995, p. 177). Indeed, Brown (1994) argues that this opportunity to discuss private issues with others accounts for the pleasure of soap opera discussion. As one of Harrington and Bielby's (1995) respondents described, talking about soaps "has the satisfaction of gossip without the guilt because the people aren't real and can't be hurt or betrayed by what one says about them" (p. 119). There are more social pleasures at play than this (covert) socioemotional discussion, but all aspects of r.a.t.s. ultimately must be understood in light of the fact that soap operas invite discussion of emotional and domestic issues that normally are deemed to be private (Geraghty, 1991).

Character Interpretation

Brunsdon (1983) argues that to engage viewers in the central narrative question of what will happen, soap operas must engage viewers in the prior question of "What kind of person is this?" (p. 80). Indeed, most of the interpretation in r.a.t.s. centers on the characters. More than half (53%) of the participants' agreements and disagreements, for example, examined the meanings of characters' behavior. The next most discussed topic generated barely one third as many messages. Livingstone (1989, 1990) shows that differences in how viewers interpret story lines are rooted in differences in how they interpret characters. Much character interpretation involves personalization. Participants discuss what they would do in characters' positions and what they and others they know have done in similar positions (Hobson, 1990).

The most interpreted character in the Carter Jones story line was the ever-imperiled Natalie, whose character was taken over by a new actress, blinded, hospitalized, and kidnapped. Although it was really Carter who set the fire in which she was blinded, for a time, both Natalie and her husband, Trevor (who rescued her from the fire [Photo 2.1]), believed that Trevor had accidentally caused it. In this post, a woman questions whether the behavior of the just-recast Natalie is consistent with "the 'old' nat." The two women who respond draw on their own marriages to question the hospitalized Natalie's coldness toward

Photo 2.1. Trevor Saves Natalie (as played by Kate Collins) From the Burning House

SOURCE: ©1998 (Ann Limongello/ABC Inc.) Used by permission.

Photo 2.2. New Nat (Melody Anderson) Holds Trevor Responsible for Her Blindness
SOURCE: ©1998 (Ann Limongello/ABC Inc.) Used by permission.

Trevor following the fire (Photo 2.2). I will return to the issues raised in these messages about fan criticism in the next chapter. At this point, note how these women bring knowledge of themselves and their husbands to bear on understanding Natalie (even as they decide they are different from her):

```
>>nat is also having a grudge toward trevor...
>>something the "old" nat wouldn't do...i do
>>not like the attitude they are putting on nat!
>>very unreal!
```

```
>I also thought that this wasn't right. If my
>husband accidentally burned down the house and I
>got hurt I really don't think I would hate him
>for it. If anything I would try and not make him
>feel guilty.
```

```
I whole heartedly agree. I know my husband would
feel terrible. For goodness sake the man carried
her out of a burning home. I would have thought he
would have left her there if he did it on purpose.
The new Nat is jot not right. (August 26, 1992)
```

The next post continues the evaluation of Natalie, who has by now been kidnapped by the abusive Carter. The first poster questions Natalie. The second explains what she would do if she were Natalie. The third writer, who has embedded edited versions of these two previous posts in her own, explains Natalie's behavior from the point of view of someone who has been abused:

```
>>After bashing his head in with a (hot) frying
>>pan (GO NATALIE!), you would think Natalie
>>would have tried to either incapacitate Carter
>>(i.e., tie him up somehow) or (if it were me),
>>finish him off completely, rather

>But anyways I would be acting like I like
>Carter. At least I'd be alive when they found
>me! What good is this trying to fight him
>thing gonna do for her?? She can't get off the
>boat! He is just gonna beat her up again and
>again! If she was nice to him sooner or later he
>would really trust her and would think it was
>ok to let her off the boat.

This is called a survival technique. If Nat was
going to bash Carter, I agree with Janis...she
should have continued until his head was MUSH. If
not, she shouldn't have tried to bash him at all.
But as far as acting nice, Carter would have found a
reason to hit her, even if she WAS nice—that's the
way an abusive person is. ("What? You don't like
tomatoes in the omelette I made for dinner?"
BLAM!!!) It doesn't matter that he thinks he loves
her—anything she did to upset him would set him
off—even VERY minor things. What would Nat have done
the first time Carter wanted to kiss her or sleep
with her? (October 20, 1992)
```

Just as interpretations of Natalie's attitude toward Trevor drew on personal marital experience, this third woman's understanding of abuse is grounded in her own experience, a point she made explicit in a post nearly a month earlier:

```
I was on the receiving end just ONCE—but it was
enough to make me get an immediate annulment from
a mistake-of-a-marraige. AMC [All My Children]
portrayed my ex to a "T" (professional, likable)—
but completely lost me when they started this
ridiculous story with Nat. (September 30, 1992)
```

This poster, Lexine, was far from alone in bringing such traumatic personal experience to bear on the public interpretation of the story and its characters. In the post that follows, Esther summarizes a thread that has involved four posters and then brings her own experience to bear. The trigger for the first of these embedded messages was a scene in which Carter, having beaten Dinah Lee, enters the room in which Dinah Lee is hospitalized and argues that Dinah Lee caused his behavior:

```
>diane:
>>>>
>>>>Boy did this ever bring back nightmare
>>>>memories...I'm not after sympathy, but
>>>>want to tell that from experience, this is
>>>>*so* typical. My ex-husband did the same
>>>>thing (he wasn't as psycho as Carter, thank
>>>>God). He only hurt me when I asked for it!
>>>>Then, just to keep the peace, I'd end up
>>>>apologizing to *him*! He was alway
>>>>remorseful, cried & said it would never
>>>>happen again, etc, etc, etc...just like
>>>>they do on tv.
>
>pam:
>

>>>diane, I applaud you for getting out of such a
>>>destructive relationship! That took a lot of
>>>courage. Waytago, woman!
```

```
>
>dan:
>
>>I'll applaud too! NO human should ever have to
>>go through that!
>
>
>debbie:
>
>there are shelters and women's networking...
>but money is tight and it is hard and scary to
>leave a relationship...even a bad one. and
>women (my mom included) have been programmed to
>apologize for things that aren't our fault...
>brava, diane...
>--

And one of the ways you can pay them back is to
volunteer to help after you have gotten back on your
feet, that's what I did and it is very rewarding
work. The shelter I stayed at gives periodic
training to do things for them, like man their
hotline. I am becoming a paralegal and plan to offer
my services after I am out of school. I, also, man
the hotline for them.

Esther (October 16, 1992)
```

What is striking in this series of messages is how quickly and easily the lines between interpreting Carter's character, discussing one's own experience, and providing social support for one another disappear. Lexine, Diane, and Esther all share their histories as survivors of abuse, whereas Debbie shares her mother's history. All of these posters affirm the socioemotional norms that making the victim feel responsible is normal but wrong and that women in this position should leave these relationships, although it is difficult to do so. In their movement from immersion in the drama to bringing the drama into real life, these participants use the soap as an opportunity to affirm their own choices and to empower other abuse victims who might be reading their messages.

Although personalization like this is an important way in which participants make sense of soap characters, it is not the only one. In this thread, for example, participants rely primarily on the understandings they have developed about the character of Carter in his time on the soap, interpretations grounded in the show's previous events rather than their own lives. First, someone excerpts a summary of an episode and highlights the ambiguities of its implications:

```
>..meanwhile Carter is still at the bar at
>closing time. He's about to go, when...
>"& this just in...the house at 95 Hudson st.
>belonging to Detective Trevor Dillon & his Wife
>Natalie has just burned down. Mrs. Dillon & the
>Baby were seriously injured." The camera focuses
>on Carter's face as he mouths the word "NO!"

I didn't understand this!
Is this just an act to look like he is concerned?
Or is he really sorry he hurt Natalie/Mo instead
of Trevor? Or is he sorry Trevor is still alive
and probably gonna kill em! (August 18, 1992)
```

Within a few hours, Jennifer has posted an interpretation:

```
*I* THINK (this is IMNSHO)[2] that he wanted to give
the Dillon clan a "threat" and didn't mean to
actually cause harm. SO FAR all the anguish he's
caused has been mental and he probably either wanted
to start a small fire, which everyone would get out
of, or he wanted to start no fire but hoped the
Trevor would come back and find the soldering iron
by the rags. (August 18, 1992)
```

Anne offers her take on Carter's motivations, which differs from Jennifer's:

```
I think Carter is also dazed and confused. At first,
I thought what he's trying to do by being at the
restauraunt and having all the "witnesses" around
was to definitely set up his alibi. As Mimi
mentioned, why he is here, he couldn't possibly be
```

```
there! And then to act shocked, saddened and
surprised, adds to his "alibi." But then Jennifer
Anton says she thinks maybe he didn't intend for
the danger to be as severe as it was, just to
"shock" or scare Trevor. I *didn't* think so.
It looked pretty deliberate to me, esp. causing
the explosion. He knew that would happen. What
was that "thing" on the ground outside that Derek
didn't see yet anyway?

But then this whole scenario of "going to confess
his sins" throws my theory off! :-( Unless he also
goes to confess to act out his "I couldn't have been
there, I feel terrible" routine. (August 18, 1992)
```

Jennifer responds to Anne, seeking to clarify her interpretation:

```
*I*'m going to still argue the point. It's not
that I think that Carter is really good deep down
and didn't WANT to actually HURT anybody—but from
the way he treated (and is treating) Galen he seems
to enjoy playing mind games. He'd rather hurt
someone mentally BEFORE he hurts them physically.
Sort of like a cat with a mouse—the cat will PLAY
with the mouse for a while until kitty becomes
hungry and decides to eat the mouse. So—Carter
wanted to scare the Dillon clan by starting a
fire—or ALMOST starting a fire and then having
Trevor "wonder" because he would have "known" that
he unplugged the soldering iron and left it on the
table. (August 18, 1992)
```

Anne responds with a compromise interpretation that seems to settle the issue:

```
Ok Jennifer, I'll give you the credit. You are
definitely right about him not having planned on
anything happening to Natalie and Mighty Mo (I like
this name for her). Carter didn't say that he didn't
want to harm Trevor tho! I still have no idea how he
could think this wouldn't hurt anyone (physically I
mean). I still think he intended bodily harm or
```

```
death to Trevor, but of course I am not sure of
this. (August 19, 1992)
```

In one sense, soap operas are a game in which the text offers clues
to how the plots will unfold and viewers use those clues to unravel the
shows' puzzles. The clues used in the preceding series of messages are
the previous scenes involving Carter and the history of his behavior that
has developed. Fans also draw on their understanding of the genre itself
to speculate on characters' intentions (Allen, 1983). Modleski (1983)
explains this further, writing in her pejorative style, "Not only are the
characters on soap operas impelled to fathom the secrets of other
people's minds, the constant, even claustrophobic, use of close-up shots
stimulates the audience to do likewise. Often, only the audience wit-
nesses characters' expressions" (p. 69).[3] Because viewers recognize the
narrative coding behind the close-up of Carter's face, they are able to
enter the play of the construction process through readings of internal
conventions. Doing this together allows participants to draw on clues
they might not have noticed themselves.

This next post illustrates a similar process. It is posted just after
Carter, disguised as "Kyle," abducted Natalie. Charlie and Stephen
(nicknamed "Dr BJ" because he is a doctor who always wears blue
jeans) discover that Natalie is missing from her hospital bed. Natalie's
son, Timmy, describes Natalie's creepy and mysterious friend "Kyle,"
who he knew visited her frequently and who he did not trust. It is
ambiguous whether Charlie and Stephen have realized from Timmy's
description that Natalie has been kidnapped by Carter. Note how the
posters draw on "exchanged looks" to interpret this ambiguity:

```
>After Timmy gives a complete description of
>"Kyle," including the scruffy beard (notice
>Carter is the only man in PV [Pine Valley]
>besides Lucas with *any* facial hair), and
>neither Charlie nor Dr. BJ figure out it *might*
>be Carter....
>
>Ron
```

```
My take on that scene was different from yours, Ron.
From the way Charlie and Steven exchanged looks over
Timmy's head, I think they *did* know it was Carter.
```

```
They were just trying not to alarm Timmy. Remember
how they wanted to take him home right after that,
but Timmy talked them out of it?
```

Note also that in proposing that Stephen and Charlie did not want to alarm Timmy, the poster finds no need to elaborate the assumption that adults would want to protect children from uncertain bad news, instead relying on her audience to share that socioemotional norm.

Speculation

Most of the interpretation we have seen here is speculative in one form or another. People speculate on the meanings behind characters' overt behaviors. One of the most common forms of speculation, which has been stressed in previous research on soap operas, is prediction of future events. Harrington and Bielby (1995), for example, argue that "collective speculation about upcoming events takes up the bulk of time spent talking about soaps and, indeed, seems most enjoyable to participants" (p. 129). Although prediction does not take up the bulk of time in this corpus (character interpretation does), prediction is a common practice. Perhaps because this group knows the genre so well, speculations do not often rely on personalization. In making predictions, these fans usually draw on the genre's narrative codes, as seen in this example:

```
>(They do still have to have Galen and Carter
>come face to face, right?)

Nope. Not face to face yet...Carter will, of
course, see Galen and give her that killer look
from behind the shrubs, but she can't see *him*
yet! (July 26, 1992)
```

Fans also draw on aspects of the genre external to the narrative. This poster, for example, draws on the show's opening sequence:

```
Hey, looks like Galen will be sticking around PV
for a while. Her picture finally got added to the
opening. (October 9, 1992)
```

We will see another example of bringing this type of extranarrative
information to bear on interpretation when I discuss the interpretive
consequences of informing.

It is quite common in r.a.t.s. for fans to speculate on what they
would like to see happen, even when they recognize that the events they
imagine surely will not occur. These story line suggestions draw on the
pretense of speculating but move beyond it, sometimes breaking the
boundaries of soap opera convention. Here is an example of an agreement about a story line suggestion concerning the desired exploits of
Timmy and his dog, Harold:

```
>While I'm fantasizing, I would like to see Timmy
>single-handledly (ok Harold can help) save
>everybody in PV from the evil Carter Jones.
>Timmy gets Carter on his way out of the room, he
>grabs his arm, he pushes it behind Carter's back
>and pushes on it real hard, Carter winces, and
>Trevor pushes in the door and throws the
>handcuffs on him, Timmy saves the day! :-)
>Ya right, but it sounds good, doesn't it?
>:-)
>
>Anne
```

```
I'm with you there, Anne. But I'd have Timmy try
to get Carter who slips away and makes it outside
the hospital. Harold then breaks free from his
leash (tied to a waiting room couch while Timmy
visits Mom), runs outside and trees Carter.
Timmy catches up with them, runs back to call
Trevor and then goes back to wait with Harold until
the PV police arrive. Carter dangles precariously
from a tree limb with Harold nipping at his heels
while we learn that Carter has a terrible fear of
dogs and becomes a snivelling blob, anxious for the
police to arrive and 'save' him from Harold.
(October 12, 1992)
```

Fans might even end up creating their own texts, as in the case of
Star Trek fans who write their own stories about the Enterprise and its

crew (Jenkins, 1992). However, as Harrington and Bielby (1995) argue, there is far less of this in soap fandom, perhaps because the story itself is unfolding daily. In soaps, some of the elaborate speculations and predictions might be taken to constitute a similar, although perhaps more text-dependent, sort of fan fiction.[4] In this example, a fan imagines an outcome for this story, drawing on the much-discussed (and decried) story line in which Natalie ("Doll," "Nat," "NotNat") was thrown down a well and left to die by her sister, Janet ("Janut," "Nut"), who assumed her identity (I have edited out the first eight points):

Next time I rewrite the script in my dreams:

9. NotNat will lose her not-so-strong-hold on her sanity. Will go totally ballistic and we will discover that NotNat really was not Nat, but was Janut being Nat because Nat really lost it when she was in the well and through "Sleight of Camera," we all missed the switcheroo! So the Doll who wasn't Doll really was Doll and NotNat is not Nat but Nut and Nut is Doll but Doll went nuts so Nat and NotNat are both nuts. And Trevor will get confused. (Depending on how the actress does in these roles, I may or may not write her out). (October 22, 1992)

This type of creative speculation arises in r.a.t.s. because there is an audience to appreciate it. Collaborative interpretation, as we will see repeatedly, offers the chance to perform for one's fellow fans.

Informative Practices

Most of the posts that are marked by genre in subject lines are informative and often are historical (although that history might be quite recent). As with interpretation, fans share knowledge of the show's history in part because the genre demands it (Seiter, Borchers, Kreutzner, & Warth, 1989). Any soap has broadcast more material than any single fan can remember. Furthermore, because soap operas are shown so frequently, many fans miss shows for days, weeks, or even years. Although the redundancy soaps use to compensate for this has been the source of countless parodies, the scripts are in fact selective in which history they emphasize and often refer to a past that is not fully explained.

Updates

Perhaps the core institution of r.a.t.s. is the update genre. Whereas newspapers and other media have long given brief daily or weekly synopses of soaps, r.a.t.s. updates are far more developed, averaging 172 lines (posts in other genres average 24 lines). Updates and the responses they generate account for 16% of the messages, making it the genre most frequently identified in subject lines. Marked by "update" and the show's date in the subject line, these posts retell the daily episodes. The *AMC* update was originated in 1984 by Anne, an administrative secretary who is one of the few remaining early participants of r.a.t.s. and one of the most prolific. Noticing that there were no posted summaries, Anne took it on herself to write them. When she received grateful e-mail in response, she decided to continue, for a time writing all five weekly updates herself.

The updates allow people who are not able to actually watch the shows to keep up with them. Marking the updates consistently in the subject lines allows readers to go directly to them. If their only need of the group is to keep up with the show, then the marked updates save them a tremendous amount of time. Many people follow the shows through the updates, seeing the shows only when ill or on vacation. Lauren, for example, tells me that "I'm at work all day, and I haven't the presence of mind to tape the show. This way, I can keep up with the stories, and for the 2 or 3 days a year I can actually watch the show, I know who is who" (1993 survey). Danielle expresses similar concerns:

> There are just not enough hours in the day, and AMC is not at the top of my priority list. Gotta cook dinner, go to the park or take a walk, get ready for tomorrow, and my husband just thinks soaps are sooooo stupid, I don't watch them much when he's there. The only time I really watch my tapes are when I am cooking dinner, so they only get part of my attention. Reading the updates on r.a.t.s. is such a time-saver! (1993 survey)

The almost daily pleas for updates from new participants (who do not realize that each day has a preassigned updater) continually reinforce the need for updates. The marking of updates also allows people to avoid them if they have the episodes on tape but have not seen them yet (as often was the case with me).

On the one hand, updates are a reflection of the soap text, seeking to summarize it as fully as feasible. On the other hand, they are necessarily transformations of that text, as their writers lift it out of television and reformulate it for the computer screen. One significant aspect of this transformation is that the retold soap text becomes loaded with the narrative style and interpretations of its retellers.[5] Updaters are storytellers as well as reporters. In translating the story from television to computer post, they choose to convey the drama as well as the events. Consider this brief excerpt from a fairly typical update summarizing the Carter Jones story line developments:

```
OK fellow amcers, here is my first attempt at a
full update. Hope you enjoy it.

Today's episode: Men on the move!!!!!!!!
{from least to most interesting}
1) Carter and Nat (AKA The Fly)

Not much new here. Carter is still playing his
mind games with the Fly. He brought her a tape
of the Four Seasons (Vivaldi), which Nat plays
in the incorrect order (going from summer to
spring). Trev also visits and the strain in the
relationship is beginning to show. Watch out
well, Nat is coming home!!!!!! (September 22,
1992)
```

The selection of which points to emphasize, the reordering of the show's temporal sequence so that each story line is grouped together, and the pervasive embedding of opinions all serve to render the retelling more engaging. One participant, Jamie, writes, "To tell you the truth, the updates are more fun than the shows. . . . It adds so much more to the shows" (1993 survey). Indeed, updates are designed to entertain those who have already seen the shows. "I rarely read the updates in-depth since I watch the show for myself," writes another woman, Carrie. "The updaters' personal comments are of more interest to me than the updates themselves" (1991 survey). Updates often are filled with group humor, sometimes in response to the show's shortcomings, and like story line suggestions, they often are a form of individual performance, points I will elaborate in Chapter 5.

Despite these interpretive dimensions of updates, informing is their primary duty. Interpretations frequently are framed as separate from the retelling. One way in which this is accomplished is by stating opinions upfront and then using a transition such as "and now on to the update." Another, more common technique is to embed commentary in brackets with or without the prefix "Ed. note:" to separate it clearly from the story, as in these examples:

```
Carter returns and tells Nat she is never going back
to PV. They are now anchored in the middle of a
river. They will stay there "forever." Nat wants to
go back to Trevor and Timmy, but Carter tells Nat
that HE is now the one she is GOING TO LOVE! [Now
guys, I don't suggest trying to woo a woman with
this approach...] Nat tries to argue, but Carter
starts getting angrier and angrier with her. "I will
MAKE YOU love me!" he says. (October 14, 1992)


2) Catatonic.....


NOT! Cater loses it and attempts to choke Galen.
After they pull off carter and shackle him, the soon
to be unemployed Ms. Henderson gets in a few digs.
Then Nat says she wants to talk to Carter. Everyone
leaves except Nat, Trev and Carter. (ED Note: Yeah,
like they would let that happen. This guy just
assualted someone. Dr. Tolan, may I see your licence
and regiestration please?) (November 9, 1992)
```

Although people occasionally will modify an update in a later post, it is more common for responses to excerpt the relevant section of the update to launch interpretations. This was seen in the discussion debating Carter's intentions in burning down the Dillons' house, where an update was used to raise the ambiguity of Carter's intentions. Other discussion of updates is more task oriented, arranging updater switches or substitutions, requesting updates, thanking the updaters for their work, or praising them for performative skill.

Spoilers

Whereas updates retell, spoilers pretell, repeating previews culled from magazines, personal appearances, and other computer networks.[6] Following a Usenet-wide convention, these are called *spoilers* in the subject line. In contrast to updates, credibility is an important issue underlying spoilers. Those that come from less reputable sources, such as the supermarket tabloid *The Star*, are explicitly marked in the post as dubiously credible, as are those that appear in reputable sources as *predictions* rather than as *previews*. This is a spoiler that proved inaccurate (although it came from a reputable source):

```
On our local morning show here in Cleveland, The
Morning Exchange (remeber Fred Griffith, Sue?) we
have the thrice weekly maven of soapdom, Lynda
something-or-other, who answers questions and
provides spoilers. This morning she said that
Natalie will get her sight back but not for a while
because her story line is going to involve a seeing
eye dog. According to the maven there has never been
a soap line involving a guide dog so AMC is going to
play it for a while. (October 7, 1992)
```

Like updates, spoilers sometimes offer interpretive reactions to the development, although many spoilers do not include opinions. By contrast, responses to spoilers are highly evaluative, voicing opinions on whether or not the events described are desirable and how they are likely to unfold. This woman, for example, responds to a spoiler with what turned out to be a fairly accurate prediction, simultaneously stepping away from the fictional reality to speculate on how the show will handle the forthcoming recasting of Natalie (it had been posted that the actress was going to be replaced). This post exemplifies the use of both narrative codes and extranarrative information in predictive speculation. Note also the poster's expertise in Natalie's marital history:

```
>Next Week:
>Carter plots his revenge. Helga seeks a remedy to
>her problem.
>
>
```

```
I predict that part of Carter's revenge will have
something to do with Nat (getting back at Trevor who
has been on his case). Nat kept going on the other
day about break ins in the neighborhood where the
new house is and I'm pretty sure they showed Carter
"lurking" outside. Then they'll get into a car wreck
or maybe there will be an explosion (ala Max on OLTL
[One Life to Live]) which will require Nat to have
plastic surgery, and wa-la, a New Nat! I hope they
do *something* to explain a new Nat, since she's
been on for soooo long and not pull one of those
"the part of Natalie Marlowe Hunter Cortlandt
Chandler Dillon is now being played by Melody
Anderson" things. (did I leave anybody out? |-)
(August 6, 1992)
```

Unlike most of the other genres, spoilers and their subsequent discussion are identified so that they can be avoided. The use of the label provides a barrier between the viewer who does not want to know what will happen ahead of time and the preview. This shield often is repeated in the text of the message with the inclusion of another warning and then a screen full of blank lines before the message or a special character (^L) which prevents the rest of the message from appearing before the reader tells it to appear. This ability to read the group without spoiling the show's suspense is appreciated. As one longtime r.a.t.s. participant explains, "I have found that reading the 'spoilers' every week detracts from my enjoyment of the show. I like being surprised by the show, not by the group! Sometimes I read them anyway, but the majority of the time I do not" (Carrie, 1991 survey). Others like knowing the spoilers. Another participant tells me, "If there is a spoiler and I already know what's going to happen, I feel more free to do chores while I'm 'watching.' It also prepares me. Reading a spoiler does not 'spoil' it for me" (Linda, 1991 survey). That many r.a.t.s. participants know the events before they happen suggests that Allen (1985) is right in his claim that viewers watch soap operas not so much to see *what* will happen as to see *how* it will happen.

Trivia

A third informative genre identified in subject lines is trivia. Here is a typical trivia post appearing with the subject line "AMC: Trivia Quiz":

```
Hi, all you folks who love amc and quizzes! I have
been discussing some interesting points with granma
to see what we could remember and thought some of
the rest of you might like searching your brains or
learning some amc history. I also thought maybe Anne
would like a chance to take a quiz for a change! (My
apologies to all if these questions have come up
before.)


1. Whose picture has been in the All My Children
   book besides Susan Lucci's? What role did that
   person play?

2. What is the link between Myrtle Fargate and
   Phoebe Wallingford?

3. Who was Charlie's biological grandmother on
   his father's side?

4. What man have both Brooke and Donna fooled
   around with?

5. What man have both Phoebe and Mona slept with?

6. Which two families have both Chuck and Erica
   been in?

7. In all the time you've watched amc, what did
   *you* think was the funniest scene?

Good luck! (February 25, 1992)[7]
```

In this trivia post, the poster and another community member thought up the questions themselves. Other times, this genre repeats published trivia questions, usually from trivia cards, games, or books and magazines about *AMC*. The questions, all of which address historical plots and characters, are posted without answers and without evaluative commentary, as you see here. Questions often are numbered, and blank spaces are left between so that people can insert their answers in replies. In contrast to updates, where updaters are expected to interpret as they inform, trivia posters limit themselves to conveying the questions and, when people have posted their guesses, posting the correct answers. However, the posted answers occasionally spin off into highly evaluative and extended discussions of the show's past. Trivia is named in the group as a borrowing from the broader culture of American entertainment in which r.a.t.s. is nested. Trivia games and game shows have formalized a genre of interactive play based on testing one's store of minute and trivial bits of information. The use of trivia lists on r.a.t.s. carries that game into the r.a.t.s. situation. This is one of several ways in which discourse in r.a.t.s. adapts genres from other fields.

Sightings

Sightings, marked as such in the subject line, are reports of having seen a current or former soap opera actor in another context. The contexts include live public appearances; roles in movies; and televised appearances on talk shows, prime-time shows, and commercials. In this case, a poster reports spotting Carter elsewhere:

```
Last night my kid rented a movie and watched it.
It was called "Neverending Story Part II." Carter
(John Wesley Shipp) is in it as the father of the
kid who is the star. Has anyone else seen this
movie? According to my kid, he is not in Part I
of the same movie, but she is only 3. However,
she is very familiar with all of the characters on
AMC. Anyway, JWS [John Wesley Shipp] looked just
like he does on AMC. The part is completely
different as he is a nice guy in this movie.
(October 12, 1992)
```

Reports of live appearances are told as highly evaluative first-person narratives. A report will include descriptions of the setting, the audience, the actor's physical appearance, and recaps of question/ answer sessions or actor performances. The teller also describes her or his emotional reactions and usually repeats a preview or two gleaned from the sighting. Reports of talk show appearances are similar but usually without the descriptions of setting and audience. Reports on other acting performances such as guest spots and commercials often focus on the actor's appearance or, as in the preceding example, on the actor's role on the soap. Responses to sightings confirm them, correct them, and elaborate on these same themes.

The Interpretive Functions of
Informative Practices

Although all four of these genres are primarily informative and seem to be marked because of their informative nature, none works only to inform.[8] When interpretation does not pervade the posts themselves, the responses they generate are overwhelmingly interpretive. For the most part, then, information is used for interpretive purposes. Updates are used to situate evaluations, and spoilers launch interpretive discussion, as do trivia and (sometimes) sightings. Knowledge relevant to interpretation may involve fans' personal experiences, narrative history, extratextual knowledge, and the like. The information culled from soap magazines, star appearances, commercial computer networks, and other sources outside of the soap opera fiction affects fans' interpretations of the show, as this post about the actors who played Trevor and the original Natalie indicates:

```
>I gotta know this: What is the story between
>James Kiberd and Kate Collins? Don't they get
>along? (I need some juicy gossip here!) :)
```

```
There have been lots of rumors about the fact that
Kiberd and Collins don't get along. It all started
WAY back when Collins found out that Nat's "new"
love interest was going to be Trevor. According to
the Soap Rags, she ran into her dressing room in
tears.
```

```
There hasn't been a lot said recently about this.
I saw Jean LeClerc (Jeremy) at a Woman's Show last
month, and he said eveyone on the set (including
Collins and Kiberd) got along just fine. LeClerc
also lavished praise on Collins for her recent
performance of Nat/Janet.
```

```
Someone who saw Kiberd last year said he hinted that
Collins was a lesbian, but again, I heard LeClerc
say he once had a "relationship" with Collins (now
they are just friends), and she is currently
"involved" with someone. Either way, it's her
```

```
business and really has nothing to do with her
ability to act.
```

```
However, it *does* seem that the chemistry that used
to be there between Kiberd and Collins (when they
play Nat & Trevor) just isn't there anymore...
They used to have a LOT more spark! (May 14, 1992)
```

As we have seen, the temporal expanse of soaps allows characters to develop over periods of months and even years, and it encourages audiences to draw on deep history in understanding current events. Retellings and resulting reminiscing about the show's past allow participants more insight into the current episodes. For example, when Brooke hired Carter to work at her magazine, many r.a.t.s. participants were dismayed. This man who knew the show's history was especially certain that Brooke never would have done this and, to support his claim, retold for the others how Brooke herself had been victimized by a stalker many years earlier:

```
How in *heck* can Brooke so easily dismiss Steve's
worries concerning Carter when she herself, a
longgggggg time ago, was stalked by a deranged man
(Remember that song he kept playing over and over
again, something by the Police— Every Move That
She Makes). (July 31, 1992)
```

Keen soap fans are aware of the external pressures on soaps, including contract negotiations and changes in writers, and are aware of how story lines are constructed around these pressures (Geraghty, 1991). The pervasive sharing of such information online allows fans to use this expertise in interpreting the shows. Thus, pooling information broadens everyone's basis for interpreting the text. One fan put it this way: "You'd be amazed at how much information these people know. It adds so much more to the shows. I could go on and on" (Jamie, 1993 survey).

Social Functions of
Pooling Perspectives

I have already argued that collaborative interpretation offers the opportunity to negotiate personal and private socioemotional issues in a public space. This is one of the appeals of r.a.t.s., and as I will discuss in Chapter 4, it is essential to the friendliness ethic that organizes interpretive practice in r.a.t.s. However, one need not always look so deep to see the pleasures of collaborative interpretation. If one understands soap viewing as a game of making meanings from clues, then the collaborative provision of multiple readings and multiple clues has obvious benefits. No longer limited by one's own time constraints and limited knowledge, the game becomes bigger and more fun to play. The more players, the better.

For people who watch the show regularly, the main reason to read r.a.t.s. is to see the variety of ways in which people have interpreted the show. "Half the fun of watching," says Laurie, a 30-year-old computer applications engineer, "is comparing notes and speculations with others!" (1991 survey). When people have access to each other's readings of the show, they are able to rethink what they have seen, interpreting it from their own perspectives and then again from others' perspectives, giving them "a different slant on the subject matter" (Erin, 1991 survey). As Kelly, a 21-year-old undergraduate student, describes, "When I think something a character said meant one thing and another poster thinks it meant another, I will try to look at it the other way. I also notice things when people point them out that I might not otherwise notice" (1991 survey). Like Kelly, several survey respondents indicate that their attention to the show is reshaped in part by access to others' perspectives. Carrie, a 38-year-old administrative associate, explains that "r.a.t.s. has definitely affected the way I watch AMC and the things I notice about characters and settings" (1991 survey). Kelly and Carrie, like most survey respondents, insist that the access to others' interpretations does not usually change their fundamental attitudes toward characters. Debbie, an active participant, writes, "I enjoy reading r.a.t.s. and hearing about . . . other people's opinions of the characters, but I have been watching since 1983, and my opinions are pretty well formed" (1991 survey). On the other hand, participants do indicate that access to others' information can alter their interpretations of characters. Zoey says, "Often, the insights of others get me changing the way I view a character or a story line (e.g., someone provides history of a show I wasn't aware of, or someone points out an aspect I didn't see before)" (1991 survey). For new viewers, this collaborative interpretation can serve as training, helping them to become more sophisticated interpreters of the genre.

Another benefit to collaborative interpretation is the possibility of expressing one's emotional responses to the show to a sympathetic audience. When participants "share these 'emotional outbursts' with the other r.a.t.s.'ers" (Jennifer, 1991 survey), they expose one another to a wide range of emotional reactions to the show as well as to their private selves. For participants, "it adds a whole other dimension to my viewing enjoyment to discuss or vent about something that happened on my soap" (Emma, 1993 survey). For those participants who get to read these emotional responses, pleasure can be enhanced through the opportunity to empathize with others' feelings. If the game of soap viewing involves reveling in vicarious emotion, then access to the emotions of other fans further enhances that game. "If there's a scene between characters Netters dislike a lot," explains Joan, a 28-year-old computer programmer, "it encourages me to read r.a.t.s. and read the anguish felt by them. It's kind of amazing to me how intensely some people feel about certain characters on the soap" (1991 survey).

In this chapter, I have considered the ways in which the soap invites participation and how the interpretive and informative practices in r.a.t.s. enhance fans' pleasure in the show, allowing them to gain more interpretations and vicarious emotional experience from the text. But r.a.t.s. informative and interpretive practices carry a range of other pleasures that cannot be fully explained by direct reference to the text. As I will further discuss in chapters that follow, participants in r.a.t.s. pursue both group and individual rewards as they interpret and inform together. In terms of the group, this ongoing process of exploring interpretive possibilities in-depth implicitly defines these practices as worthwhile endeavors. By writing these messages, the participants in r.a.t.s. are actively constructing a social environment in which taking soaps seriously is considered appropriate rather than a waste of time. From an individual perspective, these opportunities to voice interpretations and offer information are chances to demonstrate genre competence, creativity, and expertise to others, gaining social status and pleasure from the affirmations that posts receive. Before examining this social dimension of collaborative interpretation in-depth, I turn to the ways in which fans are critical of the text and how they transform their criticisms into further entertainment.

Notes

1. Readers of newsgroups will know that digressions occur and that subject lines cannot be taken as a guarantee of their contents. However, even if noninterpretive discourse of one type or another sneaks into threads eventually, the vast majority of these unmarked and responsive posts remain interpretive.

2. IMNSHO = in my not so humble opinion (one of many acronyms used online).

3. Jenkins (1992) also makes the point that fans are capable of reading the history of a program into looks, inflections, and other subtle performance cues to what the character "had to be thinking."

4. For a time, r.a.t.s. participants did create their own soap opera, *Shifting Sands*. More recently, soap fan fiction has become more common, often being published on the World Wide Web.

5. It has been noted repeatedly that soap opera fans enjoy retelling the soap narrative for fans who are less informed (Brown, 1994; Geraghty, 1991; Hobson, 1982; Jenkins, 1992).

6. Magazines cited in spoilers include *Soap Opera Digest, Soap Opera Weekly, Soap Opera Monthly,* and *Soap Opera Now.* The two commercial networks referenced are Prodigy and GEnie.

7. There were no trivia posts pertaining to the Carter Jones story line.

8. Not all informing occurs in marked genres. For example, requests for background knowledge in the unmarked (soap interpretive) genre often are answered with retelling of the shows' deep histories.

3

It's Only a Soap: Criticism, Creativity, and Solidarity

S tereotypical visions of soap opera fans assume that viewers cannot rationally evaluate the show and that they
instead mindlessly absorb all it has to offer. In Chapter 2, we saw that
even when fans are closely involved in interpreting the shows, they rely
on conventionalized generic cues, indicating that they watch from a
distance even as they immerse themselves within the story world. For
example, changes in the opening sequence or knowledge of the genre's
conventions are used to predict upcoming events. When fans step away
from the story world, as the text demands, they inevitably wind up
evaluating the construction of that world. Like all fans, soap viewers
continually assess the show's quality and their own relationship to the
genre, resulting in both positive and negative evaluations. All participants in the rec.arts.tv.soaps (r.a.t.s.) newsgroup care about the show,
are invested in it, and respect this in one another. This is clear in the
amount of time and energy exerted in contributing viewpoints to the
ongoing discourse and the general lack of challenges to these practices
(the *flame* noted in Chapter 1 was a rare exception). At the same time,

the soap opera regularly falls short of what fans would like; the story lines are flawed, the acting sometimes is poor, the writing is inconsistent, and the props are cheap. Even without the shame that stems from soaps' stigmatization, soap viewers often feel ambivalent about the show. They love it, yet they see its flaws and often feel that the writers assume that they are less intelligent than they really are (Harrington & Bielby, 1995).

The discourse in r.a.t.s., as the excerpts in Chapter 2 suggest, is highly evaluative and often quite critical. Of the 121 agreements and disagreements over the Carter Jones story line, for example, 38% contained negative evaluations of the soap opera. Just as they are used for interpretive purposes, the information one has about the soap, one's understanding of the genre, and one's understanding of reality also are used as criteria by which to continually assess the show. As we will see, criticism is not just the limit that tempers involvement; it also can be a type of involvement in its own right, one that can be just as pleasurable as the more accepting involvement highlighted in Chapter 2.

Evaluating the Soaps

Keeping an Eye on Quality

Many of the criticisms fans have of their soaps are relatively minor, even nit-picky. These criticisms might challenge their attachments to particular characters or story lines but not to the shows or genre. In the discussion of the Carter Jones story line, r.a.t.s. fans frequently challenged the worth of the story line, its characters, and its actors. Early in the story line, for example, fans already were expressing skepticism about the story and its central character, with one fan writing, "I am tired of stories of men stalking women, and this guy is such a sleaze there's no interest in it for me at all" (September 6, 1992). The characters of Galen and Stephen, both of whom were new to the show, were repeatedly dismissed as uninteresting or annoying:

> I would like to be on the "GET RID OF GALEN"
> commitee! Blah! Sqinty-eyed, pain in the butt to
> everyone and putting half the town in danger because
> she's trying to prove something. Doesn't she realize

```
how many peoples' lives are twisting around for
her?!(Whew, glad I got that off my chest!)
(September 21, 1992)
```

Fans continually evaluate the quality of the acting. Although soaps have a reputation for bad acting, fans generally recognize the pressures under which soap opera actors operate and fully appreciate the many brilliant actors on daytime shows.[1] Many fans in r.a.t.s. admired John Wesley Shipp's portrayal of Carter. However, fans also recognize weak performances, and poor acting tends to undermine their interest in the characters. In this particular story line, the acting skills of new additions to the cast—Carter, Galen, Stephen, and the recast Natalie—were continually assessed. Although people sometimes admired acting while dismissing the character (especially in the Shipp/Carter case) or suggested that a character was worthwhile but poorly portrayed, this post demonstrates how intertwined evaluations of acting, character, and story line often become:

```
I wanted to throw in my two cents to the discussion
of Galen/Carter storyline. My editor is acting up
...sorry. Anyway, I think the actress who plays
Galen, aside from being probably the worst actress
since the Angie replacement, doesn't deserve the
fine acting job done by the Carter villain.....I
think he is EXCELLENT. The best villain since the
early days of Sean Cudahy. He is definitely
unpredictable. (September 8, 1992)
```

R.a.t.s. fans also were quick to criticize the actors' appearances (e.g., the first Natalie's apparent weight gain and her replacement's immovable hair that earned her the nickname "Tweetie," Carter's stubbly beard and outdated "Miami Vice" look), the sets (e.g., the reuse of landscapes from previous story lines), and many minor details of the writing such as the scene in which the recently blinded Natalie was learning how to use the phone:

```
I may be in the minority on this one, but I like the
new actress playing Nat. The writers are screwing up
on her storyline though.
I mean, memorizing the buttons on the phone? Can she
```

```
be that ditzie to forget how to count? I could see
if she would be learning how to identify her money
by folding it a different way, but numbers on a
phone? And a touch tone at that! (September 22, 1992)
```

Assessing Realism

Much previous research has argued that soaps' realism is valued more than any other quality, and as we have seen, realism is essential for personalization, character interpretation, and speculation (Ang, 1985; Hobson, 1989). Fans are willing to suspend disbelief in many regards as we recognize that the lives of real people are less steeped in disaster than are those of soap characters and that many of the plots themselves are less than feasible. Sometimes, r.a.t.s. participants find a lot of fun in pointing out examples of soaps' lack of realism, as this post demonstrates:

```
Did anyone catch the jingle jangle the knife made
when Carter threw it overboard? I did not hear a
splash, rather a bang of the knife hitting the floor
of the studio. My roommates and I thought that this
was really funny. (October 17, 1992)
```

At other times, rather than being funny, realism ruptures are very problematic for fans. One flaw that rarely is funny is violation of the truth of the fiction established through prior shows (Hobson, 1989; Jenkins, 1992). The posts cited previously in which the new Natalie is chided for acting in a way that the first/real Natalie would not act are examples of fans complaining about character inconsistency. This post demonstrates the detailed attention that fans bring to interpreting narrative consistency:

```
On the writer-continuity problem : When Galen first
started telling Stephen about her marriage, she said
that at first he was fine, and that he started
wearing her down emotionally, and only then did he
start physically abusing her. But today she told
Stephen (while listening to music) that she hated
that song because it was playing on her HONEYMOON
```

```
when Carter hit her really hard. Which is it??
(August 1, 1992)
```

A soap depends on viewers' knowledge of its history. When that background is continually shifting, it becomes difficult and potentially impossible to bring that history to bear on making sense of the show's present. If we have invested years in getting to know Natalie, or weeks in getting to know Galen, then these shifts in their stories make us unable to predict or even understand the characters' behavior.

The other major violations of realism are those that contradict fans' understandings of their own lives and social worlds (Hobson, 1989; Jenkins, 1992). Criticisms of these external inconsistencies might be silly but still nag at viewers, as in this complaint:

```
OK, I realize I may be WAY out on a limb here, but
the scene in yesterday's show where Galen needed to
keep Carter on the line for a specified amount of
time bothered the hell out of me.

Assuming PV [Pine Valley] has modern switching
equipment, a number trace can happen
instantaneously, especially on a LOCAL call. I
realize this was done for soapetic reasons, but I
wonder if poeple who get harassing phone calls think
it takes that long to trace them down, and then
don't report them. (July 29, 1992)
```

It is worth noting that the response to this message drew on personal experience to reestablish the potential realism of the scene:

```
>Assuming PV has modern switching equipment, a
>number trace can happen instantaneously,
>especially on a LOCAL call.

My sister went through this. They said that they had
her phone tapped (she was being stalked) and every
time she received a call from the guy, she was to
write down the exact time of the call.This way, they
could look up the times and match them to a phone
number. To make a LONG story short, they *say* they
tapped it for 2 weeks. She received over 15 calls
```

```
from this guy, some right after the other. After
2 weeks they said, "Oh sorry, we can't get a
consistent phone #. Too bad for you!" Give me a
break!! He called several times in a row!! P.S. He's
still bothering her...been 2 months now! But alas,
"there's nothing they can do..." UGH! (July 29, 1992)
```

What initially appears unrealistic is brought back into line through another fan's personalization.

At its worst, the lack of realism goes beyond mere annoyance to create serious ambivalence for fans about their attachment to the genre. Without this external realism, fans no longer can rely on their own socioemotional knowledge to extrapolate beyond the information presented in each episode (Jenkins, 1992), undermining the very premise on which soaps are founded. This post demonstrates disagreement over how realistic Galen and her friends' responses to Carter's stalking were. In the initial complainer's embedded quotation, we get a sense of the types of issues for which realism becomes especially important. Note that this poster finds the lack of realism on this point endemic to "ALL soaps" and how angry about it she seems to feel. At the time this was posted, Galen was the assistant district attorney in Pine Valley:

```
>After watching Thursday's episode with Stephen
>and Carter I have to ask a couple of things:
>1) Why is it that ALL soaps think women can't
>take care of their own problems and need some
>man to totally blow things for them? 2) Someone
>else had posted something about Galen being a DA
>[district attorney], why the hell doesn't she
>just get the gosh darn restraining order put
>against Carter? AMC [All My Children] does a
>good job with real issues such as AIDS, domestic
>abuse, etc., but in my opinion, they are really
>blowing this one.

I'd have to disagree—I was disappointed at first,
when she had round-the-clock surveillance and cops
tailing Carter, but this is so much more realistic.
OK, fine, maybe the DA could pull a few strings, but
most women aren't the DA, so at least they are
accurately portraying the helplessness of the
```

```
situation. Of course, most women also probbaly don't
have a big strong doctor in blue jeans to protect
them if the police won't!!! (he's sensitive and he's
tough...what a man!) (July 31, 1992)
```

Criticizing the Show's Messages

This post about women's ability to protect themselves from stalking demonstrates that soap fans recognize that soap operas send ideological messages and that fans are able and willing to explicitly criticize the messages soaps seem to be sending: "AMC does a good job with real issues such as AIDS, domestic abuse, etc." In research on the prime-time soap opera *Dallas*, Liebes and Katz (1989) found that the viewers in their focus groups consciously discerned the show's themes, messages, and archetypes in a show, a process they call *semantic criticism*. For example, their Arab and Israeli viewers often said that the message of *Dallas* is that the rich are unhappy. Ang (1985), in her work on Dutch viewers of *Dallas*, argues that some of her respondents indicated that they understood the message of *Dallas*, disagreed with it completely, but enjoyed the show nonetheless. As many of the posts I have quoted suggest, in the discussion of the Carter Jones story line, fans repeatedly challenged *AMC*'s portrayal of violence against women and the portrayal of women as victims who can be saved only by men.

When the story line began, fans expressed their hope that this would be a *public service* story line that dealt realistically with the issue of domestic abuse, as exemplified in this post:

```
I'm coming out of lurkerdom to say that I think the
Stalker exhusband storyline for Galen has potential.
It seems like every day I read an article in the
newspaper or see a story on the news concerning women
being killed by an exhusband or boyfriend that the
police knew posed a threat to the woman's life and
were unable to stop.

If the writers are reading this. Do some research!
Get the facts straight on this issue and build the
story around the facts. It has great potential if
it's handled the right way. (Maybe Lyle has some
```

```
statistics in his bag-o-information to share.)
(July 18, 1992)
```

Despite what was seen as a generally realistic start, Carter's transformation from realistic abuser to psychotic dramatically undermined fans' faith in the story's potential. By the time Carter had kidnapped Natalie, many fans, like this man, had become quite cynical:

```
Once again, I thought Nat was going to be strong and
save herself...after all, she seems to have gained
significant intelligence since Thursday. Once again,
I should have known better...musn't give those men
and women out there the idea that a woman could
actually take care of herself...no siree, it might
upset the balance of nature! (October 19, 1992)
```

Others were downright furious, as exemplified by this post to the group (but addressed primarily to the writers) under the unusually virulent subject line "KNOCK IT OFF WITH NAT AND CARTER!":

```
This is not entertainment, it's brutal and not
pleasant to watch at all. I really don't understand
why you think women want to see this but I can
assure you that you're wrong...I for one am tired of
Natalie being brutalized and if this thing goes on
as long as the stupid well incident did then you can
count yourselves one less viewer....

[sigh, I feel a little better now. What do the rest
of you think? Maybe if we yell loud enough they'll
get the message...]

Just wanted to get that off my chest...(October 19,
1992)
```

As indicated by the threat to the writers to "count yourselves one less viewer," many of these posts criticizing the show's ideological messages ended with the fans questioning why they watch, a form of what Liebes and Katz (1989) call *pragmatic criticism* (see also Ang, 1985; Brown, 1994).

Watching Despite the Faults

A number of scholars have argued that issues about ownership of the show lie at the heart of criticism (Harrington & Bielby, 1995; Hobson, 1989; Jenkins, 1992). Many fans have watched the show longer than the current writers have been writing it, and they often "feel they know the characters and their fictional community more intimately" (Harrington & Bielby, 1995, p. 154). As a result, "Viewers and fans criticize producers, actors, and writers who are not telling the story 'correctly' and lament their own lack of control over the writing process" (Harrington & Bielby, 1995, p. 155; Hobson, 1989; Seiter, Borchers, Kreutzner, & Warth, 1989). The repeated references to the writers in the posts I have quoted stem from this struggle over ownership (as well as the possibility that the writers might be reading the group).

As often as they may make the threat, and as critical as these r.a.t.s. fans might have been, most did not quit watching. One reason that fans do not have to quit watching just because they have strong criticisms is the videocassette recorder; many r.a.t.s. participants make liberal use of their fast-forward buttons:

```
>One story line right now bothers me so much, I
>fast forward through it all the time. It is the
>Carter/Galen/Steven plot. I can't stand Carter
>and I don't much care for Galen, either...On
>the other hand, I am really enjoying the Terrence/
>Taylor/Derek/Livia/Mimi etc. story line. I love
>the repartee between Terrence and Taylor. Even
>though it is sometimes a little annoying, it is
>realistic, I think, and fun.
>So, now that I've been so outspoken, does anyone
>care to agree or disagree?

Hi Jane—I'll add my opinionated opinion too. I think
I've already complained for all to see on the net
about the Galen/Steve thing—how I wanted Dr.
Fix-it-all to mend the chronic finger pain I'm
having from pressing the FF button on my remote
through all his scenes. When I complained about how
Gloria bugs her eyes out all the time, Pam Johnson
mentioned how Galen SQUINCHES her eyes up all the
time. Well thanks Pam, now that bugs the heck out of
```

```
me too. I just plain old don't like Galen & Steve.
Separately, or together. Carter is treating his role
very campy—I don't think it's bad acting. He just
isn't taking it too seriously since he's leaving
soon. So I don't even bother forming opinions about
temporary characters since it's a waste of time
(like my time is so valuable or something HA!).
(September 7, 1992)
```

As the reference to the "Terrence/Taylor/Derek/Livia/Mimi etc. story line" indicates, a second reason why fans kept watching despite principled outrage and "chronic finger pain" is that even when one story line disappoints, there are others to enjoy. In this regard, the genre has a tremendous advantage because it features multiple story lines in each episode. Even those who hated this story line (and I confess to being one myself) found other story lines compelling, and even this story line had its moments.

The remaining two reasons to keep watching can only be understood in the social context of a fan community. As two of the posts I have quoted indicate, sharing frustration and anger about the show's shortcomings with sympathetic others lessens those negative feelings:

```
(Whew, glad I got that off my chest!) (September 21,
1992)
```

```
[sigh, I feel a little better now. What do the rest
of you think? Maybe if we yell loud enough they'll
get the message...]
```

```
Just wanted to get that off my chest...(October 19,
1992)
```

Finally, fans transform their criticisms into opportunities to let their own creativity shine. When the show fails to perform for them, they perform for one another. Jenkins (1992) argues that this combination of criticism and creativity is common in fan cultures:

The fans' response typically involves not simply fascination or adoration but also frustration and antagonism, and it is the combination of the two responses which motivates their active engagement with the media. Because popular narratives often fail to satisfy, fans must struggle with them . . . because the texts continue to fascinate, fans cannot dismiss them . . . but rather must try to find ways to salvage them for their interests. (p. 23)

Jenkins argues that fans use the rough spots in texts as openings for their own elaboration.[2]

Although soaps, as we have seen, are designed to encourage specu-lation, their rough spots offer fans additional space for creative input, a space that goes beyond that intended by the shows' producers and writers. Hobson (1989, 1990), for example, comments that fan criticism often comes packaged with suggestions for improvement that are cre-ated by fans. In Chapter 2, for example, we saw fans respond to their criticisms of the stupidity of the adults (and especially of the police officers) by imagining scenarios in which Timmy and his dog rescue Natalie.[3] As Jenkins (1992) puts it, fans do not do *textual disintegration* but instead do *home improvements.* It is not only scholars who recognize these tensions and opportunities inherent in fandom, as Steve makes clear when I ask why he participates in r.a.t.s.:

> Currently, [it is] one of the main outlets for my creative tendencies and because I know quite a bit about the shows. Further, it's an expression of fandom—some nostalgia, some lament about the current state of the art, and plenty of armchair quarterbacking on how to do it better. Plus, trying to outguess the coming events.
>
> (Nance—I just had a flash thought—it's slower but similar to watch-ing a football game. We're always trying to guess if they should pass, run, punt, call a reverse, etc., and when the play gets stopped, we're sure we could have done it better. But we all like the pay-offs—in soaps, the climax of a murder or two star-crossed lovers finally uniting, and in football, that long last-second scoring pass or breathtaking broken-field run. Though the language is different, it seems to me that the fannish aspects are quite, quite similar.) (1993 survey)

In many forms of fandom, including soaps, creative responses to criti-cism take the form of reworkings of the shows. Fans propose alternative scenes in which what did happen is replaced by what could or should have occurred (Hobson, 1989, 1990; Jenkins, 1992). While r.a.t.s. fans do this, the main way in which they deal creatively with criticism is with humor, as the scenarios in which Timmy and Harold rescue Natalie show.

From Criticism to Humorous Performance

One might think that the gravity of the social issues raised by the Carter Jones story line and the participants' discontent with the story line would lead them away from using humor. This was not the case at all. More than one quarter (27%) of the 524 posts that mentioned the story line contained at least one funny element, as measured by explicit responses recognizing funny performances, use of cues associated with humor, and my own sense of humor as a group participant. Not only was there a lot of humor, it came from many participants. Of the 128 posters who participated in the discussion of the Carter story line, 41% used humor at least once. Most of the humor in the discussion of this story line was critical; fully 75% of the humorous posts were negative, criticizing the story line, characters, writing, props, and so on. That humor should result from fan criticism is not really surprising, although it is curiously underdiscussed in the scholarship on fandom. Most theories of humor argue that it arises out of sudden incongruity or what Oring (1992) calls *appropriate incongruity*. In humor, incompatible frames are juxtaposed, resulting in "a bifurcated logical process" (Palmer, 1994, p. 96). Humorous shifts in perceptual frame cause us to simultaneously recognize "ambiguity, inconsistency, contradiction, and interpretative diversity" (Mulkay, 1988, p. 26). Thus, the contrast between attachment to a show and criticism of that show is ideally suited to humor (especially with a genre that lends itself to interpretive diversity).

To get a better sense of how criticism is transformed to humor in r.a.t.s., I turn to three exemplary messages. I begin with a post from Lexine, one of the women who criticized the show's portrayal of spouse abuse through reference to her own experiences as an abused spouse (see Chapter 2). In this post, Lexine is responding to an update written by Dan. Dan uses the motif of titles for the story lines that is common in the update genre. In Lexine's post, she picks up on one of his titles, "One of these women is not like the others," applies it to characters other than those for whom Dan created it, and elaborates its *Sesame Street* origins into a well-orchestrated joke:

```
>5—One of these Women is not like the others!

"One of these things is not like the others,
One of these things just doesn't belong...
```

```
One of these things is not like the others,
Can you find out before I finish my song?"
            [paraphrased from Sesame Street]

Things:   Natalie        Angelique

          Hayley         DinahLee

[Answer: DinahLee—the AMC writers have not yet
turned her into a sniveling, whining,
male-dependent, helpless female character yet. But
then she has only been in PV for a day... :) ]
(September 30, 1992)
```

Lexine is highly critical of the show in this post for reasons I have discussed previously. She directs her criticism explicitly at the writers, who eventually make all female characters "sniveling, whining, male-dependent, helpless." Lexine invokes what another poster called the "damsel in distress" theme, much discussed and decried in the group, to provide the punchline. Of course, to get the joke, readers must be invested enough in the characters to recognize the similarities between them. This post and the one to which it responds find some of their humor in their intertextual invocation and transformation of another television show. Here, Lexine explicitly paraphrases *Sesame Street*, even using formatting to replicate the appearance of that show's "One of These Things Is Not Like the Others" game. The use of formatting to frame and invoke humor is not common in r.a.t.s., and her choice to use it here points to the creativity involved in r.a.t.s. humor. The incongruities in this post are multiple, among them the juxtaposition of the soap opera with *Sesame Street*, the childlike quality of the "One of These Things Is Not Like the Others" game with the very adult issue of female dependency, and these fans' acceptance of the show with recognition of its flawed portrayal of women. Each of these incongruities depends on her readers sharing her close relationship to the show but also assumes that they read the show at a distance.

Lexine's post is in response to a title in Dan's update. The post that follows is a response to Dan's "Unanswered Questions," a set of 10 numbered rhetorical questions he appends to the end of each of his updates or posts alone when others write the updates. The unanswered questions find most of their humor by pointing out the limits of soap opera reality; that is, they are founded on the problematic qualities of soap realism. In this post, Patty responds to one such set of unanswered questions. I have edited the questions to those relevant to the Carter Jones story line:

```
>Unanswered Questions:
>
>5) Where is Harold?

Harassing Winnifred to let him out to go save Not
from Carter/Kyle/Psychoguy.

>9) Has Jeremy been to his Gallery lately?

No, he's FAR too busy saving blondes (except Not,
guess it only worked on Kate Collins, and was
permanently damaged before the well). (October 13,
1992)
```

Perhaps the most striking feature of the unanswered questions and their responses is the extent to which they rely on knowledge of the show's characters and past, in other words, how these questions rely on close knowledge of (and hence attachment to) the show. Dan's fifth question ("Where is Harold?") refers to Timmy's dog. The answer uses a minor character, Winnifred, a maid. Harold and Winnifred both occasionally disappear from the show for months on end; Patty is assuming that her readers are familiar enough with the show to know these characters and be entertained by the idea that when they are not on screen, they might be together. Patty's response also alludes to Harold's first weeks on the show, during which he did his canine best to save Natalie when Janet had tossed her down the well and assumed her identity. The humor in the thought of Harold wanting to go out and rescue Natalie again relies on this past knowledge. At the same time as she draws on this textual closeness, Patty invokes the "damsel in distress" and adults-without-a-clue criticisms as sources of humor, echoing the other posts suggesting that Harold and Timmy were the smartest characters on the show. Again, Patty's response implies that the dog might be an improvement on the humans.

Dan's ninth question ("Has Jeremy been to his Gallery lately?") also relies on and calls forth a response grounded in knowledge of, and hence attachment to, the show. At this point in the story line, Jeremy, a gallery owner, had spent all his waking hours protecting Galen and Dinah Lee (both of whom, like Natalie, are blonde) from Carter. Patty's response that Jeremy is too busy saving blondes invokes, yet again, the theme of women in need of male rescue; however, instead of faulting the writers as Lexine does, Patty seems to fault the character. She follows this by suggesting that Jeremy's inability to rescue Natalie might be due to the change of actresses; that is, his psychic powers worked only on Kate Collins, who played the previous Natalie (the distinction between the Natalies also is made earlier with Patty's use of the nickname "Not"). She goes from the distanced reading involved here back to a close reading when she adds the qualification that Jeremy was among the many who failed to notice anything amiss when Janet was impersonating Natalie.

In this third example, Amy responds to Margie's complaint about Galen's telephone. As seen in the embedded quotation, Margie laughs both at the show and at herself for caring so much about it. Amy picks up on her criticisms and uses them to launch her own humorous litany on fundamental absurdities of the soap opera world:

```
>Does it bother anyone else that Galen's phone
>rings way to frequently? I don't mean she gets a
>ton of calls at strange hours (which she does).
>I mean the time between rings is practically
>non-existent! Why do soaps have to fake ringing
>phone? Why don't they just have a phone that
>they can call and have it really ring? And if we
>have to be subjected to the fake ringing, how
>about slowing it down??
>
>Come to think of it, most phone in Pine Valley
>ring too fast! And another thing (boy, I'm
>dangerous when I start thinking in the middle of
>a post!), most of the one-way conversations
>(the phone conversations where we only hear one
>person talking) are done too fast as well! Like
>the person says something and then says
>something else and the time between things
>wasn't long enough for the invisible person on
>the other end to have said "boo!" *SIGH*
>
```

```
>I'm looking for phone-reality on a SOAP?!
>Someone, get me to a shrink, quick! This thesis
>is really taking its toll on me!
>
>Margie
```

```
Margie, Margie, Margie, take a deep breath. Count
to 10. Release your breath. There. Repeat IOAS,
IOAS, IOAS.
```

```
We've already discussed that there is no concept
of what we call time in soap operas. We need to
develop the soap opera theory of relativity
(SOTOR)—it relates space, time, AND production
schedules, writer's quirks, writer's failed
memories, last minute plot changes, actors
contracts, available sets, available sound effects,
etc. It's sort of like cartoon physics. It can be
used to explain why Dimitri can ride 20 miles on a
horse in the same amount of time it takes Erica to
get there by car, and why the next day Brooke and
Edmund can walk to the same place, why mail arrives
before it was sent, and why the phones ring too
fast. In fact, maybe this is the answer to the PVGD
problem too. With all of these people zipping around
faster than the speed of light, it's no wonder that
they're aging faster than normal. Of course, that
doesn't explain why it doesn't affect the adults...
we'll have to look into a corollary for that.
(August 7, 1992)
```

Amy begins with a reminder to Margie, "IOAS," a group-specific acronym for "It's Only A Soap." The phrase has been conventionalized in the AMC discussion to the point where its meaning rarely needs to be spelled out. It is used like a mantra to invoke calm in the face of hopeless soap opera absurdity, as Amy's full comment clearly shows: "take a deep breath. Count to 10. Release your breath. There. Repeat IOAS, IOAS, IOAS." "IOAS" reflects many aspects of this group's collective stance to the show, in particular the participants' recognition that the show is a flawed constructed fiction, but one to which they are legitimately attached. The show, says this acronym, is meant to be a source of pleasure; when it is not pleasing, one should distance oneself from the show instead of getting upset. "IOAS" negates irritation over the show, at the same time validating one's right to irritation. The fact that the phrase has been conventional- ized indicates for all that all readers find themselves annoyed by the show. Thus, "IOAS" represents the fundamental incongruity of being a soap opera fan, the juxtaposition of attachment and criticism.

The critical sentiments behind "IOAS" often are channeled into humor, as Amy demonstrates. She draws parallels among the telephone ring speed, the distance to Dimitri's hunting lodge (to which Erica drove while Edmund and Brooke walked), the time warp that surrounds mail, and "PVGD" (a group acronym for Pine Valley glandular disorder, the imaginary illness that explains why the soap's children age so much faster than real people[4]). Amy goes beyond listing these similar suspen- sions of soap opera realism to explaining these phenomena with "the soap opera theory of relativity (SOTOR)," which relates space and time in Pine Valley to a sophisticated survey of the realities of a soap opera's construction: "production schedules, writer's quirks, writer's failed memories, last minute plot changes, actors contracts, available sets, available sound effects, etc." Amy's post demonstrates many of the phe- nomena seen in the other humorous performances I have quoted. She selects resources from across the soap opera text and transforms criti- cism into entertainment, juxtaposing realism and absurdity as well as entertainment and frustration.

In these three examples, as in most critical humor in r.a.t.s., close readings that take the story world on its own fictional terms are juxta- posed with distant readings that stand back and challenge that world. Lexine's "One of these things" game assumes that the readers care for the characters well enough to know them, yet it turns that closeness around to point out that the writers are to be faulted for the characters' flaws. The distant view of "writers" is juxtaposed with the close analysis of characters. Patty's answers to the unanswered questions also assume close familiarity with characters and story his- tory, suggesting closeness to the text, but then turn that closeness to humor by highlighting the story's status as a (flawed) constructed fiction. This incongruity is seen in its fullest form in Amy's "SOTOR," which stands so far back from the narrative that all of its absurdities come together into one explanation: Soap time is relative. This theory means little, however, if readers are not engaged closely enough with the text to notice these temporal contradictions and find them annoying.

With critical humor, r.a.t.s. participants assert their mastery over a text they do not own and find collaborative ways in which to sustain their involvement. Participants are able to distance themselves from the soap by laughing at it, but at the same time, the laughter encourages them to stay attached to the drama. These posters describe how r.a.t.s. humor enhances or encourages involvement with the show: "The people posting here are *hilarious.* It's nice to find a bunch of people who watch soaps for the reason I do—they're funny (in particular at their most serious)" (Samantha, 1993 survey). "I enjoy reading it because the folks are so creative. I find it greatly enhances my watching of *Days* [*Days of Our Lives*] and *AMC* because I find more humor in it than I did in my pre-r.a.t.s. days" (Sandra, 1993 survey). By using the show's flaws as material with which to entertain each other, the community becomes amusing enough to hold the participants' attention through the show's lows. The humor offered by the discussion might even be the only reason why fans remain engaged during periods when the soap is particularly bad. "When one of my soaps gets dull, the Net will keep me watching—e.g., the song about Nat in the Well (AMC), funny updates, fun stuff period" (Zoey, 1991 survey). By transforming a dull, overly serious, or absurd drama into a source of humor, these fans remind one another that it is okay to pick apart the show, that there are ways in which to be a fan despite its shortcomings, and that they all are caught in this bind between enjoyment and irritation (a phenomenon codified in the phrase "IOAS"). Humor is one way in which participants negotiate what it means to be a soap fan and encourage one another's continued fan status despite the genre's flaws.

Criticism and the Creation
of Group Identity

In this examination of how the fans in r.a.t.s. discuss *AMC*, it is clear that these fans also are relating to one another. Geraghty (1991) writes,

> Community is . . . experienced in the interaction between the programmes and their audience. Soaps offer a common currency to viewers which permits the enjoyment to be shared between those who do not watch the programmes together. This effect of uniting disparate audiences goes well beyond television's capacity to provide the subject of conversation the morning after. The pleasures of soap are so much bound up with speculation and analysis that they demand that view-

ers share the experience. [The narrative strategies of soaps] are dependent on the audience's capacity to predict and evaluate the characters' actions so that there is a common participation in the problems being portrayed and the variety of solutions on offer. [Soaps] can be discussed by friends, strangers, and acquaintances in a variety of situations. Such conversations demand a shared knowledge of the history of the subject and offer a mutual pleasure in the pooling of information on significant details and the disagreement over questions of interpretation. Discussion of soap opera also involves sharing ideas about personal relationships and emotional dilemmas. . . . Such a process offers the feeling of community through the experience of shared pleasure. (pp. 122-123)

The community of r.a.t.s. is founded in more than "the experience of shared pleasure"; it is in part a group identity constructed through ongoing communicative practices. In positioning themselves vis-à-vis the soap opera, fans cannot help but take positions vis-à-vis one another. In r.a.t.s., we see that people continually position themselves as highly similar to one another and, in general terms, as highly attractive. We saw this in response to the flame challenging soap operas discussed in Chapter 1. In that case, participants explicitly reminded one another that they all are intelligent and funny.

Perhaps most significant in constructing this group identity is the way in which these posts construct their readership; inherent in all of the messages I have quoted is an assumption that the people who will read them are sophisticated readers of the soap opera. Although the stereotypes might treat soap viewers as unable to differentiate reality from the drama, these posters assume that other fans will recognize the genre's conventions, its (lack of) realism, its variable quality, and the details of its construction (consider Amy's post outlining the many forces at work behind the televised text). Given that the messages characterize their audience in this way, it is no wonder that people in r.a.t.s. characterize the group as a safe haven for intelligent soap viewers.

In addition to seeing one another as experts in soap production, these fans treat one another as experts in the show's events and its history, implicitly assuming and validating close, lengthy attachments to the show. The importance of this common expertise in generating a sense of similarity is particularly clear in the group's humor. Without detailed shared knowledge of the show, references to Winnifred or

Harold's absences (as seen in Patty's post) or to "the hunting lodge" (as seen in Amy's post) make no sense. Humor assumes similarity in other ways as well. To be funny, references must draw on contexts of shared meaning. Key to creating successful r.a.t.s. humor is discerning the interpretive bents of the other participants. New interpretations that ring true (e.g., the first use of "Not" to describe the recast Natalie) may be praised for their humor or may become resources for future humor as they are reinvoked, extended, and transformed by subsequent posters.

The sense of within-group similarity that develops through the interpretation of the soap opera in r.a.t.s. is further enhanced by the way in which posters repeatedly position themselves as dissimilar to the soap opera writers (and "TPTB" [The Powers That Be] more broadly). Many critical messages refer to the writers explicitly, usually blaming them for the show's flaws and suggesting that they underestimate their viewers' intelligence. Some criticisms are even addressed to the writers. This "us versus them" dynamic inherently defines participants as an in-group: "United in their alienation," write Harrington and Bielby (1995), fans create "a community organized through sarcasm as a form of play" (p. 150). Indeed, sarcasm and the many other types of critical textual play at work in r.a.t.s. are essential to understanding r.a.t.s. as a community, although these critical and humorous practices are just some of the organizing forces in r.a.t.s. In the next two chapters, I will turn to other ways in which the participants develop the interpersonal relationships and individual identities that help to make this fan group feel like a community.

At this point, we can see further hints of the pervasive and complex nature of building an interpersonal community while engaged in the collaborative project of interpreting a television show by examining how participants create the appearance of interpretive consensus. Just as a soap relies on viewers to know the show's history, r.a.t.s. participants rely on readers to have read the group's discussion of that history. These participants draw repeatedly on their own previous discussions to situate a point, to make a joke, to reference soap events, and to codify interpretive consensus. Much of the humor in r.a.t.s. recycles previously voiced interpretations of characters, story lines, production qualities, the writers, and other elements of the soap opera. Through interpretive discussion, consensus on these matters is negotiated invisibly, as past interpretations are selectively invoked and new ones are selectively adopted or praised. The result is a collaborative interpretation that appears to be shared. As we will see in the next chapter, this is enhanced by a general reluctance to voice disagreement.

In the discussion of Carter Jones, this is most evident in the significance generated around the character of Natalie. Patty and Amy both refer to her as "Not" (as do other posters I quote), a nickname loaded with interpretive meaning. It calls attention to the change of actress, highlighting a change that the producers would have the participants ignore and incorporating that change into her very name. Beyond calling attention to the switch, it assesses the new actress and finds her inadequate. The nickname presumably was first used to express one participant's stance on Melody Anderson. It worked as humor because it was an *aptonym* or a name that others in r.a.t.s. also found "in some way appropriate to [the character's] characteristics" (Nilsen, 1993, p. 68). The fact that it was then used by others demonstrates that they shared this interpretation of Anderson's portrayal as inadequate and transforms a single participant's evaluation into that of the group. Dissenting opinions, if voiced, likely will be qualified, as in the post excerpted in the beginning of this chapter that begins with "I may be in the minority on this one, but I like the new actress playing Nat." Thus, even disagreement can promote a sense of interpretive consensus.

Lexine and Patty both draw on Natalie's recurrent status as a victim in need of male rescue in their humor, a point other critics of the story line make as well. Lexine uses her as an example of such a woman in her "One of these things" joke, and Patty draws implicit parallels between Natalie's current and past crises in her responses concerning both Harold and Jeremy. Here, the parallel between Natalie's past and present is invoked. That Natalie's past is used to symbolize victimhood speaks volumes about the group's interpretation of the character. Lexine also pegs Angelique and Galen as "damsels in distress," enhancing the sense that this is a group that shares a common frustration with how the participants' show portrays women.

As is the case with "Not," "IOAS," and the unanswered questions, the sense of similarity among participants can become codified into ritualized forms of group-specific meanings. These codes can serve the role that artifacts might serve face-to-face, providing central objects around which the group can define itself. Group meanings are codified in other ways as well; the very forms of the spoiler, the update, the sighting, and the other genres are artifact-like instantiations of group organization.[5]

Looking at this group as an audience community leads to the understanding that when an audience becomes collaborative, it changes what it means to be a fan. The pool of relevant information is expanded, the range of interpretations on offer is broadened, genre expertise is refined and cultivated, and the opportunity to discuss the private worlds of feelings and relationships with others is enhanced. Collaborative soap interpretation on a scale as large as r.a.t.s. cannot help but transform fans' relationship to the genre. Out of this transformation grows a transformation among the participants; a sense of group identity emerges from their otherwise disconnected lives. As they interact about the soap opera, they develop and maintain relationships with one another. In r.a.t.s., this relationship is one of similarity, fostered by (among other things) sharing soap expertise, treating each other as smart and funny, developing codified ways of communicating, setting up participants in opposition to the writers, and validating each other's emotional attachment to the show.

Notes

1. For example, it always is a little jarring to remember that *All My Children*'s identical twins, Adam and Stuart, are played by the same actor, David Canary.

2. Jenkins (1992) argues that in efforts to find such opportunities, fans rewatch shows and scenes. They videotape and fast-forward (or, in the case of soaps, rewind) to focus only on particular points of emphasis. They try to spot continuity errors and/or reused props.

3. In light of fans' complaints about the tendency of soaps to have men rescue women, it is worth noting that in these alternative scenarios, it is the woman's son and dog—rather than her lover—who are cast as the heroes. I will leave the fun of this analysis to psychoanalytic critics.

4. *Soap Opera Weekly* refers to this phenomenon as "SORAS" (Soap Opera Rapid Aging Syndrome).

5. Other online groups also develop codified discourse practices that become group defining. Tepper (1997) shows how in the alt.folklore newsgroup, asking obviously stupid questions (*trolling*) became a form of joke used to

distinguish group insiders from outsiders. Cherny (1995) discusses the *whuggle,* a greeting practice in a real-time online group she called ElseMOO. Knowing how, when, and whom to whuggle clearly marked group insiders. Cherny's analysis is particularly intriguing in that it suggests the extent to which individual participants' interpretations of these group-specific genres may vary. When asked to describe the whuggle, participants offered strikingly different associations.

4

"I Think of Them as Friends": Interpersonal Relationships in the Online Community

P eople start to read online discussion groups because they are interested in the topics of discussion. When people first start reading rec.arts.tv.soaps (r.a.t.s.), they are attracted primarily to the wealth of information, the diversity of perspectives, and the refreshing sophistication of the soap opera discussion. Soon, however, the group reveals itself as an interpersonally complex social world, and this becomes an important appeal in its own right. For many, fellow r.a.t.s. participants come to feel like friends. Jamie's story of her involvement in the group parallels my own and reflects what several other participants describe:

> At first, I read r.a.t.s. to keep up on what was going on—again like a good book. But then you start up conversations with others. It's

fascinating to see all the different points of view on such a range of topics. Then you become friends with the other posters. Pretty soon, it's like sitting down to a conversation with a bunch of close friends. Even though you've never met, you make some warm and pretty close friendships with this group. (1993 survey)

My survey question about relationships within the group—"What do you consider your relationship(s) (if any) with people on the Net[1] to be?"—consistently elicited descriptions of the newsgroup's friendliness. This was even true of those who were new to r.a.t.s. or silent within it:

I haven't really formed any "relationships" with anyone on the Net. I guess I view other Netters as friendly strangers, in reality. I consider myself too new to have had any real relationships with everyone, but I do think I would like to have them as friends. (Joan, 1991 survey)

I'm a silent reader (so far :)). But I think of them as friends. (Teresa, 1991 survey)

Accomplishing Friendliness

Joan and Teresa indicate that they have no one-to-one relationships with other participants. In this regard, they probably are typical of most who read r.a.t.s. regularly. After all, only a tiny minority of any Usenet group's readers actually contribute to the group; many more participants are invisible than visible. Thus, the friendly atmosphere on r.a.t.s. raises questions that are applicable to any Net group with a social atmosphere. In the case of r.a.t.s., the issue is how a group in which thousands of strangers reading what a few hundred of them write comes to see itself as an inclusive "bunch of close friends." The more general problem is how any online group comes to construct norms, in this case about what type of relationships participants share, given that most participants stay silent and there is little one-on-one interaction.

When I asked them to compare r.a.t.s. to other groups on Usenet and other networks, nearly all of my survey respondents spoke in terms of the greater friendliness of r.a.t.s., indicating how this set the group apart:

As to other newsgroups, it doesn't compare to the other technical groups that I read. Not the same camaraderie. (Erin, 1991 survey)

People interact in this group. It is like having a conversation. Other groups have more caustic discussions. The people I have met from this group have been really nice. It's the first group I read, and it is pleasant. (Linda, 1991 survey)

The creation of friendliness in r.a.t.s. is not a given but rather a communicative accomplishment. We already have seen a number of ways in which participants in r.a.t.s. create friendliness while addressing the topic of the soap opera. Their treatment of the soaps constructs an attractive image of the participants as intelligent and witty. The use of humor not only negotiates the problematics of participants' relationship to the soaps, it also "shows our acceptance of [the others] and our desire to please them" (Morreall, 1983, p. 115). Participants also create friendship by offering one another social support on personal issues related to the soap. In the case of the Carter Jones discussion, women and men expressed their support for women who had left abusive relationships. All of these phenomena indicate that creating friendliness is ongoing, implicit, and multifaceted. Whether consciously or not, participants orient to an ethic of friendliness when they write their messages, regardless of the particular practice in which they are engaged. In short, friendliness is something a group *does* rather than something a group *is*.

Managing Disagreement

People in r.a.t.s. are particularly aware that their sense of friendliness is demonstrated largely through a behavior they avoid. The computer often has been accused of encouraging hostile and competitive discourse. The widely noted phenomenon of *flaming* (i.e., attacking others) has been hypothesized to result from "a lack of shared etiquette by computer culture norms or by the impersonal and text-only form of communication" (Kiesler, Siegel, & McGuire, 1984, p. 1130). These scholars argue that rather than being mitigated, as often is the case in face-to-face disagreements (Pomerantz, 1984), online disagreements are exaggerated. This can be a tempting argument when faced with disagreements such as this one from a newsgroup that discusses the television show *Star Trek: The Next Generation:*

```
>>Just fine by me. Personally I'd like to involve
>>Lursa and her sister (the Klingons) too. Now
>>THAT would be a fun date.
```

```
>>
>>—Jim Hyde


>Will you stupid jerks get a real life. Everyone
>with half a brain or more know that a human and
>a Kligon can not mate. The Klingon mating
>procedure would kill any human (except one with
>a brain like you). Stay of the net stoopid!


Oh really. Hmmmm. And I suppose Alexander and his
mom are just clones or something? If you recall,
she is half human, and Alexander is ¼. Romulans
don't seem any more sturdy than humans, and we
saw hybrids there as well.
Looks like I'm not the one with half a brain. Check
your facts before you become the net.nazi next time
pal. This isn't just a forum for us to all bow down
and worship your opinion you know. You might also do
well for yourself to learn how to spell, stooopid.
—Jim Hyde (rec.arts.startrek.current, Apr. 12, 1993)
```

Although flaming is common online, it generally is considered bad manners. Mabry (1997) analyzed 3,000 messages collected from many forms of computer-mediated communication (CMC) and found that more "tense, antagonistic, or hostile argumentative statements" tended to be accompanied by more intense conciliatory behavior. McLaughlin, Osborne, and Smith (1995), analyzing a large corpus of messages chastising others' behavior, argue that Usenet standards discourage the wanton insulting or flaming of others. Despite this, flaming remains common in many groups. The r.a.t.s. newsgroup is not one of them, and this is inseparable from its friendliness:

> I find this to be one of the most friendly and chatty groups on Usenet. Flames are very uncommon, particularly compared to rec.arts.startrek and rec.arts.tv. (Laurie, 1991 survey)

> Comparing [r.a.t.s.] to other newsgroups: [It is] one of the nicer ones (less flame wars for the most part). (Lisa, 1991 survey)

> The group in which I find the most flame wars (thus the least friendly and supportive, in my opinion) is a local group. . . . I would put

rec.arts.tv.soaps right under rec.pets.dogs for friendliness, support, warm[th], lack of flame wars (in Y&R [*The Young and the Restless*] anyway, which is the only soap I watch and read about), in general, overall enjoyment. (Teresa, 1991 survey)

This tendency to explain friendliness in terms of flaming indicates that it is easy to be friendly so long as everyone is in apparent agreement; it is in the points of disagreement that friendliness is most challenged. However, at the same time as r.a.t.s. does not want disagreement, the group is, first and foremost, in the business of maximizing interpretations, a process that inevitably leads to disagreement, especially considering how overcoded the soap operas are. Rather than considering friendliness as accomplished through behaviors that r.a.t.s. participants avoid, I look in this section to the behaviors they use to construct disagreements that attend to the ethic of friendliness.

The potential for disagreement to damage the group's sense of solidarity was enhanced in the Carter Jones discussion. This (extremely friendly) post to r.a.t.s. from Anne indicates the problem that participants faced with this story line:

```
You know I realize that whenever AMC [All My
Children] does a "heated" storyline, we all get
"heated" too! We all agree tho, it's all the
writers faults! :-)

>Man....I'm really p*ssed at those writers.
>This is too important a topic for them to give
>it the cosmetic-kissy-kiss treatment.

Oh and the cosmetics dept. too :-) I am truly
sorry to those of you that have been in an "abused"
relationship. My heart goes out to you. I am very
glad that you were smart enough to get out of it.
Applause!

I won't say what I think of men who do it. The
lowest of the low. This is just too deep a
subject to even talk about on a computer.
Carter is scum! But I guess John Wesley Shipp is
ok :-) I hope to see him a "good guy" sometime.
(October 20, 1992)
```

Anne's comments that the group participants all get "heated" discussing a story line concerning subjects too deep "to even talk about
on a computer" suggests that discussing this story line brought out
emotions difficult to discuss even when in agreement. Such difficulty
could only be enhanced when participants did not see eye-to-eye on the
story line. Thus, the disagreements concerning this story line offer a
revealing window into the discourse strategies that create and maintain
friendliness in r.a.t.s.

Mitigating Offense

Most disagreements contained verbal components, or message features, that functioned to lessen their negative impact. Just over 40% of
the disagreements used qualifiers that framed disagreements as resulting from differences in subjective opinion. Qualification leaves room for
the poster to turn out to be wrong and the other right, reducing the
threat to the other's position. In this example, the poster places qualifiers prior to and following the point of disagreement (the qualifications
are in boldface):

```
>>Tell me, why did Brooke give Carter Jones an
>>invite to Weirdwind, & if

>She didn't INVITE him. They showed him at the
>door and the butler
```

I may be wrong, but **I thought** Brooke did invite
Carter Jones. **I actually thought** he **may** be
covering the event as a reporter. Seeing as
how Brooke started the homeless shelter, **I would
think** that would give her some say in who may
attend a fund raiser. I do know she had a guest
list and showed it to Carter. That's how he knew
Galen would be there. Anyway, at the door, he
wasn't named as an invited guest, but he
identified himself as being with Tempo magazine.
(July 23, 1992)

From time to time, but not often, people apologize for disagreeing.
This example demonstrates the apology:

```
I'm sorry, Anne my buddy, but I have to disagree
with both you and Liz... (October 19, 1992)
```

A few participants lessened the potential offense of their disagreements by explicitly framing their messages as nonoffensive. This technique, used four times, is when the poster explicitly keyed her activity as something other than confrontational.[2] In one case, this involved prefacing a contradictory assessment with "I think this is so funny." In another case, someone wrote "no offense to *Knot's Landing*" just before suggesting that *Cape Fear* had been a greater influence on the story line.

Building Affiliation

As if it were not enough to actively lessen the negative force of one's words by showing respect and backing off one's claims, as these strategies do, many disagreers articulated their disagreements in ways that actively built social alignment between the participants. For example, they frequently prefaced disagreements with partial agreements, a strategy that has been noted in face-to-face and epistolary interaction as well (Mulkay, 1985, 1986; Pomerantz, 1984). Fully 29% of the disagreements in r.a.t.s. were prefaced by partial agreements. Partial agreements generally were followed by words such as "but" and "though" or phrases such as "at the same time" that positioned what followed as disagreement. In these two examples, this disagreement strategy can be seen. In the first, the dispute is over whether or not Brooke was tough enough when she fired Carter after catching him using *Tempo* magazine resources to develop potentially incriminating photographs of Galen hugging Trevor:

```
>Well, it seems she got some QUALITY time in
>yesterday, firing Carter Jones!
>Go Brooke! Brainslap of the Week! She held up
>to him and didn't back off or squirm! I loved
>it... :-)

I thought the same thing, too, "Finally, Brooke
is giving it to Carter with both guns." But,
then when she takes the incriminating picture,
she ONLY TAKES THE PICTURE leaving Carter with
the negative in the darkroom. You don't have to
```

```
work for Kodak to know that he can still make
more pictures which he does. (October 2, 1992)
```

We see the same pattern here in a disagreement over whether or not kidnapped and blind Natalie was handling Carter as well as she could:

```
>even watch, fast forward! It is stupid beyond
>belief! She should have tied carter up after she
>knocked him out. She knew where the bed was so
>tear strips of sheets and tie his a*s up! But
>noooo, I'll pull up the anchor then I'll drive
>the boat home, sure I'm blind, but I can do it.
>Carter should be knocked out forever. Gimme a
>break!
```

At first, I'll admit, I thought Nat was being very stupid too. But watching her in action on Monday's show, I thought she had a good tactic try and make Carter dislike her, since he only likes weak and dependent women. She seemed to try and play his psychological mind-f**k games right along with him. I was impressed, too bad it didn't work. (October 20, 1992)

Partial agreements generally promote interpersonal harmony (Pomerantz, 1984), but both of these examples illustrate a phenomenon that exaggerates this effect. Like many of the partial agreements in this sample, these indicate temporal shifts in the posters' thinking. Initially, the posters held the same position as the person with whom they are disagreeing, but then they came to interpret soap events differently ("I thought the same thing, too, but then..." and "At first...But watching her in action on Monday's show..."). Therefore, the disagreement is situated as one with their earlier selves as well as with the other, enhancing the similarity between self and other.

A second affiliative strategy in disagreement was the use of the other's name (used in 18% of the disagreements), as can be seen in this excerpt in which the poster makes explicit the affiliative quality of naming with the phrase "my buddy":

```
I'm sorry, Anne my buddy, but I have to disagree
with both you and Liz....
```

Participants also explicitly acknowledged the perspective of the other in 12% of the disagreements. Here, Liz responds to Pam's contradiction by acknowledging Pam's position before disagreeing. (Pam's message is quoted with a colon [" : "] rather than with the usual angle bracket(s) [">"] in the left margin, presumably a feature of Liz's newsreader.) Note also the use of naming:

```
[stuff where Anne and Liz say Nat kinda put
herself in this bad situation deleted]
:ENTIRELY Carter's fault for deceiving her. All
:Nat did was trust him, and she didn't have our
:benefit of knowing he's a slime!
:
:I know that neither of you meant anything by
:what you said, but I couldn't let it go—it was
:too close to Carter's rationalizing that the
:women he beat were responsible for the beatings,
:not him.

I see what you are saying, Pam.


However, some poster wrote something about Nat
not forgiving Trevor for not rescuing her
sooner—and if you look at it that way, I have
to say that Nat would have no reason to hold
this against Trevor since the whole mess was
caused primarily by Carter's mental illness
and secondarily by Nat's opening up to him /
agreeing to leave the hospital with him.
The whole thing could never have happened if
Nat hadn't left the hospital instead of waiting
for Timmy. Of course, I suppose Kyle could have
abducted Natalie more subtley—like wheeling her
out for some xrays and just continuing right on
out of the hospital!

I am not saying that Nat deserved what happened
to her or that she was responsible for the
```

```
beatings—just that if had she been less trusting
she wouldn't have made Carter's abduction plan
so easy, but then again it was her blindness
(Carter's fault entirely) which which made it
all possible.
```

```
I know it is annoying when people must be less
trusting or re-arrange their own lives or
personalities just to be able to live in a
society full of criminals and psychos, but it
is a part of life. I know this pretty well from
living in the big city after growing up in a
small town. And being a 5'2" woman doesn't help
at all! (October 21, 1992)
```

Getting Back to the Task at Hand

The single most common message feature of disagreements was elaboration, which occurred in 69% of them. The preceding paragraph of the immediately prior post is an example of elaboration in disagreement. We can see here that the poster has taken a tangent off of the original disagreement and is moving the topic onto new ground.[3] Offering reasoning to support the writer's perspective also was more common than any of the offense mitigators or social alignment strategies.[4] Reasoning was given in 61% of the disagreements. Both elaboration and reasoning usually involved personalization or speculation, as in the preceding example of elaboration and in this example of reasoning:

```
>After watching Thursday's episode with Stephen
>and Carter I have to ask a couple of things:
>1) Why is it that ALL soaps think women can't
>take care of their own problems and need some
>man to totally blow things for them?
```

```
Hey...kudos to Stephen's forceful approach/
attempt to ending this! There is just so much
one can take when the one they "love" and/or
"have special feelings for" has been and or is
being victimized! And remember... Stephen has some
hidden dark secrets that have not transpired yet.
```

**Looks like abuse may lurk in his background
somewhere.** (August 3, 1992)

Neither elaboration nor reasoning directly lessens the negative impact
of a disagreement, nor does it build social alignment between the
participants. What it does is move the interaction from disagreement
back to the practices at hand—interpreting the soap through personalization and other forms of speculation.

To summarize, instead of flaming, participants in r.a.t.s. attended
to an ethic of friendliness by playing down the disagreement with
qualifications, apologies, and reframings. They built social alignment
with partial agreements, naming, and acknowledgments of the others'
perspectives. They moved conversation rapidly away from the disagreement itself and back to the group's primary purpose of collaboratively interpreting the soap opera. It also is worth noting that there
were relatively few disagreements over the story line—just under
10%—suggesting that one common disagreement strategy was to stay
silent. The norms that protect interpretation seem to actively diffuse the
force of disagreements and perhaps lead to their being voiced less often.
This leads one to question to what extent a *meta-text* of fandom reflects
genuine agreement or fans' desire to create an affiliative environment
that will encourage the voicing of interpretations.

Much of what I have described is not much different from what
happens in face-to-face conversation. Just as most disagreements are
handled with some degree of tact in offline life, so too are they handled
with an orientation toward the face of the other online. One reason that
online relationships can feel like face-to-face friendships is simply that
both share many of the small but essential details of human interaction
used to convey warmth and respect.

Ritualized Space for Friendliness

Tangents

To this point, I have considered how the ethic of friendliness is
attended to throughout the messages discussing the soap opera. Although sticking to the topic of the soap opera has obvious benefits for
a group organized to discuss soaps, it does pose some problems for
friendship, which rarely (if ever) is so topically constrained. Talking

only about soaps impedes the group's ability to become a bunch of friends. During the early years of r.a.t.s., when the amount of message traffic was more manageable, participants handled this by simply digressing, a practice that generally was tolerated. However, in the fall of 1991, when traffic began to expand dramatically, people who barely had time to read the posts pertaining to the soap operas began to voice irritation with having to weed through messages that did not even relate to the soaps. Someone proposed that the convention of marking a subject line with "TAN" (for tangent) used in other Usenet newsgroups be imported, a suggestion that was adopted almost simultaneously and with little further discussion.[5]

TANs can cover any number of topics. They often begin with the soap opera and then turn personal:

> I like how story threads on the soap bring out story threads in people's lives that they then share on RATS (for example, stuff about children and pets in the various TANs). It's mostly light and fun. Even when it gets serious, it's still engaging. (Doreen, 1993 survey)

In other cases, the TANs share personal news. This post from one poster about another is typical:

```
Hi everybody—Just wanted to let you know that
Cindy Dold and the BH [better half] have a new
little baby boy! Cindy's modem at home is broken
so I doubt she'll be posting anything any time
soon, but you can send your congrats to her at
cd@mcl.cyi.msstate.edu. She'll get it eventually.
Here are the vitals:
Born: 6:05 p.m.
Date: October 1, 1992
Sex: Male
Name: Charles Mitchel Dold
Weight: 8 pounds, 10 ounces
Length: 21 inches
Health: Perfect
Little Charles is solely responsible for Miss.
State's win over Florida that evening. They made it
to their hospital room from recovery just in time
for kickoff! Go Bulldogs!!
```

```
Congratulations to Cindy and Norman, and welcome
Charles! (October 16, 1992)
```

A post like this one is likely to result in a flurry of congratulatory e-mail for Cindy:

> When something big happens (wedding, birth) that's made known to the Net, we do send each other e-mail. It's nice to get it, too. (Jane, 1991 survey)

The big "somethings" that people share in TANs are not always as happy as weddings or births, but the group provides social support through darker times as well. One longtime poster's surprise birth announcement told us that she had lost the baby to sudden infant death syndrome within days of her birth. When she shared her tragedy with the group in a post inspiring in its grace and strength, I was not the only one in tears. Many of us were deeply moved[6]:

> I like the personal tone of this newsgroup with people (mainly women) freely giving support and expressing care for one another. Recently, for example, Lisa's personal tragedy has touched my life most profoundly. (Doreen, 1993 survey)

Many people responded to Lisa, and it mattered to her:

> I had really looked forward to telling everyone about my baby and getting their surprised and pleased reactions, for example, and it helped to know so many people cared when she died. :-((Lisa, 1993 survey)

As another participant puts it, "We've developed a kind of family, and when good things and bad things happen, there's a lot of support out there on the Net" (Judy, 1993 survey).

Although I did not ask specifically about TANs, many people who responded to my survey explicitly pointed out their important role in personalizing the r.a.t.s. environment: "I also like the *AMC* TANs because it gives you a chance to get to know the poster and then people who post don't seem like faceless people on the other side of the country, they seem like a real person!" (Kelly, 1991 survey). Another participant's comment on the TAN offers a good sampling of the topics:

I find the subjects brought up as tangents almost as interesting as the soaps . . . for example, the cross section of r.a.t.s. who are cat lovers, Star Trekkers, etc. Some of us have shared our birthdays, our taste in beer, and our butt size. . . . We know who has read GWTW [*Gone With the Wind*]. . . . We know who has PMS [premenstrual syndrome]. (Debbie, 1991 survey)

As the mentions of "butt size" and "PMS" suggest, the tangents often are used as a forum for discussing issues of particular concern to women including experiences with violence against women, worst dates, and whether or not to change names when marrying. Less gender-bound topics might include how early participants put up their Christmas trees, other television shows, and notorious court cases. TANs offer participants a space in which to broaden their discussion and, when it is called for, to provide one another with social support. The marking and maintenance of this space can be seen as an institutional acknowledgment of the group's commitment to friendliness. At the same time, the indication that the post is tangential in the subject line lets those participants who are not interested in the group's social dimension to avoid these broader interactions.

Unlurkings

The last of the marked genres in r.a.t.s.[7] also is social in nature. Unlurkings, informally marked by the use of the terms *unlurking*, *unlurk*, and *lurker* in the subject lines, are posts in which new or rare posters introduce themselves to the group. These posts usually specify the poster's name, how long the poster has been lurking in r.a.t.s., the poster's occupation, the species and names of pets (especially cats, which are taken to be a common link among *AMC* participants), and almost always general opinions about *AMC*. This unlurking is typical:

```
It's me again. I wanted to introduce myself. My name
is Kari Barnes. I am a PhD. student at Carnegie
Mellon University in Pittsburgh. I have been
watching AMC for several years. At first, it was
during the summers in the mid to late 70's— back
```

```
when Erica was involved with Nick and her marriage
to Tom (this was while I was in high school). Then
I watched during my lunch hour. With the help of
my faithful VCR, I have not missed an episode in
about 4 years. My husband likes to watch it with
me sometimes, but he is not a big fan.
I like to read the updates and the posts, but I do
not always have the time to read them all. My
husband and I do like to know what other AMC fans
think of the storylines.

That's it for now. (September 29, 1992)
```

Unlurkings are regular but not common. Unlurkings are introductions, flagging the entry of new members into the community and providing the others with the opportunity to welcome them. Responses to unlurkings work as a welcoming committee, encouraging new or returning participants to remain active voices by letting them know that they have an interested audience:

```
>By the way, this is my second time unlurking.
>The first was yesterday when I sent a test
>message which actually made it. I don't have
>time to give you any background info on me at
>the moment—duty and deadlines call, but I wanted
>to alert everyone about the opportunity to see
>Jenny. Enjoy!! :)

Any time you have some to tell us more about
yourself, Andrea, we welcome it. (October 14, 1992)
```

For at least some posters, it was the welcoming responses they received to their first posts that made them into regular participants:

I stopped on r.a.t.s. to check out what was happening on *AMC* since I never get to watch it, and the rest is history. I was hooked. I posted, and it was great getting responses from people welcoming me to the group. I'm more interested in the Net than in the show. The members are more like friends. (Monica, 1993 survey)

Like TANs, unlurkings have become institutionalized through being labeled. That the only two identified genres that are not informational are interpersonal indicates this group's ongoing orientation toward fostering a group environment of friendliness.

Dyadic Friendships

The friendly nature of r.a.t.s. is further buttressed by a private but sometimes visible world of one-on-one friendships that have formed as participants move from public discussions to e-mail. A number of people who responded to my surveys indicated that they had formed a small number of close one-on-one friendships through the group:

> I have met [two] friends, and I have met others who I consider [acquaintances], having not formed much more than that. (Anne, 1991 survey)

> I e-mail daily with two other r.a.t.s. participants, and I consider them both close friends. Our relationships have expanded far beyond the discussion of *AMC*. I consider others on the Net-at-large to be friendly acquaintances whom I would enjoy getting to know better in a personal sense. (Carrie, 1991 survey)

Friendship pairs often develop out of Usenet groups. Parks and Floyd (1996) conducted a randomized e-mail survey of Usenet posters and found that 60.7% of them had established personal relationships through Usenet. Most had moved their interactions to e-mail and in some cases met face-to-face, as these two *Days of Our Lives* (*DOOL*) r.a.t.s. participants explain:

> I've become good friends with several people I've met on the Net. One is now my housemate; another got me into square dancing; a third loaned me a car when I visited Portland recently. I'm sending Christmas presents to one r.a.t.s.'er in New Zealand for the second year. I do a large amount of Net-related e-mail each day. None [has] become [a lover]. Yet. B-) (John, 1991 survey)

> I tell them it's a place where a group of us from all over the world sit and discuss soaps online. They look at me funny, and I try to explain,

but it's not easy! I also tell them that I found all my long-lost sisters here (the Peels from *DOOL*) and that we get together all over the country. Then they REALLY look at me strangely and say "You drive to meet people that you've never met to talk about a soap opera!!" And I say "Heck yeah!" (Lynn, 1993 survey)

Parks and Floyd (1996) found that 35.3% of their respondents used the telephone, 28.4% used the postal service, and a full third (33.3%) carried their relationships into face-to-face interaction.[8] Women were somewhat more likely than men to have established online relationships, but the best predictors were the duration and frequency of posting to a particular newsgroup. Their respondents reported "moderate" levels of commitment to these relationships (as measured with a standard scale used to assess commitment in face-to-face relationships).

Although these friendships often are conducted below the surface, they are referred to in the public discussion. For example, when one r.a.t.s. participant meets another from a different location, one (if not both) will post a report for the others to read. In smaller ways, posters might demonstrate a dyadic friendship by referring to another by name in one's message. Thus, these private pairs of more individualized friendships bubble up into the group's environment. Although this seems to enhance the general sense of friendliness in the *AMC* group, some of the survey respondents in the *DOOL* group indicated that the explicit tightness of a group of friends in that subgroup made some readers feel excluded rather than welcomed. In Chapter 6, we will see that this has become increasingly problematic as the group has grown ever larger.

The Limits of Online Friendship

The three areas of practice I have discussed—disagreements about the soap opera, social genres, and dyadic friendships—provide some answers to the question of how a group of strangers comes to see itself as an inclusive "bunch of close friends." Other ways in which friendliness is promoted are through the image of participants as intelligent and witty, humor, and the provision of social support. People create an atmosphere of friendship on r.a.t.s. by treating one another as they would treat their friends—with kindness, breadth, depth, and an accepting attitude that goes beyond what is called for by the task at hand.

That there might be no big mystery to how people can create friendships online does not mean that these online friendships are considered identical to face-to-face friendships. Whereas some posters who had not met face-to-face seemed completely content describing their relationships with the others on the group as friends, others qualified their descriptions in ways that indicated, if not the lesser worth, at least the greater strangeness of online friendships:

> I generally say that r.a.t.s. is an electronic discussion group where people can talk about particular soap operas and where strange friendships seem to emerge among people who may never have met each other but who share a common interest. (Suzanne, 1993 survey)

> It is an unusual circumstance, this whole entire thing—having "friends" you have never met. (Anne, 1991 survey)

> The hardest thing for me to explain is when I refer to someone that I only "know" over the Net but I consider a friend. I'll talk about what has happened to them or something they said, and when someone asks me who they are, I try to explain, and they usually look at me as if I'm crazy since I've never met this person and often only communicate with them in a very public way. (Sally, 1993 survey)

In addition to finding the friendships in r.a.t.s. slightly foreign in feel, some participants recognize that the text-based medium allows people to imagine others to be more attractive than they would be face-to-face:

> I think of them as decent people, some of them, as friends—just like I do with the people I know in person who watch soaps. The only exception being that I tend to form an idealized image of them in my head, which never matches the reality. But, then, that's what I expect others do too. (John, 1991 survey)

> I define r.a.t.s. as a group of folks who got together because of a single particular interest, in my case *All My Children*, but who have discovered that we really like each other as people (or at least Net personalities). (Debbie, 1991 survey)

Walther (1996) calls this the phenomenon of *hyperpersonal interaction*, in which relational partners rate one another more highly online than they would in face-to-face groups. If these newsgroup friendships are a little strange and a little idealized, they also are easier to let go of when the pressures of life intervene. Just as a soap fan might skip the soap when she or he is busy, the soap fan also might lessen or drop the social connections in r.a.t.s.:

> I was in closer contact with a couple of people before, and we talked about other things that didn't have to do with the group. I did e-mail, but some of these relationships I've had to let lapse due to less time available. (Linda, 1991 survey)

If r.a.t.s. is any indication, then online friendships are comparable to and compatible with face-to-face friendships, but at least for most participants, they do not replace them.

Influences on the Development of Online Social Norms

The range of practices I have considered in this chapter—microstrategies of disagreement, marking sociable posts, and indicating the presence of backstage friendships on the main stage of r.a.t.s.—all work to demonstrate and continually reinforce the group's norms regarding how participants ought to relate to one another. Many of the ways in which friendliness is created in r.a.t.s. draw on face-to-face interaction. The discourse strategies in disagreements, the enhanced breadth of discussion, the provision of social support, and the recurrence of face-to-face meetings share as much with offline friendship as with online friendship. This is suggestive of how friendship can come so easily in a medium so new. At the same time, some of the practices involved in creating friendliness in the online environment are unique to the medium. The use of the subject line to create particular types of social situations in the two genres of tangents and unlurkings exemplify this.

Friendliness in r.a.t.s. is just one example of the general tendency of ongoing computer-mediated groups to develop behavioral norms. Some online norms span wide groupings of CMC users. For example, Myers (1987a) writes, "There is widespread acknowledgment of a national BBS [bulletin board system] community—with both positive and negative norms of behavior" (p. 264). Werry (1996) discusses linguistic norms on Internet Relay Chat. There also are norms that span Usenet. McLaughlin et al. (1995) derived a seven-category "taxonomy of reproachable conduct on Usenet," drawing on posted reproach sequences in Usenet groups and the introductory Usenet postings distributed across the network. They identify norms regarding the incorrect use of technology, bandwidth waste, network-wide conventions, newsgroup-specific conventions, ethical violations, inappropriate language, and factual errors. Norms also develop at the group-specific level, as McLaughlin et al.'s (1995) fourth category indicates and as I have demonstrated in r.a.t.s. Users continually reinforce the norms of their groups by creating structural and social sanctions against those who abuse the groups' systems of meaning (Mnookin, 1996; E. M. Reid, 1991). Groups have differing norms about sanctioning themselves. Smith, McLaughlin, and Osborne (1997) found considerable variation across groups in the tone of reproaches for *netiquette* violations. In r.a.t.s., not surprisingly, violators are given what one respondent calls "gentle reminders."

Face-to-face experience and the medium are two influences on the norms that come to be important in organizing practice in r.a.t.s. and, I would suggest, in other computer-mediated groups. Two other important influences on emergent norms in online groups are the characteristics of the participants and the purpose of the group's interaction. The issue of participant characteristics in r.a.t.s. will be developed in terms of individuality in the next chapter. At this point, it is illustrative to consider how the fact that most participants are women may influence the group's adherence to an ethic of friendliness.

Usenet, like most CMC, is populated by many more men than women, a fact that stems in part from men's greater access to the medium. Because men have greater access, computer-mediated groups, including Usenet, are likely to exhibit male styles of communication, so that even when women have access, they might not be comfortable or interested in participating. Ebben (1993), Herring (1994, 1996), Selfe and Meyer (1991), and Sutton (1994) are among those who have shown that many of the gender inequities of face-to-face interaction are perpetuated online, where women speak less, are less likely to have their topics pursued, and are seen as dominating when they gain any voice at all.

Savicki, Lingenfelter, and Kelley (1996) found, in a large random sampling from many Usenet groups, that the gender balance of newsgroups has a modest correlation with language patterns within them (although they stress that there clearly were many other factors at play). Groups with more men used slightly more fact-oriented language and calls for actions, whereas those with fewer men were more likely to self-disclose and try to prevent or reduce tension. Herring (1994, 1996) describes an online female style she calls *supportive/attenuated,* which "idealizes harmonious interpersonal interaction" (Herring, 1996, p. 137). In this style, "views are presented in a hedged fashion, often with appeals for ratification from the group" (p. 119). Herring's description matches well the disagreement styles of r.a.t.s. participants, suggesting that the language practices in this group likely are influenced by participant gender. Given the concerns about gender inequities online, it is notable that r.a.t.s. is not only a place in which female language styles prevail but also a place in which there is considerable self-disclosure and support on the very types of female issues that provoke flame wars (if raised at all) in so many other groups.

The fact that so many women would come to this group in the first place stems from the gendered nature of the form around which they rally. Many aspects of the normative structure of r.a.t.s. come right back to the soap opera. Interpreting soaps is, after all, the group's primary purpose. It is hard to underestimate the influence of this purpose on the normative structures of r.a.t.s. For example, if one looks to the disagreements and compares the disagreements over interpretations to those over facts, one finds that all of the message features that lessen the threat of a disagreement and enhance friendliness are more likely to occur in disagreements over interpretations (see Appendix C). Disagreements over facts—what did or did not occur—challenge the participant's memories on truly minor issues. Disagreements on interpretations challenge the others' socioemotional standards and reasoning, a far greater threat. Loading such disagreements with protective wording demonstrates the group's orientation toward making it safe to voice interpretations.

One would not necessarily need safety to voice interpretations, but soaps, as the previous chapters have shown, rely on their audiences to interpret them through reference to their own feelings and relationships. The discussion they stimulate often is quite personal. As messages quoted in Chapter 3 indicated, there is a good deal of private and sometimes painful self-disclosure in the course of interpreting the soap opera. The richness that those disclosures provide is necessary for the soap's fullest collaborative interpretations. Thus, the group is invested in supporting these disclosures. This helps to explain how this group developed its social support function. That social support has grown into tangents indicates the seriousness with which the personal is honored in r.a.t.s. as well as the pleasure that shared personalizing offers.

This group's purpose of interpreting the soap opera encourages the friendly relational norm seen in the tendency to treat one another well, especially when debating interpretations, and to promote an environment in which people would be willing to come forth about personal traumas when it would help to interpret the show. At the same time as it promotes particular practices, the orientation toward interpreting sets limits on the friendliness of the social environment in r.a.t.s. The fact that tangents are marked explicitly in the subject lines indicates that some people do not want to partake in r.a.t.s. when it goes beyond the soap. Although the establishment of the TAN genre sanctions a space for purely social chat, its marking also marginalizes it as outside the group's primary arena. Even one of r.a.t.s.'s most sociable participants thinks that there should be limits:

> I am one who began talking about "life" things, or things just that I felt, not related to my particular soap, *AMC*. . . . This is how the TAN subject header became used. I like it! I don't think we have to talk about *AMC* all the time, but I also don't believe someone should continually talk about anything other than *AMC*; otherwise, they don't belong in the group. (Anne, 1991 survey)

One sees other affirmation of the overriding importance of interpretive practices in the frequency with which disagreements leave the issue of disagreement and reorient to the task of interpreting.

To summarize, the ethic of friendliness that pervades r.a.t.s. discourse is influenced by multiple forces, as are the norms that organize interaction in other online groups. Face-to-face interaction offers language and models of its use, the medium offers novel ways in which to organize communication, the characteristics of the participants influence how they are likely to interact as well as what they are likely to communicate about, and the purpose of the group limits and shapes the group's topics and treatment of those topics. However, none of these influences is a sole governing force, and exactly which aspects of any of them came to be important in the underlying normative structure of r.a.t.s. could not have been predicted.

Appropriation and the Creation of Community

Norms provide much of the tradition that organizes online communities. In social worlds where objects to tie people together simply do not exist, normative traditions are particularly important. The friendliness practices I have discussed are structural in that they are routine and systematic features of the language that is r.a.t.s. At the same time, they are "varied and improvisatory" (Miller & Mintz, 1993). Because posters have to meet the demands of the particular situations that inspire their messages, their specific behaviors always are open to variation. As Hymes (1975) writes, there is a "continuous tension between tradition and situation, tradition defining situations, situations displacing traditions, both inevitably and mutually changing" (p. 355). Over the long run, as practices become routinized, they become incorporated into the structure of the group (tangents are an excellent example). That structure is then recreated through ever-dynamic practice, which continually challenges the group's structure, changing it over time (Duranti & Goodwin, 1992). Tradition, as Bauman (1992) explains, should be understood not as "an inherent quality of old and persistent items or genres passed on from generation to generation" but as "a symbolic construction by which people in the present establish connections with a meaningful past and endow particular cultural forms with value and authority" (p. 128).

Thus, the structures that organize online groups are emergent, an unpredictable outcome of the tensions between the many preexisting influences on people's messages and the linguistic and cultural resources they choose to draw in putting their messages together.[9] Rather than seeing participants in online interaction as operating in ways dictated by the available resources or rules, an understanding of online social structure as emergent implies that participants pick and choose from what is available, at times using things in unexpected ways and at times not using some of the possibilities. Some of what happens in r.a.t.s. can be explained by the forces out of which it forms. Some can only be explained by reference to the endless variation that comes from its participants as they selectively and creatively appropriate what is offered every time they choose their words.

Notes

1. At the time this was posted (in 1993), most people in the group were using the term "Net" as a synonym for the newsgroup rather than for the Internet as a whole. Some respondents, however, explicitly differentiate between their (friendly) relations in r.a.t.s. and relationships conducted elsewhere on the Internet.

2. In using the term *keying*, I draw on Goffman (1974).

3. In the coding, *elaboration* was defined as something that fit best into the sentence form "I disagree and _____."

4. Reasoning and elaboration often were difficult to differentiate. For coding purposes, *reasoning* was defined as something that fit into the sentence form "I disagree because _____." More important than the division of examples into one category or the other is that they serve similar functions in the group's disagreement practices.

5. This is a nice example of how interactive and easy the creation of ongoing group traditions can be.

6. Indeed, 5 years later, knowing that she has since had two healthy children, I still get choked up writing this.

7. For a discussion of the other genres, the reader is referred back to Chapter 2.

8. Hellerstein (1985) found this relational movement offline in a study of a university online systems as well.

9. The idea that CMC groups are emergent is shared by Contractor and Seibold (1993). In their work on group decision support systems, they draw on Giddens to argue that participants appropriate rules and resources from pre-existing sources of influence through social interaction. They base appropriations in members' perceptions of the group's rules for structuring discussion and in the content and pattern of group interaction. Structuration theory and self-organizing systems theory are used to explain that the group members' interactive appropriation of the preexisting rules and resources creates structure beyond that which already exists. The generative mechanism of a group's structure lies in the recursive interplay between structure and interaction. The patterns of appropriation that emerge in computer-mediated groups may attain stability, may occur cyclically, or may fluctuate, depending on the fit among the multiple influences on them.

5

The Development of Individual Identity

The rec.arts.tv.soaps (r.a.t.s.) newsgroup is held together by its clear focus on interpreting the soaps, its group identity, and social norms that influence every message. All of these factors shape the sense that this group is a community. But it would not feel like a community without the individual personalities that emerge out of the endless parade of messages in r.a.t.s. These "net.personalities" allow r.a.t.s. participants to feel that they know one another, even if they do not post or have personal relationships with each other. Just as the norms of r.a.t.s. interaction and the intelligent/witty group identity are interactive accomplishments, so too are the individualized identities that emerge within the group. Individual posters are influenced by several factors and use a variety of discourse means, which I will review in this chapter, to develop their group-specific identities. Whereas this process of creating identities is inherently individualistic, the acceptable means of establishing identity, as well as what constitutes an acceptable identity, is socially defined, revealing another layer of emergent social norms.

To Post or to Lurk

One cannot create a recognizable identity in any group without posting. Like any voluntary online group, some people in r.a.t.s. are far more active posters than the rest. Indeed, analysis of how frequently people post to r.a.t.s. reveals dramatic differences in the participation rates among participants. Most posters rarely contribute, merging into an anonymous collective. Other people's messages appear again and again. These heavy posters become particularly responsible for personalizing an otherwise anonymous environment and for setting the tone of the group.

Most people in r.a.t.s. do not post at all, choosing not to seek active voices, let alone identities. Brian Reid calculated the estimated readership of r.a.t.s., as well as of the other Usenet groups, between 1986 and 1994. In 1986, he estimated that r.a.t.s. had approximately 1,100 readers. By December 1988, that estimate had risen to 6,400. By December 1990, he was estimating that as many as 28,000 people might read r.a.t.s. By the summer of 1993, the estimate reached 48,000. The accuracy of these numbers is dubious given that there is no real way in which to measure nonposting readers, but any way one slices it, there are far fewer posters than readers. During the 10 months I collected messages in 1992, there were only 2,503 posters, surely a small fraction of the participants.

There are a number of reasons that one would opt not to post, among them uncertainty about how to post, a sense of not knowing enough about the group to speak, the feeling that one has nothing new to contribute, and a lack of time, as these survey responses indicate:

> I follow another newsgroup religiously (misc.kids) and just can't keep current with r.a.t.s. I have posted once or twice lately but don't really feel I "know" a lot of the new regulars. I have a massive kill file but still get 100-200 *AMC* [*All My Children*] messages that I have to go through when I get a chance to read. (Danielle, 1993 survey)

> I'm mostly a lurker now . . . because I don't have time or because i feel that my POV [point of view] is just what someone else said, and I don't want to waste bandwidth just to say "me too." (Lisa, 1993 survey)

> I suppose I'm just lurking (although not completely—I just posted one note) because I don't have the time to spend writing long, amusing

TABLE 5.1   Participation Rates in rec.arts.tv.soaps During 10-Month
Corpus

Number of Posts Written	Number of Posters and Percentage	Number of Posts and Percentage
1	828 (33)	828 (3)
2 to 9	898 (36)	3,671 (11)
10 to 49	626 (25)	7,477 (23)
50 to 99	78 (3)	5,482 (17)
100 to 199	50 (2)	7,262 (22)
200 to 299	16 (0.64)	3,909 (12)
300 to 399	2 (0.08)	763 (2)
400 to 499	1 (0.04)	420 (1)
500 to 599	2 (0.08)	1,108 (3)
600 to 699	1 (0.04)	636 (2)
700 to 799	1 (0.04)	752 (2)
Total	2,503 (100)	32,308 (100)

NOTE: Percentages are in parentheses. Percentages do not add to 100 due to rounding.

letters about all this. (If I had time, I would not be having to wean
myself off the one soap I was watching—which this newsgroup has
helped immensely with. I *know* nothing is happening on the soap, so
why bother to watch it?) (Samantha, 1993 survey)

Even among those who do post (like some of these self-proclaimed
lurkers), there were enormous differences in the amounts of posting. In
an analysis of one month's posts from 1991, I found that 10% of the
posters wrote half of the group's messages (Baym, 1993). Similar differences emerged in my analysis of 32,308 "from" lines collected during
the 10-month corpus. Table 5.1 summarizes the results of this analysis.

A third of the posters wrote only once in 10 months. This group of
very light posters wrote only 3% of the total posts. As seen in the
quotations from survey responses, some of these very light posters
considered themselves to be lurkers. The 1,602 posters who wrote
between 2 and 99 posts constituted nearly two thirds of the group and
wrote just over half of the messages.[1] The group's 73 heaviest posters,

those who each wrote more than 100 messages in the corpus, wrote 46% of the posts.[2] This dominance of the voices of heavy posters is even more striking when one considers the many thousands of lurkers. The heavy posters' greater interest and commitment to r.a.t.s. is indicated not just by their greater posting frequency but also by the fact that they were most likely to respond to my questionnaires. Of the 51 responses I received to the first two surveys, 10 were from heavy posters, 33 from light posters, and 8 from lurkers. Furthermore, the only posters anyone mentioned by name in my survey responses were heavy posters, strongly suggesting that these frequent participants are most likely to develop recognized personas in the group.

As the reader likely has figured out by now, the exemplary heavy poster is Anne, an administrative secretary at a major American technical institute, creator of the update genre, and general prominent persona. Anne has been participating longer than nearly every other participant. During the 10-month corpus, Anne wrote 2.3% of the messages herself, more than 75 a month (all sent from her office computer). Anne has become known not just for the frequency of her messages but also for her style, marked by its extreme friendliness and use of others' names, which has become instantly recognizable:[3]

```
>BTW [By the way], Anne, you really crack me up
>sometimes!

Belinda, the feeling is mutual and we are so glad to
have you back! (July 22, 1992)

>These spoilers are from Soap Opera Weekly.
>Carter plots his revenge. Helga seeks a remedy
>to her problem.

Hi sandy, thanks for posting these. (August 6, 1992)

Hi all you new posters! keep 'em coming! :-))))
(August 5, 1992)
```

Indeed, Anne posts so frequently, and with such personal and cheery affection for the others, that one might trace the friendliness ethic that characterizes the group in large part to her early and continued presence. The affection she doles out is returned, and the recognition she has obtained perpetuates her participation:

> Anyway, reading the group encouraged me to post more and become more involved! You were right in your assessment that maybe I just realized that folks found me fun and entertaining or enjoyable, and being appreciated made me feel so good. Actually, probably seeing my name in some sort of header or quoted made it even more exciting for me. The more I became involved, the more addicted I got! :) (Anne, 1993 survey)

Thus, the heaviest posters, who also seem to be the most invested in r.a.t.s., gain the greatest opportunities to develop unique and recognizable styles and may play particularly influential roles in creating the group's social environment. *Additional voice for the soap*

The Computer Medium as an Influence on Identity

All posters, whether heavy or light, find their ability to shape identities influenced by the medium. For example, Usenet's ongoing temporal structure allows for the possibility of becoming a heavy poster and, hence, provides the very opportunity to construct an online self. The asynchronous temporal structure of Usenet, where participants have time to think about what to write before posting, can enhance their ability to strategically manage the impressions they create (Walther, 1996). Identities such as Anne's could not emerge in a real-time short-term chat room. Rather than focusing on temporal dimensions, most research into online identity has emphasized that the cues on which we rely in face-to-face meetings are *filtered out* (Culnan & Markus, 1987). I will address the issue of anonymity in a moment. For now, I want to show how even without face-to-face cues, the medium does allow a number of structural ways in which to create consistent identifiers to fill this void. We might not have faces, but we can have unique identifying marks. Most important among these are names and signature files.

Enhanced Naming

The obvious starting point in creating an online identity is the choice of a name. Names can appear in the from line of the headers as well as in the signatures at the end of messages. Whereas users of many systems choose evocative new names, people in r.a.t.s. usually identify themselves using their real names.[4] Myers (1987b) describes the power of naming in anonymous computer systems, writing that names are "transformed into trademarks, distinctive individual smells by which their users are recognized as either friends or enemies within an otherwise vague and anonymous BBS [bulletin board system] communication environment" (p. 240). Walther and Burgoon (1992), studying a non-anonymous computer-mediated communication system, found that even when participants had access to one another's real names, they still developed nicknames and used embellished signatures. Walther and Burgoon suggest that the creative enhancement of naming counteracts the inordinately high levels of uncertainty about one another in computer-mediated space. This is further supported by reports that names are enhanced to define identity in other disembodied communication media including citizens band (CB) radio (Dannefer & Poushinsky, 1977; Kalcik, 1985) and urban subway graffiti (Castleman, 1982).

The use of real names in r.a.t.s. is partially attributable to the systems used by these participants to read and write to the group. Most people access r.a.t.s. through work-related accounts that identify them using their real names. The preference for real names is normative as well as structural. Participants on r.a.t.s. actively discourage anonymity. Although some take on nicknames, most who use nicknames also promulgate their real names within the same messages. One prominent r.a.t.s. personality, for example, uses her initials as a name, but her full name appears in the headers. Similarly, one popular poster is known as "Granma," yet she makes no effort to hide her real name. When a poster's from line is a seemingly random collection of letters and numbers, the poster usually will sign off with a name. When there is neither a name nor a signature, people often will ask for a name in their responses. In general, then, r.a.t.s. has an aversion to anonymity in identity construction, an aversion likely rooted in the demands of soap opera discussion. The use of real names helps to create a trusting environment in which the type of personal disclosure so important to collaborative soap interpretation can be voiced.

Signature Files

In addition to signing off on their messages, participants using most newsreaders can use signature files (or sig files), attached automatically to the bottom of posts by the senders' newsreaders. Because they appear in the body of each post from a given sender, sig files are one of the most immediate and visually forceful cues to identity. Sig files demonstrate a variety of strategies for building recognizable identities. They usually include a name, an e-mail address (and now a Web address), and a quotation (often chosen because it indicates the poster's value system), as seen in these examples:

```
--
Pam Evelyn Johnson      pamjohn@frank.northville.edu
I myself have never been able to find out precisely
what feminism is; I only know that people call me a
feminist whenever I express sentiments that
differentiate me from a doormat.Rebecca West, 1913
```

```
--
                        *******************
Amy                     Since I gave up hope,
                        I feel much better.
                        *******************
```

```
--
Lisa D. Anthony         "Practice random kindness and
Assistant Staff             senseless acts of beauty"
Unnamed Important Laboratory
anthonyl@ll.bigu.edu
```

Some sig files include personal information about one's hobbies and, hence, serve as an explicit forum for self-disclosure:

```
--
Jennifer Anton (jenn@university.edu) Collegetown,
State Catx2 Owned, Square Dancer, Leaper, Ballroom
Dancer in training
```

Sig files often take advantage of another opportunity provided by the computer medium, the ASCII illustration, which is built out of punctuation marks and letters, as in this smiley face:

```
--
Marge E. Sussman      | So many bad drivers,
Computer Co. Systems  | so few hand gestures.
555-555-1212 (work)   |    o o
marges@cc.com         |    \___/
```

Or this one, used by a participant who nicknames herself "kitten":

```
***********************************************************
conan the librarian a.k.a. kitten  /\ /\debbie lynn
"my life's a soap opera,          {=.=}
    isn't yours?"                    ~
lynns@library.university.edu
```

In one of my favorite files, Lexine kept us posted on her pregnancy by counting down to the due date. When her son was born (a little late), she started to use this sig file:

```
--
"The Babeling"—born July 5th | Lexine Andrews
(also known as....)          |
                             | E-mail:
O_\__/←Jamie Peter Andrews   | lexine@unix.com
```

In addition to disclosing posters' values and hobbies, the quotations and even illustrations used in r.a.t.s. sig files often are directly related to the soap opera and may change frequently to keep up with the soap's latest funny lines. In these cases, identity construction is built in part off of the soap opera text (a practice that has become increasingly important, as I will discuss in Chapter 6). These two quote *AMC* characters:

```
--
Bill Phillips     "Would you just calm down,
bill@uv.cc.com     you're supposed to be
                   innocent!" Edmund to Dimitri,
                   breaking in on a 'business'
                   meeting at Erica's
```

```
--
Lyle Mays
lmid@isp.COM    "But Bri, we have so much in common...
GE Mail: lm4    ...for one thing, we're both mammals..."
Vox: (555) 555-1212       —Hayley, pressing her luck
```

This one includes both a reference to the *AMC* character Tad and a creative rendition of the outrageous ties for which the character Trevor is known, indicating how identities thrive on creativity even when built from materials provided by the show:

```
--
What, You don't sit around  |  V  David J. Lincoln
in a loin cloth and turban  | /%\ E-mail: dj8493@univ.edu
chanting around a beezwax   | |&| sodif78@univ.edu
candle for Tad to come back?| \@/ <= Trevor tie
```

Perhaps recognizing the significance of having a sig file but not knowing just what to do with one themselves, some opt for delightfully self-referential versions:

```
--
!!!!!!!!!!!!!!!!!!!!!!!!!!!!!!!!!!!!!!!!!!!!!!!!!!!!!!!
Emily
ajcu1947@unix.stateu.edu

...with nothing particularly witty to .sig...
```

```
--
s. robinson
------------------------------------------------------
= How the heck do ya get that .sig to work =
=                anyway !!!???                =
------------------------------------------------------
```

The names and sig files in r.a.t.s. both demonstrate that at the same time as they are shaped by the medium, they also are greatly influenced by the social context of r.a.t.s. in which these structural possibilities are used. The group's naming conventions encourage the creation of identities in line with offline personas. It is bad Usenet manners to include sig files more than five lines long, and most adhere to this norm. Sig files also are conventionalized in their inclusion of quotations. That most of these files are humorous is in keeping with the r.a.t.s. norm of wit, which we have seen in other group practices. At the same time as these names and sig files are shaped by the medium and the group's social conventions, each is distinctive in its own way and, with repetition, becomes an instantly recognizable marker of its unique user.

Offline Identities

The personalities on r.a.t.s. also are shaped by the offline identities of their idiosyncratic participants. As we have seen, people generally use real names, which create congruence between on- and offline identities. Furthermore, people in r.a.t.s. use a good deal of self-disclosure, which is one of the main ways in which they let other people know who they are. Participants slip self-disclosures into their posts in many (sometimes subtle) ways, as is the case here where an updater sneaks in a mention of her efforts to become pregnant:

```
As we open the show, Trevor and Nat have gone to bed
for the evening and are starting to heat things up
when Mighty Mo becomes Mighty Mouth (scenes like
this make me question the sanity of my trying to get
pregnant—I like uninterrupted sleep!). Trev says
he'll take care of it, but Nat shows how she can
manage just fine. (October 28, 1992)
```

This self-disclosure, like many in r.a.t.s., results from personalization of the soap. However, people often self-disclose simply to let more of themselves seep into their messages and to promote the interpersonal atmosphere I described in Chapter 4. The exemplar of this is Granma, one of the women referred to repeatedly in my questionnaires as an especially wonderful poster. Her humorous self-disclosures have revealed that she is a grandmother, a college undergraduate, and (among other attributes) a former stripper. Granma even shared with the group her joy and excitement when the daughter she had given up for adoption years ago came, with her own daughter, to live with her. These two excerpts from one of her posts demonstrate her unique disclosing style:

Did they put in yet another Junior? (I know I know,
my mind is playing tricks on me! Hell, at my age, my
mind is the only thing still active! Ha!)

BTW, I liked Lyle refering to Carter Jones as CJ.
Reading this post made me feel like I actually had a
life! (Excuse me, but studying, working, studying,
working, cleaning, cooking, studying, studying,
studying and then studying isn't exactly my idea of
having a life!)

Granma CJ (October 19, 1992)

Many self-disclosures are offered to explain the inability to keep up with
the soap or absences from the group:

BTW, I'm back!!!!!! Just coming at you from [big
company] instead of [big university] now that I've
graduated and gotten a job. It's great to see all
the new posters, especially since with the new job,
I won't have much time to post. (August 3, 1992)

Still others are slipped in to situate soap-relevant comments:

I got a new 21-speed ATB [all-terrain bicycle] two
weeks ago, and have been riding like a madman (food
to bike by: cold Creamettes w/Miracle Whip, and
PowerBars). Last week, around the time people were
noticing the winter attire on PV [Pine Valley]
citizens, I saw this bodacious brunette in a Miata
on Lake Shore Drive, wearing a bikini, w/ a bumper
sticker on her car that read: "Beyond Bitch." I was
laughing so hard I had to stop for a sec. :) I got a
mental image of Gloria wearing it, and rode around
for the next two days matching bumper stickers and
t-shirts to AMC characters. (August 3, 1992)

In other words, posters find a variety of ways in which to situate their
self-disclosures, but they share the common characteristic of being
grounded in the lives they live offline. Although it is possible that some

of these self-disclosures are phony, disclosing an imaginary self clearly is not the norm.

This stands in contrast to the dominant discourse on online identity, which emphasizes how anonymous users can switch genders, appearances, sexual orientation, and countless other usually integral aspects of the public self as well as taking on multiple identities (Carpenter, 1983; McRae, 1997; Myers, 1987b; E. M. Reid, 1991, 1995; Stone, 1995; Turkle, 1995). E. M. Reid (1991), for example, writes that Internet relay chat users "are able to express and experiment with aspects of their personalit[ies] that social inhibition would generally encourage them to suppress." In general, the work on online identity demonstrates a scholarly fascination with how anonymity can be used to invent alternative versions of one's self and to engage in untried forms of interaction, theoretically problematizing the notion of "real self." Turkle (1995) and Stone (1995) both connect online identity play to a postmodern condition in which identities have become more fragmented and flexible.

Somewhat ironically, this emphasis on the disjuncture between on-and offline selves ultimately situates the online self vis-à-vis the offline identity who creates it, even while arguing that there may be no such thing. In her analysis of identity formation in real-time multiuser domains (MUDs), for example, Turkle (1995) argues that these groups can operate much like therapy. The identities that people construct in Turkle's model come from a combination of the anonymity afforded by the medium and the psychological histories of individual users. Of one user, for example, she writes,

> Julee shaped her game persona to reflect her own deep wish for a relationship with her mother. Playing her ideal of a good mother allowed her to bring mother and daughter together in a way that had been closed off in real life. (p. 188)

Of another, she says, "Ashamed of his father in real life, he used the MUD to play the man he wished his father could be" (p. 191). Turkle might well be right that such psychological issues are behind some of the identity construction that goes on in online spaces, but analyses that emphasize anonymity and identity play do not lend a good deal of insight into what we see in r.a.t.s., where people seek to build identities congruent with those they present face-to-face; therefore, the analyses are problematic as general models of online identity. Instead, we need to understand how online identities are shaped by the online contexts in which they are created.

The extent to which identity play is an anomaly in r.a.t.s. can be seen in this thread, which plays with the potentials for multiple identities and the realities of meeting real people offline. It originates in joking about a married couple, Martin and Beth (both of whom participate in the group), and evolves into the suggestion that all the people who post from Champaign-Urbana, Illinois (including me), are in fact the same person. Embedding quotes from the Martin and Beth thread, Jennifer writes,

```
>Yes folks, there really is a Beth H.! (Hi Martin,
>Hi Beth). We met in Cleveland last year and had a
>wonderful time discussing AMC, RATS and all of our
>net buddies over some delicious Vietnamese food at
>Minh An's on Cleveland's near west side.

NOW—How do you know that Martin didn't HIRE someone
to PRETEND to be his wife?? :] :] :]

>Now, as to whether there's really a Martin
>;-)))))))))....well, I'll just have to take
>Beth's word for it...and those were some pretty
>wonderful words as I recall :-)))))))).

HEY—how do we know that Martin isn't just a figment
of Beth's imagination and she didn't just get a
second account with her "fictious" husbands name??
:^} :^}

(And—how do any of you know that *I* really exist.
Actually there's only one person in Champaign
Urbana—and she's I mean I'm schizophrenic and
sometimes I post as Debbie and sometimes I post as
Nancy and sometimes I post as Annie and :] :])
(June 1, 1993)
```

Dan (from Chicago), who recently had joined all the Champaign-Urbana r.a.t.s. participants (including me) at a get-together at Jennifer's house, responded,

> >(And—how do any of you know that *I* really exist.
> >Actually there's only one person in Champaign
> >Urbana—and she's I mean I'm schizophrenic and
> >sometimes I post as Debbie and sometimes I post as
> >Nancy and sometimes I post as Annie and :] :])
>
> And Jennifer can, quite amazingly, project several
> different images of herself as the pseudopeople that
> she posts as when out of towners show up at CU
> [Champaign-Urbana] get togethers. How do you do
> that????? :-) :-) (June 6, 1993)

Debbie chimes in to further the joke, ultimately bringing it back to the recurrent soap plot of multiple personalities:

> >(And—how do any of you know that *I* really exist.
> >Actually there's only one person in Champaign
> >Urbana—and she's I mean I'm schizophrenic and
> >sometimes I post as Debbie and sometimes I post as
> >Nancy and sometimes I post as Annie and :] :])
>
> yeah, jennifer (i mean i) am really tight with
> the cs [computer science] dept....multiple accounts
> and split personalities....
>
> actually, c-u is merely a figment of someone's
> sick imagination...
>
> yeah, that's it....jennifer/debbie/nancy/
> annie.... it's the old multiple personality
> story line again...
>
> *giggle* (June 6, 1993)

The rampant use of smiley faces throughout this thread and Debbie's "*giggle*" all indicate how much it is taken for granted that people in r.a.t.s. are who they claim to be and the absurdity of suggesting that it might be otherwise, especially given that so many participants do meet offline. If people in r.a.t.s. really did play with their identities, then there would be no humor in playing with the idea of playing with identities. This is not to say that no one in the group has ever pretended to be something he or she is not, but such play is an anomaly in the group.

To summarize, users' offline identities are an important influence on the identities they form in r.a.t.s. Participants' self-disclosures and the interpretations they bring as they personalize the soap stem from offline experiences (see Chapter 2 for a discussion of this). The offline meetings between participants (see Chapter 4), which often are discussed in r.a.t.s., further buttress the congruity between the group's on- and offline selves. I will develop, in a moment, the ways in which a participant's skill with words and wit are important in creating identity in r.a.t.s. At this point, I just note that if one brings these talents to r.a.t.s., then the potential surely exists offline as well (although it might not be demonstrated as frequently or in quite the same ways). The fact that offline identity is brought so straightforwardly to online interaction in r.a.t.s. cannot be understood as a function of the medium or even of offline identities, for these individuals might well take on playful personas in other online contexts. It is the group's value structures that have normalized the congruity between on- and offline selves.

Situating Online Identity in an Online Community

The social context of an online community is perhaps the single most important influence on the identities constructed within it. In r.a.t.s., the need to interpret soaps through reference to personal experience encourages a group norm of (relatively) honest self-representation. Collaborative soap interpretation is best enhanced when we are given access to others' real-life experiences. Thus, this central group need influences the norm of presenting "real" selves in r.a.t.s. In general, the individual self is inseparable from the group in which it is situated. Rogoff (1990) makes this argument when she writes, "Even when we focus attention separately on the roles of the individual and of the social milieu, those roles are defined in terms that take each other into account" (p. 28). Emphasizing the role of communicative practice in the interplay between social whole and individual identity, Miller (1994) argues, "Selves, like cultures, are not so much preserved . . . as they are created, reworked, and revised through participation in everyday . . . practices that are embodied in and responsive to shifting interpersonal conditions" (pp. 175-176).

The Dialogic Self

In other words, people in r.a.t.s. and other online communities define themselves not just in relation to their offline selves or to the medium but also in relation to one another and to the group as a whole. Bakhtin, writing during the 1920s (although he was not translated into English for another 60 years), was among the first to reflect on the ways in which individual identity is shaped by interaction with others. He emphasizes the role of *voice*, problematizing the issue of with whom speakers' utterances originate and arguing that most of our words and positions come from others in our environment: "The unique speech experience of each individual is shaped and developed in continuous and constant interaction with others' individual utterances" (Bakhtin, 1986, p. 89). Any voice within a community is *heteroglossic,* combining others' voices in individualized ways. In so doing, speakers position themselves relative to other voices in their communities. The most blatant level on which this is seen online is in direct quotations, as when people in r.a.t.s. build the posts through which they develop their identities directly off of others' posts. Appropriations of others' voices also may be more subtle:

> The transmission and assessment of the speech of others, the discourse of another, is one of the most widespread and fundamental topics of human speech. . . . Our speech is filled to overflowing with other people's words, which are transmitted with highly varied degrees of accuracy and impartiality. . . . Every conversation is full of transmissions and. interpretations of other people's words. (Bakhtin, 1981, pp. 337-338)

Examples of this are seen in the subtle adaption of previously voiced interpretations, themes, and vocabularies in r.a.t.s. The assessments of Natalie, discussed in Chapter 3, offer a particularly vivid example.

Kamberelis and Scott (1992), drawing on Bakhtin, suggest that individuality "gets defined in and by the effects of appropriating, transforming, and resisting particular discursive practices in particular ways" (p. 373). This is seen clearly in the humorous performances in r.a.t.s. where other voices in the soap opera, other popular cultural genres, the r.a.t.s. community, and other communities are appropriated, transformed, and resisted in individualized ways. Lexine's *Sesame Street* post in Chapter 3 exemplifies this. She appropriates the voice of a previous poster (Dan), quoting him explicitly. He has appropriated voices from *Sesame Street* ("one of these women is not like the others") and transformed them to work with those of the soap opera. Lexine reappropriates the *Sesame Street* reference, transforms it, further incorporates voices from *AMC*, and uses the whole to resist the *AMC* text, criticizing the ideological agenda in the writer's representation of women, a criticism that reinvokes numerous voices in the community who have made that complaint before. What is Lexine's is the choice of other voices, the affective reaction to them, and the creativity with which she combines these voices into her own perspective. Thus, finding a voice in r.a.t.s. is largely a process of making oneself distinct from the others through the creative use of existing discourse.

Community Values and Interpersonal Status

As I have argued, in addition to being built in relation to and out of other voices in the community, individual voices also are influenced by a set of community values, in this case values that grow out of the needs of this group as a soap fan community. The norm of honest self-presentation in the name of enhanced interpretation is one such value. These values also lead to differential valuing of identities. While in theory all participants in a Usenet group are equal, in fact group values make some forms of *cultural capital* more valuable than others and, hence, lend those with such capital greater status. Hobson (1989) discusses how information about soap opera events can serve as a form of such capital among soap opera fans. A second valuable form of cultural capital in r.a.t.s. is performative skill. Each of these can be understood in terms of the processes outlined in Chapters 2 and 3, particularly the goals of maximizing interpretations and creating entertainment for one another in discussing a medium that does not always entertain as it should. I will discuss these two forms of cultural capital in r.a.t.s.—information and performative talent—in turn.

INFORMATION

I already have discussed the importance of providing information in r.a.t.s. To be involved in r.a.t.s. at all, one has to be aware of what is happening on the soap. Without knowledge of the latest characters and twists and turns, one cannot follow even the simplest of r.a.t.s. discussions. Appropriating the importance of information to build their own personas, some posters become known for their ability to remember the shows' histories or electronic soap opera archives. This *Santa Barbara* fan demonstrates how one can gain an identity by identifying one's self with expertise in the show's history in this excerpt from a longer post (all ellipses are the posters' own):

> Also...I keep a SB [*Santa Barbara*] archive, in it I
> will copy this file. If anybody is interested, I
> have archived a copy that somebody had of all the
> soap opera actors' birthdays (all soaps included),
> where to write to SB, history of Brandon, Channing,
> SB parentage. Just e-mail me if you're interested.
>
> Here's an sample, it may be outdated by now:
>
> here's a partial santa barbara family tree...
>
> pamela & cc were married & had mason. pamela had
> an affair with hal clark (scott's uncle). she & cc
> divorced but she was carrying cc's child (the
> writer's never quite explained why it wasn't hal's
> kid). nevertheless, unbeknownst to cc, pamela had
> his daughter, elena. she was raised by dr. alex
> nikolas (cc's enemy who always loved pamela).
> cc finds out about her about 30 years later when
> she starts terrorizing the acknowledged capwell
> children (esp. eden & mason). this story gets really
> convoluted so i'll just point out the highlights.
> around the same time jeffrey & alex came to town
> for revenge on cc (because of his treatment of
> pamela) jeffrey & kelly fell in love & married...&
> divorced. elena was shot & cruz was accused...turned
> out she comitted suicide. alex left town after he
> realized he could never have pamela (BTW [by the
> way], pamela showed up during cruz' trial).
> i hope this helps...(November 22, 1991)

Another way in which people stake out identities is by identifying themselves with informative genres. We have seen that the discourse of r.a.t.s. is categorized into genres, many of which are informative. Among these are updates, spoilers, trivia, and FAQs (frequently asked questions—and answers). Updaters, spoiler providers, and trivia and FAQ posters all gain their identities in part through the increased visibility of their informative contributions.

The update is the most prominent informative genre through which an individual can gain prominence. In r.a.t.s., each soap opera has a single person responsible for writing updates each day of the week. For each soap, then, there are no more than five updaters at a time (although substitutes may fill in when a regular updater is unable to post). Each updater becomes known for a day of the week (e.g., Jennifer is *AMC*'s Monday updater, Margie is the Thursday updater, and Lyle got the privilege of writing updates for Friday, usually the soaps' most exciting episodes). As I have discussed, updates were originated for *AMC* by Anne, who began by writing all 5 days herself:

> As you know, I started doing the updates on a daily basis. People were not doing any updates at the time, and I remember I just started doing them. I had a lot more free time back then *and* privacy. I could never have time to do it now unless I had a computer at home. I haven't parted with the $1,200 or so it would take to have one at home. If I did, I would most likely still be doing updates, probably once a week, [although] I may have taken some sort of hiatus at one point. (Anne, 1993 survey)

When Anne stopped updating, others volunteered, and she handed off each day. The person who is incumbent in the role of updater continues to select a successor or, when needed, a temporary replacement. Updating is a time-consuming task, and the updaters make a substantial commitment to the group. One of the rewards is the enhanced recognition of their identities.

Although there are generic similarities among updates (see Chapter 2), each updater develops a personal style that clearly differentiates his or her updates from others. I will return to this performative aspect of updating later in this chapter. At this point, I want to emphasize how updaters' special role in providing information about the show's latest twists and turns grants them special status within the newsgroup. Participants also may become affiliated with the genre of spoilers if they post them regularly and consistently. Similarly, trivia posters may become identified with that genre. Lisa took on the job of writing and regularly posting the group's FAQ, making her the unofficial group *norm keeper.* These r.a.t.s. participants who serve in the role of updaters or who provide spoilers, trivia, or other inside information gain greater social recognition than do most posters, not just because of their enhanced visibility but also because these informative commodities matter in this community. As one woman says,

> My favorite r.a.t.s. posters are the ones who post summaries and interesting tidbits about "my" two soaps since I don't generally tape or watch them and that's my only way of keeping track of what's happening on them. :-) (Angela, 1991 survey)

PERFORMANCE

Important as information is in r.a.t.s., the ability to write intelligent, witty, insightful performances is the most significant form of cultural capital, one that buys a good deal of visibility and status in r.a.t.s. Bauman (1975) explains why performance has special potential to increase the status of the performer:

> Through his performance, the performer elicits the participative attention and energy of his audience, and to the extent that they value his performance, they will allow themselves to be caught up in it. When this happens, the performer gains a measure of prestige and control over the audience—prestige because of the demonstrated competence he has displayed, control because the determination of the flow of the interaction is in his hands. (p. 305)

In addition to gaining increased recognition and admiration, the virtuoso performers in r.a.t.s. also might have more power to shape the perceived group consensus than do the other participants. For example, if someone generates a clever nickname that becomes widely used in the group (e.g., "Not" for Natalie), then the poster has codified a group interpretation that might not have become institutionalized without that poster.

We saw in Chapter 3 that r.a.t.s. participants transform their criticisms to entertainment through humorous performance. Fan performances serve to create the group's identity of intelligent wits and to perpetuate soap viewing. They also serve to demonstrate virtuosity, allowing some participants to stake out identities as expert performers. Many of the posters identified by name in the survey responses are the performative funny ones: "Lyle is great! There are a lot of really funny people who post to *AMC* r.a.t.s. Anne and Brian PRZOIUHIHPI-HOIHPOI (well, you get the idea) are funny too" (Laurie, 1991 survey). Dan gained his online identity in part through his invention of a fun new performative genre, the unanswered questions (see Chapter 3). With only rare exceptions, he remained its sole practitioner as of 1998.

As you might expect, one of the main platforms for humorous performance is the update. Brian "PRZOIUHIHPIHOIHPOI" (he has a long Polish surname that few seem able to remember), for example, writes his updates in other people's voices. In this excerpt, he speaks as fashion critic "Mr. Blackwell":

```
AMC—7/21 update from MR. BLACKWELL—

That's the update, but let me give you my thoughts
on the other ladies who didn't do much today. Gloria
looked okay, but the color was too bland. Phoebe
looked great in a seafoam suit, Mona looked dreary
in red, Ruth's outfit was a great midnight blue, but
the bows should be in a young girl's hair, and Enid
looked like her personality: prim, proper, and
BORING! I took off points for anyone in long sleeves
under fifty (Opal, Ang.), wearing a shawl (Erica,
Natalie, Vivian), or wearing a suit (Livia). Ladies,
it's summertime, not October! Well, that's it for
now; see you at the next social event! (July 23,
1992)
```

The effectiveness of this identity-building strategy can be seen in this excerpt from a post Anne wrote 3 months later:

```
Nadine and Granma, what did you Mr. Blackwell's
think about the clothes at the wedding? Where's
Brian P. anyway? he's the "real" Mr. Blackwell...
(October 14, 1992)
```

In this update, Brian takes on the voices of Peter Jennings and other ABC News reporters, mocking live news coverage:

Hello, this is Peter Jennings here at Madison Square
Garden, where we are awaiting the latest news about
the goings on in Pine Valley. Let's quickly take you
too the floor where Jim Wooten is standing by. Jim?

Thanks, Peter, and the latest news is that Edmund
has asked Brooke to marry him; however, Peter, she
is having many doubts. It seems she has had it with
his childhood agonies; he has tried to blow off all
her excuses, and told her about what Dimitri said
about growing up and getting over his pain, but she
still won't buy it and has said she can't marry him.
Right now, Peter, he is at Phoebe's house talking to
her, and she's explaining how hurt Brooke has been
by the death of her daughter, Laura; so much so that
Phoebe says she is terrified of life. Oh, I just
received word Brooke is at Phoebe's agreeing with
her. Peter, I have word, unofficial, that Edmund has
asked Brooke again to marry him. I hope to have
further developments on this story soon.

Keep us informed, Jim, as we go to Lynn Sherr. Lynn,
do you have the latest on Angelique and Jack?

Yes, Peter, as you know, Angelique is remembering
her childhood when Jack comes in with the budget
figures for the shelter. She tells him she's been
having odd feelings dealing with the missing years
during her coma, and he decides to take her to a
drive-in restaurant, one of those places constantly
playing oldies with waitresses in poodle skirts.
While there, he tells her he will be her guide into
the 21st century. We can see that he is falling for
her, but she has no idea. He shows her an old
picture of himself and they talk about their youths;
they also make a pact not to "grow old." As they
leave, she asks if she can drive his sportscar,
which at first has her hitting the wrong buttons,
then getting caught by police for speeding, which
she gets out of. The last we know, she was going
upstairs to bed, and he was feeling mighty pleased.
Looks like nothing much going on right now, but

there could be some real news later on. Back to you,
Peter.

Thank you, Lynn. Now we go back to Jim Wooten for an
update; Jim, what's the latest you have?

Peter, Brooke has apparently said yes to his
marriage proposal. Now, whether this goes through
still awaits to be seen, but it's a good sign, so
far. Peter? (July 15, 1992)

Probably the most immediately recognizable performative style is seen
in Lyle's updates:

```
Storylines [A,C]:
-----------------
```

Carter, unaware his sister's phone has been tapped
by Trevor, feeds her false 4-1-1 on Nat (on
houseboat willingly; wants to leave Porkchop), and
freaks when he learns she told Trevor that he had
previously called. TweetyNat, meanwhile, is in the
galley fumbling around for a butcher knife [looked
like a Ginsu, actually], and praying once again for
Trev to find her [[shades of The Well] maybe we
should start a new lotto: how many times a year will
Natalie be kidnapped??]. She decides to hide the
knife under a pillow.

Midship, Psycho figures out Dillon has tapped the
line and starts talking directly to him: "Speak up,
Dillon!...you actually thought I'd tell you where
your wife is?!...Trace this!!...See you in hell!"
[as Pam noted, a line from *Cape Fear*] Trevor:
"You're a dead man." Click.

Not sweettalks CJ, and gets him to sit beside her on
the bed. She reaches for the Ginsu, but he spots the
movement, and as she tries to deliver a killing
blow, Carter blocks and spins her on her back,
screaming, "You lying, _two-faced_ WHORE!!" He

throws the knife overboard, takes off his belt,
wraps it around his hand and whops Not in the face
(twice), declaring, "this is for your own good." He
takes off the belt/wrap, grabs Nat by the hair, and
once again starts beating the crap out of her,
VICIOUSLY punching her in the face with his bare
hand [one of the most graphic (albeit cleverly
shot), unnerving scenes in AMC history; if that was
my wife, he'd never make it to trial].

When she regains consciousness, Not begs confusion
and forgiveness (Carter: "So you tried to stab me
because you were _seasick_??!"), and breaks out
Psyche 101, as she tells him she loves him, and
wants another chance. CJ bites, and hugs her (as she
grimaces from the pain). In a beautiful shifting of
gears, Not (sniffing) asks what's cooking, and
insists on helping. Carter leads her to the hot
skillet (thank God for cast iron). Nat grabs it,
flings the contents in CJ's face, and as he reels in
pain (and temp. blinded), proceeds to BEAT THE
LIVING S**T OUT OF THE GUY, knocking him
unconscious. She searches frantically for the
cellular, but only manages to knock it off the
ship's railing into the water [the writers are
playing us like an accordion, ain't they? :)].
[Meanwhile, Jer and Trev have stopped by Carter's
sister's place again, where Trev informs her that
"if she doesn't give them the location, and CJ hurts
Nat the way he hurt Galen, he's going to have to
kill her brother.]

Realizing she has to get the hell out of Dodge
(and fast), Tweety recalls CJ telling her about a
rowboat at the back of the houseboat. She also
remembers somthing about "dangerous currents" and
"not making it to shore," triggering a FutureFlash
of Trevor telling Timmy about her death. She regains
resolve and starts pulling up the lifeboat, but
Carter regains consciousness, scampers madly towards
her on all fours (did that remind anyone of the

```
just-hatched alien in "Alien"?), and grabs her,
screaming like a banshee!

TAXI!!!!!

CLIFFHANGER! (October 18, 1992)
```

Lyle's highly individualized use of nicknames, wording (e.g., "FutureFlash"), and brackets pervades all of his posts, not just his updates:

```
>I'm sorry, Anne my buddy, but I have to disagree
>with both you and Liz. It's not Nat's fault that
>she's in this situation, it's ENTIRELY Carter's
>fault for deceiving her.

I question the character's judgement for accepting
the ride to "31 Flavors." She and Psycho weren't
that close.

[ Wait. I think I heard something: "...How close do
you have to be to someone in order to accept a ride
to an ice cream parlor??? Answer: Depends on how
many times you've been shot, kidnapped and tossed
down a well. ;)) ] (October 20, 1992)
```

Jennifer's updates also have a distinctive personality and demonstrate a style very different from Lyle's or Brian's. Hers relies on capitalization and the embedding of what she calls her "cynical (or insightful) comments," as seen here:

```
Dimitri sees Nat and asks if she can forgive him and
if they can have a life together. Nat says that she
HAS forgiven him, but they can't have a life
together because she doesn't love him. { I don't
know—seems like a good reason to me. } She says that
she NEEDED him and that she was dependent on him,
but she never really LOVED him. Dimitri thinks she
wants to get back with Trevor and such { DIM—BUY A
```

```
CLUE—she don't LOVE you. } She says she needs to be
self-sufficient { watch out Nat—you're heading into
very unfamiliar territory }. Later Dimitri is in the
park and is thinking, maybe, just maybe, he needed
to save someone and Nat needed to be rescued.
(February 25, 1992)
```

Although updates are a convenient platform for performance, any post can be performative, as seen in Granma's self-disclosures and the humor mentioned in Chapter 3. A number of participants, like Granma, perform in part by making fun of themselves in their posts, creating a sense of who they are while making the others laugh. One of the most adept at this is Roseanne, as seen in these two posts complaining about being a day behind and the realism of the kidnapping story line:

```
>>I, like a lot of you, live in the Austin area,
>>and am quite upset at the fact that our local
>>station managed to get us a day behind.

>>Call them and tell them you are royally P.O.ed,
>>and if they don't do something, you'll watch AMC,
>>as well as the rest of your ABC viewing choices,
>>from the San Antonio station. If they ask, LIE.
>>Tell them you live south of the city, and have
>>a **really** big antenna.

>Sorry, Steve, this one won't work. I *do* live
>south of Austin and *do* watch the SA [San Antonio]
>stations at times and they, too, are one day
>behind on AMC.
>I imagine KVUE knows that. Maybe a northern city:
>Waco? Temple?

see!!! i told you!!! it IS A CONSPIRACY!!! THE
STATION MANAGERS ARE PROBABLY SECRET Y&R [The Young
and the Restless] OR B&B [The Bold and the
Beautiful] WATCHERS TRYING TO DO IN AMC. THEY'RE
PROBABLY ALSO CONNECTED TO THE PEOPLE WHO DECIDED
TO DO THE GNAT IN THE WELL _____ ON THE
HOUSEBOAT STORYLINE...
```

```
(wild rantings continue as couple of men in the
white coats break into her apartment, sedate
roseanne and place her in her calming pale green
straight jacket, the cat midnite is looking on
with wide eyes and a puffed up tail...)

roseanne "i'm not paranoid" paulson (October 17,
1992)
```

The use of capitalization, spacing, parentheses, and multiple exclamation points marks this post as a performance. In the next case, it is the degree of detail, comments such as "a long line of people with iron bladders," and her description of what she would do if she were Erica that mark this post as a humorous performance regulars would recognize as Roseanne's even without the headers or signature. Note how she signs her name with a self-descriptor in quotations, following the same distinctive format, although with different content, as in the post just quoted:

```
ok, i know we've discussed this bathroom stuff
before when nat was in the well, but i've noticed
it two times recently...

first of all, let me say i don't want the men
walking down the hall in the hospital tugging at
their zippers or the women entering an office
adjusting their panty hose. i would just like a
dose of reality in these long siege situations.

for any and all nurses out there, the little bit i
know about catatonia does not include trips to the
bathroom. doesn't the person just sit or lay in
basically one position? i come from a long line of
people with iron bladders, but i don't think i could
have lasted the amount of time carter was supposed
to be laying in his cell then hospital.

my mind is also a bit fuzzy, but did they switch
carter to a hospital gown? i can't remember his
attire when he lunged at galen. let me tell you,
```

i have had a cathater (sp?) once, and now if a nurse
tells me to pee, i ask her where and how much!

["iron bladder" paulson had decided that she could
wait a couple more hours because of still being
affected by anesthesia and the pain from a 6 inch
incision. the nurse decided that this was not to be!
i certainly learned my lesson!!! :)]

and now we have edmund and erica in the wine cellar.
they've been there from the time erica was
kidnapped, through dimitri's discovery, through
informing angelique et al, through a night time
flight to budapest, through calls during the day.

being conservative here, let's say 24 hours.
24 hours?!? yikes! if i were erica, not only would
i have wet my pants, my butt would be asleep from
siting on that wooden chair. i'd be cranky from
lack of caffeine, my stomach would have been
growling so loud that it would have been on
brooke's answering machine, my hair would be
stringy, well, you get the idea...

i'm not expecting total reality, but the only times
i've seen a bathroom on the show is when someone is
listening to a conversation on the other side of the
(stall) door or a pregnancy test. if they want the
kidnapping scenarios to be more believable, take the
people to a place with a bathroom (house boat).
after all, most of the lengthy kidnappings we've
seen have involved feeding the captive.

roseanne "potty mouth" paulson (November 19, 1992)

Just as Roseanne and the others sneak self-disclosure into these performances, the performances—even without explicit self-disclosure—
can build on previous self-disclosures, indicating the ultimate insepa-
rability of these varied means of constructing identity. If we reconsider
Lexine's *Sesame Street* post, for example, we see that her use of a
children's television show reinforces her identity as a mother. As I have

indicated, Lexine's motherhood has been the subject of much discussion within the group. She told the group when she learned she was pregnant, used her sig file to count down to the baby's due date, and included an ASCII illustration of him when he was born. This is further played out in this message posted to the group by Anne and responded to by Lexine:

```
Anne-mania writes:

>Subject: Re: AMC: This is a test
>
>WO, WO, WO! Two missing AMC ratsters back in
>ONE post! I'm in my glory! [. . .] Lexine, get
>Jamie on that keyboard NOW :-) if it says
>dkbkdsfkdkfsajweif
>fcbjasdkgfsdafjwa;fjasdjf;sdajfawejftawcdjkvasjgasfj
>across the screen that's ok! :-)

What?! Jamie has already mastered the keyboard at
the grand-old age of 14 weeks!!! Didn't I tell you
I had a genious baby? :-)

Hmmmm. . . . does anyone know how to clean
baby-drool off a keyboard? :)

Lexine
(who is spending much of her time these days playing
pat-a-cake) (October 18, 1992)
```

Community Affirmation of Identity

People in r.a.t.s. continually reinforce group values by validating and honoring some identities but not others. People affirm identities by responding to the posts of individuals who demonstrate desirable qualities, by identifying noteworthy individuals by name in their posts, and (perhaps most important) through praise. Anne's comment that "probably seeing my name in some sort of header or quoted made it even more exciting for me" indicates the importance of responses in affirming identities and encouraging ongoing participation. In this post, a woman's postscript clearly identifies particular posters I have discussed as especially valued, implicitly letting them and others know that their posts demonstrate the types of qualities (in this case, humorous performance) that attract positive attention:

```
P.S. Sure was great seeing posts from Granma &
Roseanne again! And to echo Anne—Where's Brian these
days? Hope that he didn't get so burnt out at that
scrabble tourney that he's forgotten how to spell
AMC:-) (October 15, 1992)
```

Posters also often are rewarded with explicit praise. This poster praises Lyle for his performative nicknames:

```
>Yogi and Boo-Boo (Brian and Dix) bop chez hospital
>>and learn from Gloria that Nat has been kidnapped.

ha ha ha ha ha! Love the names!

>Dix and Jethro X blow off Pops and blow Dodge to
>pick up Junior (who has grown two feet and is now
>five-years-old) chez Chandler.

Jethro! ha ha ha! (I DO hope coffee runs right
through this key board, or I'm in trouble big time!)
(October 19, 1992)5
```

In this post, Anne is praised for having correctly predicted upcoming events, demonstrating her competence in reading the soap genre:

```
Anne wrote:
>
>I don't know if any of you noticed or not
>(Lexine did, thanks Lexine!) but *I* predicted
>Carter was going to Corinth before I knew!
>Really I did...! :-))) I did post it before I
>saw last week's show or any of the ad's I've seen
>after I predicted it...I'm so proud.... :-) :-)

I remember that, Anne! You're amazing. (October 20,
1992)
```

Praise itself can be performative, as this post praising the *AMC* updaters for carrying out their duties during Natalie's boring well saga demonstrates. The song parody here takes off on a group-authored parody of the story line (sung to the tune of "The Farmer in the Dell"):

```
I wish to dedicate the following verses to Jennifer,
Carol, Andrea, Marge, Lyle, and the subsitutes.

You put up with some uttterly boring shows
You put up with some uttterly boring shows
Hi ho the dreary-o
You put up with some uttterly boring shows

You still did the updates
You still did the updates
Hi ho the dreary-o
You still did the updates

We thank you very much
We thank you very much
Hi ho the dreary-o
We thank you very much (October 8, 1991)
```

To summarize, participants in r.a.t.s., and other online groups, have a wide range of interrelated discursive strategies to individualize themselves despite the apparent limits of the medium. They can post frequently so that their voices will gain distinction, if only through their volume. They can mark their posts with names and sig files that give insights into their values and affiliations. Their repertoires of show-relevant knowledge can distinguish them, as can their self-disclosures, which might or might not bear direct relationships to the show's content. They can take on distinctive roles, taking advantage of the group's genre system. They also can develop identities through performances that build distinctive styles.

Although these identity-building resources might seem neutral, the ways in which (and success with which) they are used are deeply rooted not just in the influence of the medium and offline identities but also in the community in which they are mobilized. Online identities are built out of, and situated in response to, a group of other voices and a value system that makes some types of voices more appealing than others.

The value system that shapes identity construction in r.a.t.s. emphasizes honesty, information, insight, and wit, all of which can be attributed to the group's purpose of interpreting the soap opera and the problematics of being intelligent fans of the genre that sometimes suggests otherwise. Such values are continually reinforced through the selective affirmation of the many identities put forward in the group. Perhaps one *can* be anyone he or she wants to be online, but if one wants to be admired or even liked, then he or she would be wise to attend to the very real social constraints that groups develop.

Notes

1. I fell into this category, authoring 41 messages.

2. The phenomenon of heavy posters has been shown in other analyses of online interaction as well. The works of Hellerstein (1985) and Myers (1987b) suggest that some of the heavier computer-mediated communication users thrive on the relational possibilities of the medium. The heavy users of the University of Massachusetts system studied by Hellerstein (1985) said that their primary use of the system was to communicate with friends. They reported spending more time in computer-mediated social interaction than on the phone or in face-to-face communication. Myers (1987b) found two types of experts among his heavy users, one technologically astute and the other relationally astute, both of whom dominated the message flow. Those he called the *social experts*, who focused on relational concerns within the group, gained their power from their ability to nurture and direct the flow of online relationships. They saw the computer as a community and the communication networks as based on social relationships. They interpreted the communication content as the expression of values and saw the result of communication as the creation of roles.

3. Mark Huglen, who had never read r.a.t.s. but helped me to code the disagreements and agreements, remarked on how quickly he came to recognize her style (and how likable he found her to be).

4. Or at least names that sound ordinary enough to be real.

5. Besides its singling out of Lyle and its clear valuing of humor, this example also is noteworthy for its invocation of an embodied reader sitting at the computer whose laughter can damage her computer. This common praise strategy also appears in this post from another poster: "I'm going to have to be careful what I eat while reading notes now that you're back...not everything cleans off the keyboard/screen easily :-)" (October 29, 1992)

6

Futureflash:
5 Years Later

I have been describing rec.arts.tv.soaps (r.a.t.s.) at a particular point in the Internet's history. The Internet of the early 1990s was undergoing incredible expansion, but that growth pales in comparison to what has happened since then. At the time I stopped collecting data in 1993, to have access to the Internet one generally needed to have a job that provided an account, to be a student at a university that provided accounts, or to have a spouse with an account. The overwhelming majority of users were male. America Online, which had more than 13 million subscribers in late 1998, was a small new business that connected to the rest of the Internet only through e-mail. The World Wide Web, which for many has become synonymous with the Net, barely existed (although early versions of Mosaic, which became Netscape, were beginning to circulate). Most people who read Usenet were on UNIX mainframes, using UNIX-based newsreaders such as *rn* and *nn*. In a very real sense, the Internet of that time was only for the educated elite. As r.a.t.s. participants looking back describe it:

> This sounds incredibly snobbish, but 4 years ago, to read a newsgroup, you had to have some level of competency with a computer. I don't think that's true today. (Carine, 1998 survey)

175

There are a lot more different types of people subscribing. It used to
be that it was mainly "computer knowledgeable" people. (Darla, 1998
survey)

As Carine indicates, these days anyone with enough money to
afford a low-end computer and a modem, or a WebTV, and approximately $20 a month can have an account on the Net. It still is a minority
of the American population—let alone the global population—that is
online, but the Internet is dramatically more accessible today. Usenet
can now be accessed through America Online, other commercial Internet service providers (ISPs), and the Web. The most used Web browsers,
Netscape and Internet Explorer, both have built-in newsreaders. One
Web site, DejaNews,[1] now archives Usenet posts back to 1995, allowing
anyone with Web access to read and post to Usenet; one need not even
have a newsreading program.[2] Whereas there were approximately 5,000
Usenet newsgroups in 1993, there are well over 20,000 as of this writing
and likely many more as of your reading.

For r.a.t.s., like most newsgroups, the rise of ISPs, WebTV, and
cheap(er) computers meant a huge increase in traffic. When America
Online opened its (one-way) floodgates to the Internet at large, the
impact was felt immediately on Usenet as thousands of new participants joined its groups. The huge numbers of posts in r.a.t.s. became
unmanageable. Running a KILL file to cut out posts for the soaps one
did not follow could take half an hour alone, to say nothing of the time
it would take to read the posts that remained. To handle this problem, r.a.t.s. subdivided into three newsgroups—rec.arts.tv.soaps.abc,
rec.arts.tv.soaps.cbs, and rec.arts.tv.soaps.misc—in 1994. Each of these
three groups now carries more messages daily than r.a.t.s. did at its
peak. Immediately following the split, enormous amounts of new posters logged in to each of these three groups, irreversibly changing the
community. As Lisa puts it,

The community has definitely changed, more rapidly than it would
have if it had been left as r.a.t.s. That happens when you get a
sudden influx of people. I would say that at least 50% of r.a.t.s.a.
[rec.arts.tv.soaps.abc] became "newbies" in the community, all in the
first month or two of the newsgroup split. (1998 survey)

I had stopped reading r.a.t.s. in 1994, before the split. There were
more messages than I could read regularly, and ironically, I was spend-

ing so much time writing about r.a.t.s. and the soaps that I had far less time to keep up with either. In 1998, when I logged on to r.a.t.s.a., the group that now houses the *All My Children* (*AMC*) discussion, it was like returning to the town where I went to college after a long absence. Many of the same people and institutions were there and thriving, but there were new people and traditions that everyone seemed to know but me. Anne and Lisa still were there, if posting less often, but others such as Lexine, Lyle, Granma, and Roseanne were gone (although Lexine turned out to be lurking, as did several other old-timers). New voices had become firmly ensconced as the heavy posting regulars. Joellen, a 40-year-old special education teacher who began reading r.a.t.s. in 1992 and left a few years later, echoes my experience in her description of returning to the group as "like leaving home and feeling uncomfortable trying to go back" (1998 survey).

This final chapter examines both the continuity and changes in this online community in light of the many changes in the Internet. In addition to the time in which I have been reading r.a.t.s.a. (as a lurker rather than a participant[3]), I have visited a number of Web sites that have emerged around r.a.t.s.a. The bulk of this analysis rests on 41 responses to a survey I posted to the group and e-mailed to people recommended by Anne and Lisa as particularly important current or former participants (see Appendix A). These responses painted a surprisingly consistent portrait of the group and its evolution.

The respondents to this survey, like those who responded in 1991 and 1993, were predominantly female (35 females, 6 males) and held a wide variety of occupations including graduate student, secretary, system administrator, software engineer, childbirth educator, and editor (among approximately 13 other occupations). Of the 41 respondents, 26 had been reading since at least 1993 (and, therefore, were participants during the time I have described). Of the 41 respondents, 5 also had responded to my earlier surveys. The age range of respondents was 23 to 54 years, with an average age of 37. Although there is no way in which to assess the representativeness of this sample, it is consistent with another series of nonrandom demographic assessments of the *AMC* r.a.t.s.a. contingent conducted by Sean Griffin (personal correspondence, May 14, 1998). Of the 219 people who had responded to the weekly polls he posts, 87% were female, 57% were age 36 years or over, 31% had at least some graduate education, and 66% had incomes over $35,000. One suspects that despite the openness of the Internet, the group remains biased toward the high end of the educational, age, and income spectra. According to Griffin's data, the group also is approximately 87% White, with the largest minority group being "Chicano/Hispanic/Latin American."

Consistency Over Time

Conventions and Conventionalization

Many conventions on r.a.t.s.a. have changed very little from the group's earlier incarnation as r.a.t.s. The genre system that was in place by 1991 still is the same; there are labeled updates, tangents (TANs), and spoilers (although the new convention of *spoiler space*—a screen full of empty or nearly empty lines—has replaced the "^L" that used to make the spoiler harder to read by accident). Unlurkings have gained the more formal title of "newbie introduction," at least within the *AMC* group, but their content and function remain the same. Speculations and other interpretations still comprise the majority of the messages and still go unlabeled. The group remains filled with abbreviations, in-group jargon, and nicknames exclusive to the group.

New conventions also have emerged (among them Griffin's weekly poll), indicating that the dynamics that led to the conventionalization of discourse practices still are very much in force. Most notable—and controversial—among these new conventions are the FACs (favorite *AMC* characters) and corresponding FOCs, FGCs, and FPCs for *One Life to Live (OLTL), General Hospital (GH),* and *Port Charles (PC).* Participants claim FACs, FOCs, FGCs, or FPCs and then usually indicate those affiliations in their sig files, so that many participants' online identities are marked by alignment with specific soap characters (even when they are not discussing those characters in the contents of the posts). The F*Cs differ in significant ways, indicating the continuing differences among the four main subgroups of r.a.t.s.a.: "The four groups are pretty distinct, even as to modus operandi; rules for acquiring FACs, FOCs, FGCs, [and] FPCs; and attitudes toward TANs, language, etc." (Tia, 1998 survey). This is the description of FACs from the *AMC* "Newbie Sponsorship Program" (to which I will return shortly):

> We have a concept on the group called a FAC
> (Favourite Allmychildren Character), which is
> your Pine Valley Alter Ego, if you want to have
> one—you certainly don't need to. You don't have
> to pretend to be it if you're not a pretender,
> but a lot of posters like having a FAC in their
> signature, at the very least. A FAC can be a
> character, a place, a prop, a set, an annoying
> personal habit...the sky's the limit. We have
> a FAC Erica but also a FAC Janet's Lovely Locks
> and a FAC Pine Valley's Treacherous Roads. The
> main rule is 1 FAC per Person, and 1 Person
> per FAC.

As this indicates, FACs can be—and are—used for role-playing, a practice that some enjoy more than others. For example, one participant who has come to be well known has developed his online persona in part through his humorous portrayal of a "drunken Brooke."[4] *AMC* participants may maintain a one person per FAC rule, but the possible FACs are left so open that there are plenty to go around. By contrast, FGCs are limited to characters. The first person to claim an FGC becomes the "CEO" of the FGC and can allow others to use that FGC at her or his discretion. As one might expect, the apparently exclusionary small-group FGCs have caused many conflicts in the *GH* subgroup.

A second noteworthy new convention is the "Frango Awards" given out within the *AMC* group. When I was participating regularly, several r.a.t.s.'ers mentioned their love of Frango chocolates (sold at upscale department stores). Several years later, this led to

> a TANgential discussion about them, which led many posters to
> sample, taste, bring to get-togethers, and send to other r.a.t.s.a.['ers],
> then at some point Whitney decided to give out awards to posters for
> creative types of posts, whether in their signature lines, subject mes-
> sages, witty responses to flame bait (as a diversionary tactic), or
> predictions that turn out to be true, etc. Hence, the "Frango Awards"
> were born. I believe they are now in their third year. Whitney asks for
> volunteers once a year to select the best of the best, and the awards are
> given out in January, I believe. The Frango Awards ceremony (set up

as in any other awards ceremony, Emmys, Oscars, etc.) for 1998
can be viewed at http://www.interchg.ubc.ca/budgplan/
frango98.htm. (Anne, 1998 survey)

Among the Frangos awarded is the Lifetime Achievement Award.
The first went to Lisa for her years of maintaining the group's FAQ
(frequently asked questions), and the second went to Anne.

Core Values

As Anne's description of what merits an award suggests, the
group's general purpose and values have remained constant, if occasionally challenged, over time. Participants' descriptions of what they
like most about r.a.t.s.a. draw on all of the themes so important to the
r.a.t.s. of the early 1990s, emphasizing intelligence, diverse perspectives,
friendliness, humor, and fun:

> [I like] conversations with intelligent folks who offer well thought-out
> insights. (Ariel, 1998 survey)

> [I like] the general camaraderie . . . and the fact that I can discuss my
> soaps and ask questions without being put down or looked down
> upon. (Courtney, 1998 survey)

> I LOVE the sometimes warped senses of humor. Also, I like hearing
> all the different perspectives. (Agnes, 1998 survey)

> [I like] the camaraderie, the humor, and the opportunity to discuss
> soaps with a group of unabashed, intelligent, and informed friends.
> (Tia, 1998 survey)

> What I like most about r.a.t.s.a. is that I have made many friends across
> the miles, including even outside the U.S. . . . Not only do we talk about
> *AMC*, but we get support from our friends in times of good and bad.
> It's remarkable! I also like the diversity of the subscribers; each and
> every one has a uniqueness about [her or him] and a different point of
> view so that one's perspectives are widened from others' points of
> view. And it very often is done without the least bit of hostility, more
> as in "Well, I understand your point, but I think a bit differently about
> it. . . ." There is genuine respect of others in many r.a.t.s.a. folks. I also

like the voluntary contributions that various posters make. Whether it's an update or a preview or a spoiler (provided [the participant has] posted it correctly) or a tidbit from a soap magazine or a trivia game, or any *AMC*-related game, the creativity inspires us and makes lots of fun for everyone. (Anne, 1998 survey)

The relationship that these fans have with the show now seems consistent with what it was then. They feel a mix of love and frustration. The genre still is viewed as inconsistent, leading fans to make pleasure for one another when the show does not. The fans have an extraordinary collaborative knowledge base regarding the show, one that has been enhanced by the creation of fan Web sites devoted to particular characters and shows. (However, not all Web sites are exactly devoted; for example, one fan maintains a site for people who hate the *AMC* character Brooke.) One fan likely is on the mark when she suggests that one reason for r.a.t.s.a.'s stability is "possibly because watchers/readers/ fans are pretty stable in what they want from the show" (Hannah, 1998 survey).

The r.a.t.s.a. participants seem to be stable not only in what they want from the show but also in what they want from each other. The importance of self-disclosure, social support, a welcoming attitude, and genuine friendship comes through as clearly as it ever has. People still disclose about their private lives in discussing the soaps and bring personal areas of expertise to bear on interpretation. Gloria's rich description of this phenomenon could easily have been written in 1991:

> Though we are all watching the same show, we see it [through] very different filters based on our life experiences, our priorities, and our professional backgrounds. When a medical, legal, [or] social issue comes up, those with the most experience, or any experience at all, weigh in with their takes on the situation. It is interesting to hear real-life solutions or complications that add depth to a very superficial story line. My husband asked me why I read the [newsgroup], and when I told him about the medical or legal perspective posted by one reader and the camera/television knowledge imparted by another poster [regarding] a specific scene, he said "Wow, so these are not just housewives looking to be carted off to Fantasyland." After I hit him (tho I knew he was teasing me), I knew that that was a major part of r.a.t.s.a. . . . As I read the [newsgroup] more and more, I learn much about the personalities, childhoods, current family situations, and life

experiences of the individual posters. These help me to form a picture of the person and help me to better understand not only their views but [also] the reasons for those viewpoints. (1998 survey)

The connections among maximizing interpretations of the soaps, self-disclosing, and providing social support for one another still seem to be in place. Like r.a.t.s., r.a.t.s.a. creates an atmosphere in which self-disclosure is safe, and in so doing, it encourages people with show-relevant personal experiences to offer their interpretations:

> It's amazing how open-minded people on r.a.t.s.a. are. A few years ago, when [AMC] started its homophobia story line, some newbies came on-board and made a juvenile stink about it. The responses from the many gay men (and the few lesbians) on this group ranged from defensive to humorously educational, but what surprised me [was] the amount of support and understanding that came from other demographics within the group. People who might not seem to fit the mold of socially progressive were angered by the intolerance and quite protective of the feelings of lesbians and gay men. (Bill, 1998 survey)

The r.a.t.s.a. newsgroup also has maintained its welcoming attitude toward newcomers, especially in the *AMC* subgroup. But as will become apparent, the relationship between old-timers and newbies is more strained than it once was.

The network of e-mail and offline friendships I described in Chapter 4 continues as well. Although many survey respondents say that they have no personal relationships with other participants, many others describe close e-mail relationships and friendships that have moved from the Net to offline life. At least one romantic cross-continental couple has formed through the group (although if his immigration visa is granted, the couple will not be cross-continental forever). Some who have left the group have maintained a number of friendships formed there:

> I made a few very close friendships through r.a.t.s., and for that I'll always be grateful. . . . I go to lunch once or twice a month with a couple of women who work at my university that I met through r.a.t.s. in 1993 or so. Another r.a.t.s.'er was coming to town from Oregon for a visit and posted ahead of time, asking if any [city name]-area

r.a.t.s.'ers wanted to get together for lunch. So we did, and the habit continues. We also do other things together (go to the movies, baseball games, and such). The funny thing is that discussion of the soaps is always more of an afterthought these days. (Joan, 1998 survey)

Although I still read the group, I have an ongoing "net.friendship" with someone who no longer posts, but we [have kept] in touch weekly for the past 4 [to] 5 years. [I] will be meeting her for the first time this summer! (Tabatha, 1998 survey)

The network of offline friendships continues to work as a community-enhancing force in the group, even for those who are not involved in such relationships. Asked why she thinks that the group has remained so consistent over time, one relative newcomer explains,

The old-timers started reading r.a.t.s.a. when Usenet was a reserve of academia and other learned professions. They have built relationships and friendships, encompassing not only their time online but including physical visits to each other's homes. (Gloria, 1998 survey)

The physical visits to which both Joan and Gloria refer have become increasingly ritualized and publicized within the group, further strengthening the role that they play in preserving the friendly relational atmosphere of the group. Regional groups of participants have organized; those in Chicago call themselves "Chiratsa," and those in Dallas call themselves "Big Dratsa." Photographs taken at these and other get-togethers are posted on the Web for all to see. (In general, the Web has become a way in which to associate faces with names in the group.)

In summary, r.a.t.s.a. perpetuates the purposes and accompanying values so central to r.a.t.s. These organizing principles have been kept in place by enduring conventions, a consistent relationship to the soap opera genre, and a network of personal relationships with one another, all of which manifest and become codified through an ongoing stream of dynamic communicative practice. In addition to these forces, many participants attribute the group's consistency over time to those long-time posters who have remained committed to the group:

A lot of the old-timers have stuck it out through the years, and they help maintain the tone of the group. (Amanda, 1998 survey)

Well, Anne is *still* part of it, too! People come and go, but there is a core group of people who have posted regularly all along, and I think that goes a long way toward continuity of style within the group. (Lark, 1998 survey)

New Tensions

"Old Fogies" Versus "Young Turks"

Although much of this community's practices have remained in place, their preservation no longer is as simple as it was in the old days when just about everyone who came in liked the group just the way it was. Many new participants have adapted eagerly to the norms, values, and conventions that defined r.a.t.s., and their participation is enthusiastically supported. In comparing r.a.t.s.a. to a private soap discussion on Internet Relay Chat (IRC) with which she was involved, Ariel, a 37-year-old graduate student, comments on the importance of "new blood" in any group:

At one point last year when [the] chat room had been *particularly* inundated with idiots, a bunch of the daily chatters (myself included) opened up an IRC channel. What I found out quite quickly was just how insular and closed an obscure little IRC channel can be. There was *no* new blood at all! And, while it kept trolls to a minimum, it also created a very stagnant atmosphere. By the end of a month, we all knew each other's likes and dislikes and I found it, quite frankly, totally boring. An open, public forum like r.a.t.s.a. has a constant influx of "new blood." . . . Some of it is "bad blood," . . ., but at least it's *different* blood! (1998 survey)

Indeed, although many of the old-timers seem to agree that the influx of new participants is necessary to prevent stagnation and that new participants often are wonderful additions to the group, a new type of newbie has appeared since Usenet became so accessible, and the once taboo flame wars have erupted in their wake:

Once AOL [America Online] "opened" the Internet and Usenet to millions, we were inundated with dozens and dozens of newbies and flame postings each week. (Lexine, 1998 survey)

It seems that over the past year or so, there have been more and more people getting online who are ignorant of rules of grammar, spelling, capitalization, etc. But even worse, they have nothing worthwhile to contribute. Sure, for years there were people darting in posting stuff like "I THINK BJ ROOLZ!!!! IF U DONT AGRE U SUK!!!!." But for a long time, they were drowned out by the intelligent conversation. Now, this sort of idiocy seems to be becoming the norm, while intelligent conversation is getting lost. Of course, this is happening across the Net and is not an isolated phenomenon. (Violet, 1998 survey)

I'd blame it on AOL and WebTV and other "services" that have made the Net extremely accessible. Some of these newbies have spilled over to Usenet, where many of them don't know (and, what's worse, have no desire to *learn*) the basics of netiquette. I have nothing against new users who need some help, but I really detest idiots who "storm the gates" and think the newsgroup should be turned upside down to accommodate them. (Ariel, 1998 survey)

The central problem to which these women allude seems to be that too many new posters neither understand nor care that this is a group with long-standing traditions which are highly valued within the community. While many quickly learn and adapt, others "want the world (i.e., r.a.t.s.a.) to change to their specs because it's inconvenient otherwise" (Lisa, 1998 survey).[5]

These violations and challenges to convention, once treated with gentle reminders, now result in flame wars that make the "rules" explicit. These flame wars were mentioned repeatedly when I asked what people like least about r.a.t.s.a. This was exemplified by an enormous flame war over who could and could not join a particular *GH* FGC.[6] Ariel describes this flame war:

There seems [to] have developed a split along the lines of "old fogies" versus "young turks." The recent FGC flame war (that I'm not ashamed to admit having participated in!) is a case in point. There were a lot of accusations that established, long-term posters were clique-ish and wanted to control r.a.t.s.a. It seemed to me that the people voicing the complaints were only interested in tearing down 10 years of well-developed traditions to suit their own (rather ill-defined) needs. What happens is that everyone jumps on the flame wagon and there end up being more posts about what's wrong with r.a.t.s.a. and its posters than what's happening on the shows themselves. . . . I think this shows that the newsgroup has really lost its initial focus (and I'm just not all that interested in the new focus—discussing the inner workings of r.a.t.s.a.). (1998 survey)

Marla, a 42-year-old secretary and part-time editor, shared with me a post she had contributed to this flame war that speaks specifically to the issues of maintaining community in the face of such onslaughts. In defense of the old-timers, she wrote,

```
As a community, we are diverse. Some have been
around forever, some like me since the early 90s,
and some are new. As in any community, there are
people we look to for advice and assistance. These
are the people who have EARNED this right. They have
helped "newbies," offered encouragement, and when
someone was in distress taken the opportunity to
talk via email with them. These are what most
cultures would call "elders" and deserve your
respect. They are also the ones who have struggled
and organized and founded and defined what the
culture (or community) is like. They are the ones
who keep the "written" records (lists and faq) and
can at the drop of a hat give direction to where
the information can be found. They are the
"storytellers" or "leaders" of the community
and you can't do anything about that.

There are also customs and traditions that belong to
a community. While people moving into the community
may not be happy nor those who feel their rights are
infringed upon may feel slighted, these are things
that will always remain the same. They bring a
consistency to any group. This, to me, would include
the FGCs and the net.parties. Both of these have
been a fact of life on RATS (then RATSA) ever since
I've been around. (March 12, 1998)
```

Thus, there is ongoing tension between the old ways of doing things, exemplified by the old-timers, and the attitudes of the new people, who either do not know these traditions or do not like them. Although the resulting flame wars are disliked, several participants acknowledge the flame wars' value in community preservation, as Gloria's response indicates:

> I dislike the tendency of the old-timers to band together against what they perceive to be attacks from people who are not part of the long-standing r.a.t.s.a. group. I understand the defensiveness and the need to protect or defend those who you have developed enduring relationships with. But sometimes it is not necessary for everyone to jump on a newcomer who has stepped "out of line." The onslaught can be very brutal sometimes, when perhaps an admonishment from one offended party might be sufficient. But I must admit that r.a.t.s.a. has seemingly held on to its light, respectful (for the most part), and friendly atmosphere in the face of a Web that has become a haven for those people who see anonymity as permission to be obnoxious. Perhaps it is this tight control and "take no prisoners" attitude that has fostered this. (1998 survey)

Back during the early 1990s, there were occasional *trollers,* or people who came into the group solely to disrupt it (although there was not a word for them then). The post in Chapter 1 accusing all participants of being pathetic and without lives exemplified this. However, now trolls are a more frequent phenomenon, as are newbies who simply do not want to play by the rules. As a result, there is more flaming and more clear ostracizing of people than ever before. The norms of the community are perpetuated, but at the occasional expense of the friendliness it so values.

Conflicts of this sort between the established and new voices have emerged over time in other Internet groups as well. Stivale (1997), writing about a multiuser domain, says, "The ambiguity of what is appropriate or not suggests, once again, the ongoing struggle between centripetal and centrifugal dialogic forces, i.e., forces that seek some unified, central 'command' versus those seeking to contest such unification from the margins" (p. 139). Arguing that "newcomers must authorize themselves to stand up to the seeming authority of established groups in order to save those groups from their own ossification," Connery (1997) writes that "the freedom of a group as a public sphere can only be revitalized by unruly newcomers who flout the conventions and the authorities which inevitably evolve in long-lived groups" (p. 177). Whereas many r.a.t.s.a. participants surely would agree with Connery's argument that new blood, even bad blood, helps to keep a

community vital, others would disagree that the disruption of convention always is necessary for group vitality. Indeed, r.a.t.s.a. seems to
have done an admirable job of remaining vital, hanging on to its core
conventions as well as developing new ones, even if some of the
newcomers have been left disgruntled.

The *AMC* r.a.t.s.a. contingent has developed a highly institutionalized way in which to handle the problem of well-meaning but unaware
new blood that the participants have called the Newbie Sponsorship
Program (NSP). Organized through a Web site, this program functions
both to socialize newcomers and to enforce the traditions that old-
timers have developed (thereby affirming their authority as a group,
if not as individuals). Anne describes its genesis:

> The Newbie Sponsorship Program was created by a poster (who is not
> around much anymore) from Dallas, Mona. Too many newbies were
> posting incorrectly, making inquiries as to the suggested netiquette of
> the newsgroup, asking questions, etc., and Mona idealized the NSP.
> At some point, an idea was developed to incorporate the FAQ and
> many other pointers for newbies, including getting a sponsor, into a
> Web page. Shelly and Whitney developed the page along with a
> committee of volunteers in r.a.t.s.a., in which I was one. I was assigned
> to get the links and graphics for the page. It is available at http://
> www.terindell.net/ratsa/nspmain.htm, where all the infor-
> mation about the NSP is supplied. (1998 survey)

Here is an excerpt from the NSP's main page:

```
The newsgroup rec.arts.tv.soaps.abc, otherwise
known as RATSA, is one of the friendliest groups
on the internet! (Well, we think so, at least!).
Here at the Newbie Sponsorship Program (NSP) for
All My Children (AMC) viewers, we have all the
FAQs (Frequently Asked Questions) to help make your
experience in RATSA an enjoyable one. If the FAQs
don't answer all your questions, one of our friendly
sponsors probably can.

How to Get a Sponsor

It couldn't be more simple. If, after reading these
pages, you are still a little lost, please e-mail us
```

```
to request a sponsor. We will gladly guide you
through the RATSA waters.
```

Besides providing a link to an individual volunteer who will socialize the newbie personally into the community's norms, the site provides an overview of those norms and a number of other points to make becoming an acceptable member easy. The four rules the site high-lights are "lurk first," "use spoiler space," "attack ideas, not people," and "get a sponsor if you need one." The section titled "lurk first" exemplifies much that I have sought to describe about the *AMC* par-ticipants in r.a.t.s.:

```
We suggest you lurk for a while (read without
posting). Get used to how we do things. When you
think you're ready to jump in and post, a brief
description of who you are may be a good place to
start. As you have probably noticed, we're a very
friendly group and discuss more than just the soap
itself, so any personal tidbits that you'd like to
share would be most welcome. (There's a guide on
the next page for how to put together a little
self-intro.) If you lurk on RATSA long enough, you
will notice that we are a politically, socially and
sexually diverse group and bring a great deal of
our life experiences into our discussion of soaps,
and we think that's wonderful. The only thing we're
not so tolerant of is intolerance—so if you come to
RATSA intending to fan the flames, we'll use a cold
shoulder to put the fire out.
```

It's impossible to assess the extent to which the NSP has been responsi-ble for the continuity of the friendly tradition in r.a.t.s.a. (*AMC*), but it is mentioned repeatedly as one of the most important changes by those who responded to my survey:

The [NSP] has made enormous changes. I have seen people who never would have posted otherwise make great contributions to the group. (Carine, 1998 survey)

I love the fact that we have the [NSP]. It welcomes new people and helps them get around. Often when you join a new group, you feel at sea and unwelcome if no one responds. This way, you know you are being noticed and you can ask those dumb questions to just one caring person instead of a whole group. We developed a Web page for the newbies, and that was a huge improvement. It meant people could go to the page and see the answers to their questions right away and then come to us if they were still confused. (Shelly, 1998 survey)

On the one hand, the NSP exemplifies the tradition of friendly community in r.a.t.s.(a.) On the other hand, as Samantha, a 41-year-old computer programmer and longtime poster, points out, when r.a.t.s. was a smaller group, one did not need this type of program:

It was a real community then. You didn't have to fuss around with newbie sponsorship, introductions, all that crap. You got to know people as they posted, and there was always someone trying to mediate the flame wars. (1998 survey)

The very existence of the NSP indicates how much this community has been threatened by its own success, even as it indicates its enduring strength.

Cliques

The NSP also illustrates another new tension in r.a.t.s. besides that between newbies and old-timers, that is, the emergence of what some see as *cliques*. The well-known old-timers often come off as an exclusive in-group to more recent posters:

My least favorite thing is the tendency for new-ish people to hatefully refer to the "regulars," the "status quo," etc., and resent that group (which nobody can define) for imposing all kinds of net.practices on them. (Heather, 1998 survey)

I think it is very much a community for longtime readers. Like I said before, they visit each other; they e-mail each other; they exchange friendly barbs, recipes, and advice. Newcomers (those coming in [within] the last 2 years and lurkers) are like new neighbors, getting the welcome basket but still waiting for the invitation to the private party. (Gloria, 1998 survey)

A more embittered response from Samantha, who has been a participant since 1992, shows the bad feelings that can accrue around this
phenomenon:

> It seems lately that if you delurk and actually post something, there
> are few responses if you're not within the golden circle. Or someone
> out of left field questions who the hell you are and you must be a
> newbie, get a sponsor, etc. If you haven't posted in the last few months,
> you're assumed to need your hand held or something. It's disappoint-
> ing. I really enjoyed the equal playing field the groups represented in
> their youth. (1998 survey)

In general, as Heather suggests, what exactly makes a group a clique,
or makes a poster a member of one, seems to be an undefinable matter
of perception. Participants describe a number of types of discourse
evidence for cliques. Samantha's discussion of the automatic assumption that unrecognized names need help is one. Amanda echoes other
respondents in her description of how "lots of 'in posts' that are only
meaningful to a few people clutter up the group" (1998 survey). The
most clear-cut evidence for cliques seem to be the invitation-only mailing lists that have formed out of the newsgroup, but these are not visible
within the public discourse of the newsgroup.

In addition to the vagueness over what constitutes a clique, it is not
at all clear who exactly is and is not a member of any particular clique.
Lydia, a 31-year-old library assistant, writes that she is not a member of
the r.a.t.s.a. clique, although she has "at least partial respect and good
favor" from them and has "been here a long time and posted so much,
though, that it might seem to lurkers or newbies that I am" (1998
survey). Indeed, none of the respondents identifies herself or himself as
a member of a clique, although several indicate that there are such
cliques. Anne might be right in her suggestion that cliques are not as
exclusive as they appear:

> I have heard others mention "clique." I think it is all in their head! It
> may seem like it is on the surface, but it's just not really true. If you
> want to be in the clique, you just insert yourself in, respond to those
> you think are in it, and post something outlandish. You can be in the
> clique if you want to! :) (1998 survey)

Tabatha, a 43-year-old secretary who has been participating since 1994, indicates that for some of the more recent participants, the cliquishness is not a problem, but for different reasons:

> Sometimes an accusation bursts forth that there are "cliques" on r.a.t.s.a., and I agree that there are, but I feel that they are harmless. If a poster cannot simply just take r.a.t.s.a. for what it is and join in the fun, I don't respect that person and don't care what he/she thinks. This is not reworking the Bill of Rights; it's dishing the soaps!! (1998 survey)

Showing Off

The final new tension that has emerged in r.a.t.s.a. is between clever individuality and group openness. As we have seen, cleverness always has been highly valued in r.a.t.s., both for how it entertains the others and for how it allows for the development of individual personas. However, some feel that this latter function of creativity too often overpowers the first these days. People sometimes are now seen as being clever solely to build their personas rather than to entertain the others. As Bobby, an Australian, puts it, "Some posters tend to big note themselves" (1998 survey). Although most participants do not seem to mind at all (judging from the survey responses), others think that the balance between group and individual has shifted too much to the latter in this regard. Even Anne, whose status within the group probably is more firm than anyone else's, writes, "Some seem to post such creative ideas, it makes the rest of us (me, for instance) feel as if [we] have nothing witty to contribute and don't end up posting at all" (1998 survey). Another old-timer, Kristin, a 36-year-old engineer, does not feel intimidated but does feel repelled:

> I don't like the way r.a.t.s.a. evolved from r.a.t.s. There is too much creative writing and one-upmanship there now. I think people are too busy tooting their own horns and showing off, and [there is] lots of babbling while not much is being said. (1998 survey)

In sum, r.a.t.s.a. has maintained its values and practices, but new tensions have arisen that have simultaneously challenged and enhanced them.

Coping With Change

For a number of old-timers, these less pleasant group dynamics have saddened them and, in some cases, even driven them off the group. Kristin elaborates on her strong feelings about the group now:

> I don't like r.a.t.s.a. anymore. I guess the only redeeming factor is that I can go get updates there when *AMC* is reeeeeally bad and I fast-forward through parts of the show. I can go to r.a.t.s.a. to read the updates to find out if I really missed anything. (1998 survey)

Like Kristin, Maddie, a 42-year-old administrative secretary, still hangs in there but laments,

> I wish it was the way it used to be a long time ago. . . . Unfortunately, things change . . . not always for the better. Our little r.a.t.s. community is no more! (1998 survey)

Although a number of old-timers express this sort of sentiment, they do not seem to realize how many others agree with them. In one of the funnier moments of data collection, two women wrote nearly identical comments back to me when I told them that I had heard a good deal of commentary echoing their own:

> You mean I'm not just becoming a crotchety, middle-aged, not with it anymore witch? I'm *really* glad to hear I'm not the only one who feels this way!!! (Samantha, 1998 survey)

> That's kind of a relief to hear. I thought I was just getting old, grouchy, and unchangeable. ;-) (Kristin, 1998 survey)

Other old-timers do not mind these changes and do not understand why they have become problems for others (when they realize that they have). When I told Anne that a number of old-timers seemed to think that there were tensions between newbies and old-timers, she responded,

> For some reason, people on the group feel threatened in some way by newbies, as you say, [especially] WebTV users. I understand the way things have developed as indicated by other, older r.a.t.s.a.'ers but I believe all of this is in their perspectives, dare I say heads? :); They think that these people are "out to get them" and to violate r.a.t.s.a. as

they know it. I don't think it's true; I think it's just a development that has happened—good, bad, or indifferent. I don't resent WebTV users (I guess i've really learned to roll with the punches); I skip by half of the postings if [they have] HTML code or even spoiler space. My life has just become more important! When people get *so wrapped up* in r.a.t.s.a., I wonder what else is going on in their [lives]. From my own point of view, those days are gone for me. I also think that it's the older posters who are set in their ways [and] just do not like the way the Internet has grown at an enormous rate. I was just listening to the population of Internet users; it's huge and growing every second. I think old-timers, as in life, see it one way and want it to remain that way. (1998 survey)

Lisa seemed downright surprised that old-timers would think less of r.a.t.s. now than they did then:

It's interesting that most of your respondents have said that r.a.t.s.a. changed for the worst. Are they still reading it? I may have said the same as they did when the changeover started, but now that r.a.t.s.a. has been in place for a number of years, I don't think that way anymore. Maybe it just had to do with the settling in of a community. (1998 survey)

Whereas Anne, Lisa, Samantha, Maddie, Kristin, and many other old-timers have stuck with r.a.t.s.a., for other old-timers, these tensions ultimately have driven them away. Joan, who was one of the heaviest posters in 1992, describes her reasons for leaving the group. I quote her response at length because it brings together themes that recurred in the responses of former participants as well as disgruntled continuers:

I finally stopped [2] or [3] years ago for several reasons. The primary one, I guess, was that it quit being fun. . . . I don't think the group was ever the same after the big Internet explosion . . . when all the AOL'ers and others got online. There were just too many people wanting to take *take* TAKE without ever giving. And once the group was split, there was no going back. People got too serious. Too many rules were introduced. Too many people were too easily hurt or too quick to fly off the handle when someone didn't agree with their opinions.

And then there's *spam*. It became too much of a hassle to post because you'd immediately get put on 15 idiotic mailing lists, from get-rich pyramid schemes to "hot babe" picture providers. Who wants to deal with all that? I still get spam sent to e-mail addresses I haven't used in 4 or 5 years. (1998 survey)

Besides spam (mass advertisements sent directly to e-mail accounts culled automatically from Usenet headers) and the loss of fun, other reasons people left included the loss of access through their places of employment, the lack of time (my own reason), and bosses who began to monitor employee Internet use more closely.

From Village to City

Is r.a.t.s.a. the community r.a.t.s. was? The answer seems to be that, for the most part, it is. Most traditions have endured, as has the process of traditionalization. Many old-timers still are there, and the orientations toward the soap and toward one another have endured. As Tabatha writes,

> The FAQ describes the type of community that, I guess at the time of the FAQ's inception, r.a.t.s.a. wanted to be (i.e., attack ideas [and] not people, ignore trolls, respect opinions even if they do not match your own, etc.). R.a.t.s.a. has remained very true to this, and I think the term "community" does indeed apply. (1998 survey)

Lark, a 43-year-old telecommunications research assistant ("That's *not* a fancy word for operator!" she insists) and one of the earliest participants still active, agrees. But she suggests that the increased size is not without its drawbacks:

> There are rules, written and unwritten, about how to behave in "public" on r.a.t.s.a. People learn to live with and adjust to their neighbors. They call the r.a.t.s.a. police on people who misbehave, form welcome wagons for newcomers, and [form] committees for projects (such as the r.a.t.s.a. yearbook). There are clubs for ideas, such as BABE for Banding Against Brooke English. There is even community theater (FACs). It's like a giant coffee klatch. There are more and more traffic jams as more people join the r.a.t.s.a. commute. I find myself missing people who have "moved away." (1998 survey)

Beyond traffic jams, there are other new strains on r.a.t.s.a. that r.a.t.s. rarely faced, among them people who "appear in the newsgroup to 'flame' and annoy others" (Lexine, 1998 survey), "people who seem to be perennially on the outs" (Louie, 1998 survey), and (at least seemingly) exclusive cliques (be they BABEs or old-timers) and overly rampant individualism. Nearly all survey respondents agree that the word *community* still fits, but it is a more complicated community than it once was. In the words of Ariel, who began reading r.a.t.s. around the same time I did, "It's becoming less like 'Happy Valley' and more like East L.A.!" (1998 survey). The small towns of the Internet are becoming urbanized.

Notes

1. http://www.deja.com.

2. DejaNews also prevents many people from posting because they know that they will be archived and can be searched out by bosses or any other prying minds.

3. Although I had not been reading or participating, I still thought of many of those old-timers in r.a.t.s. as friends with whom I had fallen out of touch. It was enormously gratifying to find, in returning to do this survey, that I was not only remembered but still considered one of them by several of the old-timers.

4. The character of Brooke has become extremely controversial in the group.

5. Other newbie problems are technical. WebTV apparently requires modifying a specific setting to allow the use of both upper- and lowercase letters, so many WebTV posters use all capitalization, which makes it seem as though they are shouting. Other people who access Usenet through the Web post in HTML, which looks great on the Web but fills the screen with extra characters if one is using a non-Web newsreader. Both of these are highly annoying to old-timers and others who recognize the distinction between Usenet and the Web.

6. Many in the *AMC* discussion were unaware that this flame war was going on over FGCs. In general, the *AMC* discussion seems less marked by these problems than does the *GH* group. Carine, for example, describes r.a.t.s.a. as comprised of *multiple communities* and tells me that although she watches *GH*, she does not read those posts: "Even people [who] I know from one show are very different when they're talking about another show. For example, even though I watch *AMC*, *OLTL*, and *GH*, I primarily post to *AMC*. I actually have *GH* KILL-filed because I don't enjoy the dynamics of that group, even though many *AMC* people [who] I like participate in it" (1998 survey).

Conclusion:
Tune In Tomorrow

The three stories I have told about rec.arts.tv.soaps (r.a.t.s.) as an online community, as an audience community, and as a community of practice are really one. It is the tale of how, through shared practices, a group of people who rarely (if ever) meet, whose ranks are ever changing, and who share little in common besides their comfort with computers and interest in soap operas built and continue to support a social world that, for many, feels like a community. Looking at r.a.t.s. as an online community puts the attention on the medium. When we think of r.a.t.s. as an audience community, the attention shifts to the text around which this particular group coalesced. Thinking of r.a.t.s. as a community of practice orients us to the participants' routinized yet dynamic patterns of action. In each case, r.a.t.s. offers only one example of an enormous range of phenomena. The r.a.t.s. group is just one of nearly 30,000 newsgroups. Add to that the thousands, perhaps millions, of mailing lists, multiuser domains (MUDs), multi-user domains object oriented (MOOs), chat rooms, Internet Relay Chat channels, America Online folders, Web message boards, and other online groups, and it is apparent that r.a.t.s. is just one ripple in an online sea or even in the online pond of soap opera discussion. By the same token, r.a.t.s. is one audience community developed around one mass media genre. All communities—whether they are formed through computer networks, telephones, face-to-face encounters, or any other means and whether they discuss television shows, geographically local issues, occupational concerns, or any other topics—are based on shared practice.

It would be silly to think that the story of r.a.t.s. maps on to other communities in any direct way. Indeed, part of the reason for looking so closely at the *All My Children* (*AMC*) subgroup in r.a.t.s. has been to show that the social world that emerged was an unpredictable combination of forces and flukes rather than something that close analysis of the computer network or soap genre would have allowed us to predict. The uniqueness of r.a.t.s. does not mean, however, that there are no general conclusions to be drawn from its study. In this conclusion, I bring together lessons learned, offering some final thoughts on the study of online community, audience community, and communities of practice. I said in the introduction that this book is meant as one turn in what I hope will be a lengthy conversation. In closing, then, I pose questions I hope will stimulate further discussion.

Studying Online Community

One of the most troubling shortcomings of the many analyses of online community to date has been their reliance on personal anecdote and hypothetical theorizing in place of close study. Although these strategies might offer us new ideas, they offer us little in the way of real insights and have instead led to overly simplistic understandings. A central goal of this study has been to demonstrate the advantages of empirical grounding in thinking about the phenomenon of *virtual community*. When we look closely and holistically at the actual behaviors of online communities, it becomes clear that these groups develop complex and distinctive identities, identities that result unpredictably from combinations of preexisting factors, participants' appropriations of those factors, and the emergent forces that those appropriations generate. We cannot understand these complex dynamics by just thinking about them. Online social worlds are accessible to researchers in ways that few other worlds are. If we want to understand them, we need to look with rigor and detail.

What Forces Shape Online Communities?

Early research suggested that there was only one force that was important in influencing computer-mediated interaction, and that was the medium. Although in many ways research has become more sophisticated, the continuing debates over the nature and worth of the virtual community belie an ongoing presupposition that there are two types of communities, one authentic and the other virtual. The distinction rests on the untenable assumption that the medium through which community is constructed provides its defining quality. It is true that the medium is essential to the r.a.t.s. story. The removal of geographical constraints allows people who might otherwise never meet to come into contact. The asynchronous ongoing structure of Usenet has provided the time for conventions (both generic and normative) to develop as well as the time and means for people such as Anne, Lexine, Granma, and Lyle to develop distinctive and recognizable identities. The ASCII text format of messages allows people to manage (or hide) their identities in ways that might not be possible offline. Signature files and naming strategies are encouraged and facilitated by the medium. The newsreader-mandated headers are a major source of organization and convention, as the soap opera and genre labeling practices in r.a.t.s. indicate. In more ways than I can summarize here, the medium shapes the worlds that grow through its use. However, even if we limit the influences on online community to the medium, that medium still offers several varieties of interaction. To pick just a few examples, the asynchronous, header-organized, interest-specific structure of Usenet is considerably different from America Online's real-time, nontopical, two-line message chat rooms. MUDs and MOOs, where users interact in fictional spaces that might or might not have guiding goal structures, offer still different possibilities and challenges.

But imagining the medium to be the only—or even the most important—influence on online community is shortsighted. The case of r.a.t.s. reveals how many other forces are at play. Hanks (1996) points out the importance of joint projects in his definition of community. In online communities, as in many offline communities, joint projects manifest through the topic around which most discussion revolves. Despite its centrality, topic is a woefully understudied influence on online community. In the case of r.a.t.s., the topic of soaps brings with it a purpose—interpreting—and because soaps are emotional, relational, and talk oriented, the fulfillment of this purpose ideally needs a particular type of environment, one that is welcoming, is supportive, and allows for self-disclosure. The academic mailing lists in which I participate have completely different joint projects; they are concerned primarily with informing, seeking scholarly advice, and clarifying points of domain-specific ambiguity. The only time in these groups that people talk about personal matters is when they have inadvertently sent a message to the list rather than the individual for whom it was intended. These groups do develop distinctive conventions, norms, and personalities, but they do not develop the atmosphere of "a group of friends" that characterizes r.a.t.s. The Internet's many hate groups, organized in the joint project of promoting White supremacy, are as different from academic and soap groups as these groups are from one another. In short, the topics and purposes around which online communities organize are at least as important as the medium in shaping a group's communication patterns.

Who participates, including the dominant gender of those participants, also is a strong influence on online communities. In the case of r.a.t.s., one finds mostly highly educated American women, most of whom are employed outside the home. The topics they raise, the experiences they share, and the values they bring to the group (including their language patterns) undoubtedly are influenced by this background. Indeed, all participants in any online group bring their offline experiences to bear in some way within the group, even if only to turn those experiences on their head by creating alternative worlds and identities.

The r.a.t.s. newsgroup also demonstrates the influence that particular individuals can have in shaping their communities. One reason that r.a.t.s.(a.) has evolved as it has are new posters, who have created new traditions such as the F*Cs (favorite characters on various soaps), the Newbie Sponsorship Program, and the weekly polls. At the same time, one reason that r.a.t.s.(a.) has remained as close to its earlier incarnations as it has are those heavy posters who have remained active. Anne exemplifies the influence that a single person can have on a community. She was one of the very earliest contributors to r.a.t.s. and for over a decade was its most active participant. She began the update genre that has become the group's informative core. Her extremely sociable and welcoming style has helped to set the interpersonal tone for the group and has single-handedly welcomed countless new participants. Her distinctive worth to the community was recognized explicitly when the other participants voted that she receive the Frango Lifetime Achievement Award. Would r.a.t.s. have updates and be friendly without Anne? Probably. Would it be just like it is? Probably not. How would it be different? That is anyone's guess.

Another important influence on online groups is the offline contexts in which participants live the rest of their lives and that permeate the group, a topic to which I will return. What I want to emphasize about all of these influences—the medium, the topic, the purposes, the participants, the individuals, and the offline contexts—is that online communities do not emerge formulaically from their combination. If we had known all about Usenet, had known all about soaps and their social status, and had biographies of each participant, we still would not have been able to predict the social world I have described. Each online community is an ongoing creation, manifested, challenged, and recreated through negotiations that occur implicitly in every message. As people write, they draw selectively on the features of the medium, the joint projects available, their personal histories and experiences, and the group's history in ways that collaboratively coconstruct the values, relationships, identities, and conventions that make a group feel like community. The wording of every message gives and reflects information about who the sender takes the readers and the group to be. Every response affirms or challenges those assumptions. Any group can take new directions at any time because of the influence of a single contributor. As we look closely at more online groups, we likely will find that they share systematic patterns and dynamics, but conceptualizing all online communities as a single phenomenon because they share a medium is like reducing all towns, cities, and villages to a single phenomenon because all of them are built on earth. At this early point in their history, we should be trying to understand the complexity of online groups by examining their differences, not trying to explain them away with their one commonality.

What Forces Shape Online Identities?

The issue of identity has garnered more attention than have most other aspects of online interaction. The dominant discourse on the topic, exemplified by Turkle (1995), has argued for understanding online identities as emerging from the combination of offline history and the anonymity of the medium. The case of r.a.t.s. shows us that not all online selves are fantasy beings and that not all online communities are constructed as places to be alternative people. There might be enhanced uncertainty about one another in r.a.t.s., and there might be a great potential for anonymity, but as a whole, the group has developed a norm that prefers relatively straightforward self-representation, manifested in the use of real names, self-disclosure, face-to-face meetings, Web pages with photographs, and so on. No one in r.a.t.s. masquerades as soap characters, for example, unless under the guise of a FAC (favorite *AMC* character), and even then, the person behind the character appears as well. On those rare occasions when people have tried to pull off more fantastic identities, they have been ostracized.[1]

This illustrates one of the more important lessons from r.a.t.s., that online personas are developed in group contexts that offer differing types of resources and value systems for building and affirming identities. Online identities are inherently social creations, situated within the online social whole. In creating identities, people work within the genres of a group's discourse and echo others' voices (both within the group and in entirely different genres). An individual's voice is affirmed and responded to by the others, depending on the values of that group. Those who affirm the communal values are likely to be praised, quoted, and otherwise supported, whereas those who try to present other identities are likely to be disconfirmed, even in systems that have no ways in which to exclude anyone from participating. Despite the range of possibilities, some identities will do better in a group than will others. There is a delicate balance between individuality and the needs of the group in which individual identities are created, and both sides of this tension deserve equal consideration.

How Do Online Communities Evolve Over Time?

The Internet is undergoing changes faster than anyone can foresee. When I began studying r.a.t.s. during the early 1990s, I had to explain to everyone what the Internet was. Now, I usually can get away with a quick explanation of Usenet. Most everyone knows about the Internet, even if, like my 90-year-old grandmother, they think that it works by magic. How do online groups weather the growth of the Internet? What determines how they fare when thousands of new people join their ranks? The r.a.t.s. newsgroup suggests some of the issues and tensions that are likely to emerge. First, it is clear that publicly accessible groups already have lost their status as refuges for the educated elite. The new people coming online include not just well-educated, computer-savvy folks but rather a wide range of more diverse people. As of this writing, most still are White and relatively affluent, but that likely will change over time (one hopes). Even if the Internet of the late 1990s is accessed primarily by a relatively privileged sector of the global population, it already is a more diverse population than it was. As this change occurs, the Internet's groups will have to cope with increasing amounts of difference among participants.

If r.a.t.s., the group Connery (1997) describes, and other mailing lists I have participated in are any indication, then one result of increased diversity will be increased fragmentation as groups spin off into subgroups, sometimes accessible only by invitation. Even within the public domains, subgroups or cliques are likely to form, exacerbating tensions between new participants and longer term ones or those with differing attitudes. The extent to which these groups manage their continual transformations in ways that are satisfactory to most participants will be rooted in the extent to which they are able to agree on a set of core values and then balance the persistence of what they value most with the need to change in ways that new participants will find pleasing.

The r.a.t.s. newsgroup suggests how this can be done—by maintaining and fighting for a clear value structure manifested in multiple conventions while finding ways in which to help new participants understand and feel at ease with the group's conventions. Communicative practice in any group needs to balance tradition and improvisation. The groups best able to grow successfully will improvise new ways in which to incorporate new members while maintaining what they can of their historical continuity. The Newbie Sponsorship Program developed in the *AMC* subgroup, in which all the information one needs to become a competent participant is collected in one Web site and new participants can be paired with more seasoned mentors, might have a few critics but offers a particularly innovative model that other groups might emulate.

How Does Online Participation
Connect to Offline Life?

Closely related to the assumption that online community is a single phenomenon is the often-voiced concern that this type of community is bad because it serves as a substitute for the offline lives that its participants would otherwise be having. One fear is that those who cannot build successful identities or social lives offline will turn to the (socially isolated) computer to find a world in which they fit. The stereotype of the social loser who can only make friends online is in many ways quite similar to that of the soap opera viewer who watches because the characters are easier to befriend than are neighbors. A second concern is that increased online interaction will decrease engagement in face-to-face relationships offline (Kraut et al., 1998). Again, these concerns seem to be based in oversimplifications of how people engage the medium that have stood, so far, in place of empirical analysis of the many complex ways in which online communities and offline lives may intertwine. Not only are there no signs that r.a.t.s. is doing so well because its participants have no offline lives, but there also are many signs to the contrary.

We see in r.a.t.s. a wide range of ways in which participation in the group connects to, rather than supplants, offline life. The behavioral norms about how to treat one another come directly from offline life. People in r.a.t.s. can treat one another as friends (e.g., by prefacing a disagreement with a partial agreement and adding the person's name) because this is something that they already know how to do. Participants' interests and concerns reflect those that matter to them off-line; indeed, the discussions of relational and socioemotional issues so crucial to r.a.t.s. revolve entirely around offline social worlds. Furthermore, people's self-disclosures in r.a.t.s. indicate diverse and full offline lives that are brought into the group, giving it life. Their online identities are congruent with those that they stake out offline. Research in other online contexts also has indicated a continuity between one's online and offline connections to others. Those who are lonely offline seem to remain so online, whereas those who plunge into online interactions also are highly sociable offline (Cody, Wendt, Dunn, Pierson, Ott, & Pratt, 1997; Joe, 1997).

The real web of connections between offline and online life that exists in r.a.t.s. stands in sharp contrast to Nguyen and Alexander's (1996) theoretical description of going online, one that exemplifies the dichotomy that many assume. They write,

The cardinal points and life's materiality disappear into the weight-
lessness of cyberspacetime. One initially experiences a bodiless exul-
tation that may shortly settle into the armature of addiction. Going
online "flatlines" a person. That is, it immobilizes the body and
suspends normal everyday consciousness. (p. 102)

The many ways in which "normal everyday consciousness" is manifested in r.a.t.s. should put this type of groundless global theorizing to
rest. There are more nuanced questions to be asked. If some people do
become disconnected from offline life when they go online, we should
ask which people these are, in which groups this tends to happen, and
what is going on with these people and groups that might promote this
type of disjunction. For the rest of us, we should be seeking to understand the many ways in which offline life is brought online rather than
imagining that we always (or even often) leave embodied reality behind
when we log on.

The offline life that is brought online is complemented by the ways
in which online life feeds back into offline life. People in r.a.t.s. learn
different ways in which to view relational and emotional issues that
they see around them and experience in their own offline lives. When
good or bad things happen online, the emotions they create play back
into participants' offline lives. To give just one example, the death of
Lisa's daughter, an offline experience, was brought online through her
self-disclosure and fed back offline to the many people, like me, who
never again will view sudden infant death syndrome as something that
only happens to other people. The online group also can provide social
support for people experiencing difficult times offline, as the proliferation of online support groups demonstrates. Furthermore, relationships
that develop online can—and do—move offline, sometimes outlasting
their participants' involvement in the groups through which they met.
Online worlds develop affective dimensions and experiences, and these
feelings, situated in the bodies of group members, do not distinguish
between *virtual* and *real*.

How Do Online Communities Influence
Offline Communities?

For many pop theorists such as Rheingold (1993), online communities have near utopian potentials in that they free us from physical
constraints and allow us to organize by interests, enabling us to find
kindred spirits and liberation. From this point of view, online commu-

nity offers a nonproblematic improvement over offline community. At
the other extreme are the many dystopian warnings that once we are
grouped by interest rather than by geography, we will lose our connections to *real* (i.e., geographically local) community, and these more
important communities will suffer as a result. To an extent, these
debates result from different uses of the term *community*, a problem that
can be averted through more concete descriptions of what we discuss.
As Fernback (1997) points out,

> Community is a term which seems readily definable to the general
> public but is infinitely complex and amorphous in academic discourse.
> It has descriptive, normative, and ideological connotations . . . [and]
> encompasses both material and symbolic dimensions. (p. 39)

The set of connotations that lies at the heart of many critics of online
community is exemplified by Doheny-Farina (1996), an advocate of
using computer networks to enhance local communities but avoiding
them otherwise. He writes,

> A community is bound by place, which always includes complex
> social and environmental necessities. It is not something you can easily
> join. You can't subscribe to a community as you subscribe to a discus-
> sion group on the Net. It must be lived. It is entwined, [is] contradic-
> tory, and involves all our senses. (p. 37)

Using a similar model of community, Healy (1997) argues that real
community entails more than "the voluntary association of like-minded
individuals" (p. 61).

Central to the skeptics' argument is that we seek community online
because we feel its absence offline. Healy (1997) and Stratton (1997) both
locate the romance of Internet community in a nostalgia for the homo-
geneous small town. Stratton writes, "The American mythologization
of the Internet as a community represents a nostalgic dream for a
mythical early modern community which reasserts the dominance of
the White, middle-class male and his cultural assumptions" (p. 271).
Lockard (1997) puts it more bluntly: "If the offline/Black streets have
turned mean, go plug into online/White optic fiber" (p. 228). From this
point of view, we should be worried that seeking comfort in White male

homogeneity online will have deleterious consequences for morality and ethics in the multicultural geographical world.

Despite their surface appeal, both utopian and dystopian ways of thinking about online communities obscure more issues than they raise. The r.a.t.s. newsgroup might be about as close to the utopian ideal of an online group based on shared interest as there is. It is fun. It offers refuge from the shame of viewing soaps so prevalent offline. People offer genuine support and care for others that they might never meet face-to-face. The group has an affective quality and value system that many of our geographical communities could use. But r.a.t.s. is not a utopia. There are conflicts and cliques. Some people come to disrupt, and old-timers leave disappointed. The idea of the shared-interest community as a utopia ignores the tensions and contradictions that evolve in any ongoing community where new people continually come into a world rich with traditions they did not create. Shared interest need not mean like-minded.

Furthermore, although r.a.t.s. is a warm and loving community based on shared interest, it is not a paragon of White male homogeneity, nor is it disconnected from "entwined, contradictory, sensual" communities. As we have seen, r.a.t.s. is a realm in which men abide by a value system traditionally associated with women, where women's concerns are centralized and taken seriously, and where diverse viewpoints on some of life's most important matters—things such as how people ought to treat one another—are considered an asset. Online communities can expose people to differences that they would not encounter offline. For example, an Australian participant told me about one of the things he likes most about the group: "There are so many different people at r.a.t.s.a. [rec.arts.tv.soaps.abc] that I normally wouldn't get to interact with. I'm 23 (male), and it's really great to chat with people with different life experiences and points of view" (Bobby, 1998 survey). If we are going to understand the role that the Internet will play in affecting geographically located communities, then we need to develop more sophisticated understandings of what these online communities entail.

We also will have to develop greater understanding of how people's involvement in online communities influences their involvement in offline communities. A basic assumption behind the fear that online community will damage offline community is that the time spent in online interaction would otherwise be spent building community with our neighbors if we were not online. The fact is that we know very little about what the millions of people who participate in online groups would be doing if they were not online. The r.a.t.s. newsgroup was at its most active between the hours of 9 a.m. and 5 p.m., strongly suggesting that its readers would have been killing time at work if they had not been posting.[2] There also are indications that people who spend time online watch less television. A study conducted by Nielsen Media Research for America Online found that households with connections to the Internet watch 15% less television each week ("Viewing Notes," 1998). It is quite possible that online communities of interest can enhance offline community. For example, the value system promoted in r.a.t.s. might strengthen geographically situated communities. Consider Esther's post, quoted in Chapter 1, where she spoke of her own involvement with women's shelters and urged other women to become involved in such work. My own experience was that I met people in my local community through r.a.t.s. who I would not have known otherwise, an experience echoed by other r.a.t.s. participants. Connections formed through the group allowed me to break through the university boundaries among departments, graduate students, and staff, privileging our commonalities over the institutional differences ingrained in the local social structure.

It also is important to understand that the people in r.a.t.s. recognize and articulate the differences between the community and friendships of the group and the community and friendships they experience offline. They do not see them as identical or interchangeable. Even Anne, the heaviest and longest term poster, thinks that the term *community* fits "only to a certain degree. It does feel like a community, yet it doesn't. It's kind of hard to explain. A group seems better. To me, a community is a group of people all physically in the same area" (1998 survey).

The r.a.t.s. newsgroup is not perfect, but it is a model of a pretty good online community. It shows that online groups can embrace difference, can embrace women, can be polite, can foster discussion that improves offline life, and can adapt to change without falling apart or becoming too elitist. Whereas r.a.t.s. does little (if anything) to harm offline community, and might in fact benefit face-to-face communities by creating greater interpersonal understanding and tolerance, other groups could have negative consequences for offline communities (hate groups are an obvious example). The medium is not what matters; it is the practices a community promotes that benefit or harm offline community. Our thinking about online communities is not furthered by painting them in simplistic extremes or in contrast to offline community. As Gurak (1997) writes, "People are already moving back and forth from physical to virtual community; the issue is how to shape and use these new structures" (p. 132). Online communities are not going to go away. If we are worried about a declining sense of community in contemporary life, then we should be thinking in concrete terms about what types of affective involvement and value systems we want in all of our communities and then asking what practice might promote these moralities both online and offline.

Rethinking Audience Community

This study raises many of the same issues about audience communities as it does for online communities and for similar reasons. Even as it has come to rely on the term *community*, audience research has shied away from the close examination of the discourse through which communities are built, obscuring many important aspects of what these groups involve. The r.a.t.s. newsgroup began as a group of individuals oriented to the same television programs. Through their connection to soap opera texts, they built a range of practices that function to pool information and collaboratively interpret the show. In this sense, r.a.t.s. clearly is an audience. But although this connection to the text is essential, it offers us an inadequate understanding of what it means to be an audience community. Out of the textually oriented practices, r.a.t.s. also developed interpersonal practices and connections that came to be equally (and sometimes more) important to its participants. If we are going to take the term *community* seriously in audience research, then we need to take on the unfamiliar task of examining interpersonal communication.[3] We cannot understand social relationships if we look only at group-text interactions. Being a member of an audience community is not just about reading a text in a particular way; rather, it is about having a group of friends, a set of activities one does with those friends, and a world of relationships and feelings that grow from those friendships. In general, we have far too little understanding of the spontaneous interpersonal interaction and social relations that make an audience a community, although these interactions are crucial to being a fan and incorporating mass media into our everyday lives. The Internet allows us an unprecedented (although not the only) route into these communities.

How Do Mass Media Texts Give Rise to
Particular Types of Interpersonal Interaction?

Some of what happens in r.a.t.s. probably would not happen in audience communities that form around other genres, raising the question of how interpersonal dynamics may be shaped by textual dynamics. It seems evident that some of what transpires in r.a.t.s. stems from the distinctive features of soap operas, in particular their reflection of socioemotional life, focus on female protagonists, and multiplicity of characters and interpretations. These qualities give rise to the group's purpose of maximizing interpretations and the topics discussed in service of that goal (e.g., feelings, relationships). They probably also influence the types of people who are drawn to the genre and audience communities surrounding it in the first place. After years of wondering, I have come to understand that my own attraction to the genre comes from my interests in relationships, talk, and emotion, interests that have guided my career choices as well as my viewing choices. Although different members of the audience surely get different rewards from watching soaps, I suspect that people disinterested in feelings, relationships, and talk are likely to choose other genres around which to coalesce.

I have argued throughout this book that because soaps dwell on these topics, their discussion necessitates the creation of a particular type of interpersonal environment, one that is open, supportive, and trusting. If people are afraid to voice their interpretations for fear that they will be attacked, then the group will fail. This is enhanced when those interpretations rely on private personalization. Thus, the fact that they discuss soaps makes it particularly important to treat one another with kindness and support. The friendly atmosphere, heavily influenced by the needs of discussing the genre, makes it easy for genuine caring and strong friendships to form out of the discussion.

The tendency of soap operas to fall short of what their audiences would like on so regular a basis also gives rise to another interpersonal dynamic—critical humor done to please one another. These people create a fun and funny environment for one another in part because the soap does not always do this as well as it should. The supportive,

friendly, and fun relationships, influenced by the genre, support continued engagement with the genre as people keep watching soaps to be
able to participate fully in the community. The shortcomings and stig-
matizing of soaps also led this group to create a particular group
identity, one that privileges not only humor and friendliness but also
intelligence. The temporal structure of soaps, which always offers new
conversational fodder, also influences what happens in this audience
community. It might be that the interpretive consensus forged in r.a.t.s.
is more dynamic than those formed in audience communities for
weekly episodic shows, movies, canceled shows, musicians, or other
media. The general questions I would pose, then, concern how particular media create particular types of relationships among their interacting fans. How are the ways in which fans treat one another influenced by media? To what types of interpersonal networks do different
media give rise? Do differences in media make some audience groups
more or less inclusive? Nearly all of this interpersonal negotiation
within the fan community takes place implicitly; as people negotiate
interpretations, they negotiate relationships. Thus, answering these
questions will entail looking not just to the content of fans' interpretations and information but also to the ways in which those interpretations and information are expressed.

How Are Communal Meta-Texts Influenced by Interpersonal Forces?

Much of the American work on fan community has focused on the
communal *meta-text* (Fiske, 1987; Jenkins, 1992) created by fans through
their discussions of the show. It certainly is the case in r.a.t.s. that the
group discussion affects people's interpretations of the show. Deep
histories are told, perspectives are pooled, and what individuals see
when they watch reflects the discussions they have had or read within
the group. Being a member of r.a.t.s. entails watching soaps not just as
an individual but also as a member of this audience community. It also
is true that out of the many interpretations voiced, some come to seem
like the group's. In other words, a meta-text develops that includes soap
events, histories, and group evaluation. What r.a.t.s. shows us, however,
is that the construction and nature of an interpretive community's
consensus is shaped by the interpersonal dynamics of the group.

Soaps lend themselves to multiple interpretations, and r.a.t.s. thrives on multiple interpretations. The group also thrives on friendliness. For these reasons, r.a.t.s. generally is motivated to protect individual interpretations. People do not claim authority when they post their perspectives. Indeed, the linguistic details of their disagreements show us that they respect different interpretations and qualify the certainty with which they express their own. Perhaps because of the need to protect interpretations, there is a general reluctance to even voice disagreement; with so many possible interpretations on offer, it seems doubtful that 10% of the messages about the Carter Jones story line really represented the full amount of disagreement that there was in the community. The sense that there is an opinion that is the group's, evident in comments such as "I may be in the minority on this one," surely is enhanced by the downplaying of disagreement. The agreement that seems to result, on the other hand, is purposely left somewhat open. When one interpretation seems to have become the only possible one, as with the animosity that has emerged toward the character of Brooke, it puts off fans who disagree, and the purpose of the community—maximizing interpretations—is undermined. What seems like consensus really is a delicate balancing act between the motivations to share diverse opinions and to respect the views of others.

Consensus, or the appearance of consensus, also emerges from other interpersonal dynamics. The perspectives that influence the group often come from the experiences and expertise that particular individuals have gained in life and that they choose to share. Those most likely to share, and perhaps most likely to be heard, are the heavy posters. The voices of the group's most skilled performers are particularly privileged. Humor has special force in creating meta-texts because it can codify meanings so easily and in such memorable ways (e.g., the nicknames for characters), so those with a gift for humor are particularly potent authors of meta-texts. At the same time, the humor and most of the group's messages selectively reinvoke past discussion through quotation, repetition, and other means. From a full platter of potentials, particular messages and themes are used repeatedly. My point is that which of these are used might have less to do with who is most agreed with among all fans than with who is funniest, best known, and the like. In short, meta-texts are an important element in getting a group to cohere as an audience community, but we need to better understand to what extent those meta-texts really reflect consensus and in what ways a community's unified take on a show is an illusion, influenced by a varying range of interpersonal concerns.

How Does the Performance of Audience Connect to the Rest of Life?

Just as being a member of an online group is only one element of one's life, being a member of an audience, even for die-hard fans, is only part of being a person and usually a fairly small part at that. In contrast to research on online community, work on audiences has done a better job of recognizing the importance of one's social situation. Nevertheless, its focus on class and gender issues has obscured other ways in which audiencehood and the rest of life intersect. First, r.a.t.s. should wipe out the idea that all soap opera fans, or all women who indulge in fiction, are in need of smarter people to tell us what our experience really means or to show us what we should be doing instead. The women and men of r.a.t.s. clearly are in control of their indulgence in pop culture texts. Spending time watching soaps and reading or writing to r.a.t.s. is a conscious choice made for valid reasons; it is not evidence of unfulfilled needs. Furthermore, these soap fans engage both the soap and the newsgroup at varying levels. At one extreme are those who never watch the show and use the group only to read updates. At the other extreme are the heavy posters who watch every episode and spend hours each day keeping up with and contributing to the newsgroup. Most fall somewhere in between. One size of audience member does not fit all. Although it is true that soaps are a form of escapism for many fans, we cannot assume that being a soap fan is primarily a way in which to disconnect from the rest of life. Indeed, even for those who use soaps as an escape, the catharsis and stress relief they experience are in direct response to the life they lead that is not soap related. Escapism and catharsis are but two of many ways in which non-fan life connects to audiencehood, just as online identity play is but one of the ways in which offline and online selves can connect.

The r.a.t.s. newsgroup also shows us that part of being a fan is continually assessing whether or not it is appropriate to discuss the object of one's affection with the diverse range of people one encounters in everyday life. At a committee meeting I attended recently, a high-ranking university administrator made reference to *NYPD Blue* but then immediately pointed out that "one hates to admit that one watches TV."

(My response was that he should try admitting he watches soaps.) Fans of many media are stigmatized, and that stigmatization plays a role in many of our encounters as we continually judge to whom we can and cannot reveal that we watch soaps (or love *NYPD Blue* or whatever it is that moves us). When we hide our passion, we hide important parts of ourselves from the others in our lives. When we tell the wrong people, we risk ridicule, even when those people are intimates—husbands, wives, lovers, parents, and the like. Thus, our status as fans is an important component of all of our interpersonal relationships as we decide whether or not to tell. When we tell sympathetic people, our performance of audience membership helps us to strengthen existing connections. The people we meet through membership in audience communities can become our friends, leading us to share our lives in ways that have little to do with our status as audience members.

In the case of this soap fan community, we see a number of other ways in which participation connects to the rest of life. The answer to the key soap question, "What kind of person [character] is this?" (Brunsdon, 1983) depends on the prior question, "What kind of person am I?" (Livingstone, 1990). As people personalize the soap to interpret the characters, they draw on an enormous range of non-soap experience, some pertaining to general or expert knowledge but most pertaining to emotion and interpersonal relationships. As community members discuss their takes on characters, they expose the others to different points of view on these issues. Although not always in agreement, the others can—and sometimes do—take these greater understandings of others' perspectives back into their own lives. My participation in r.a.t.s. has given me insight into what it is like to be beaten by and to leave one's husband, to be stalked, to be the subject of nasty custody battles, to be reunited with lost parents or children, and many other experiences I have not had but others have shared as they became relevant to interpreting the characters. Discussion of soaps is not the only way in which to develop richer understandings of others' points of view on socioemotional issues, but it is a convenient one, especially given that soap fans are so diverse and soaps are so easy to discuss.

Throughout our discussions of these issues, we are affirming, protecting, and exploring the value systems that guide our conduct in interpersonal relationships, something that is very difficult to do with casual acquaintances without the facade of soap characters. Just as these discussions can teach members of an audience community about emotion and relationships from others' points of view, these discussions can lead to very real social support when people have to live through emotionally trying times themselves. In short, the boundaries between the discussion of characters and non-soap emotional and relational experiences are fluid, each influencing the other. Far from being exhaustive, these are just a few of the ways in which one's status as soap fan and member of soap fan community can connect to the rest of life. Far more questions than answers remain about how other types of audiencehood connect to life, how online audience communities connect to and differ from those offline, how interpersonal relationships grow from textually oriented alliances, and the range of interpersonal situations in which the expression (or nonexpression) of fandom becomes important.

How Does the Internet Change What It Means to Be an Audience?

The Internet did not invent fan groups; they were thriving long before computers existed. On the other hand, the Internet has changed them, and for those with Internet access, it has changed what it means to be a fan. The full ramifications that the Internet will have on other mass media remain to be seen, but a few implications are apparent from r.a.t.s. First, the Net has allowed audience communities to proliferate. Where geography might not have allowed the critical fan mass to let a community coalesce, the removal of that boundary lets fans of even the most obscure shows, films, bands, and the like find one another. As fans access one another with greater regularity and frequency, interpretations of the media are increasingly collaborative. Indeed, being a member of an audience itself is becoming an increasingly social practice. The Internet also allows fans to participate in audience communities at their own comfort levels. Those who are not interested in attending fan conventions or collecting every product can read online groups as frequently or rarely as they like. Thus, the Internet makes audience communities more common, more visible, and more accessible, enabling fans to find one another with ease, regardless of geography, and enhancing the importance of the interpersonal dimensions of fandom.

The Internet also makes audience communities more visible for mass media producers, who can log on anytime to get instantaneous feedback. As Harrington and Bielby (1995) note, there is no systematic evidence that soap producers are consistently monitoring the Net. On the other hand, there is a good deal of evidence (most of which is collected in the r.a.t.s.a. FAQ [frequently asked questions]) that they are well aware of it and that some writers, actors, crew, and other behind-the-scenes personnel are reading and participating in r.a.t.s. and other online groups. Producers and writers of other shows have been far more explicit about engaging their online communities. How the online discussions will feed back into media texts remains to be seen, but it is clear that, at least in the case of soaps, the writers might be wise to pay some attention to what these fans are saying. As soap ratings are slipping, these fans are sending strong and consistent messages about what they do and do not like in the medium.

The Internet also has begun to shift the balance of power between media producers and consumers in a number of ways that the industry might rightly find disconcerting. The producers remain in control of the scarce resource of airwaves, but online, fans can create sites as impressive as can the major studios. The World Wide Web has become filled with fan-authored sites. Whereas ABC has a site for each of its soaps, the shows' fans have created many sites for those soaps, often for particular characters on those soaps, and fans can visit those fan-created sites as easily as she or he can visit the network-created sites. This is one example of what we see throughout the discussion in r.a.t.s.; the Internet gives fans a platform on which to perform for one another, and their informal performances might please fans more than the official ones do. Fans also amuse one another with fan fiction, writing their own soap episodes and story lines that are collected and posted to Web sites. As media converge more and more, and as more and more audience members go online, the absolute control of producers over their products might erode further. And if it does not, then fans might well develop alternative products that gain greater audiences. Scholarship so far has barely scratched the surface of the interplays between media producers and online fans.[4]

Studying Communities Through Practice

One goal of this book has been to show the utility of the practice approach for research on both online and audience community. Close examination of the routinized ways in which such communities organize their social lives allows us to see them as wholes while simultaneously viewing the details and dynamics that lead to their constant evolution. We can see their social relationships, identities, value systems, and ongoing tensions as well as the strategies that participants use to maintain and negotiate their structure. Practice can serve as an organizing framework through which these communities can be examined and compared.

The analysis of r.a.t.s. also suggests some areas that practice theorists might pursue in other communities as well. There has been a strong focus in practice research on the cognitive. Chaiklin and Lave (1993), for example, tout practice theory as a way in which to ground cognitive theory in social context. Miller and Goodnow (1995) point out that there have been relatively few developmental studies that take a practice approach to affect compared to those that focus on cognition. Ortner's (1984) argument (on which Miller and Goodnow draw) that the motivational and affective side of practice is relatively undeveloped compared to the cognitive remains true as of this writing. Practice in r.a.t.s. certainly can be understood in cognitive terms. The questions of how members learn the group's norms and develop the types of knowledge and ways of thinking that allow them to be competent members clearly involve cognition. But r.a.t.s. practice also illustrates the importance of the socioemotional in organizing community. People in r.a.t.s. are not just working with how to think, they also are negotiating how to feel, both in this community and in the others they inhabit. The strong emphasis on humor in r.a.t.s. shows us the extent to which emotive elements can be essential to shaping and negotiating a community's core values. Elaborating the affective dimensions of practice also will allow us to better develop the connections between practice as situated cognition and practice as embodied experience.

As a community of interest rather than a geographical culture or subculture, r.a.t.s. also raises the issue of how different communities intersect through practice. People on r.a.t.s., like all of us, move between multiple communities, importing and exporting practices along the way. Our understanding of all communities will be enhanced by understanding not just how they operate as coherent wholes but also how they interact with other wholes. As we come to live in an ever-expanding array of specialized communities, the issue of how those communities interweave is crucial to understanding culture. This is an issue that the practice approach is particularly well suited to address.

Toward a Convergent Future

Our lives are increasingly mediated by technology. Our senses of self, our relationships with others, and our communities all are shaped by our daily interactions with and through machines. Online communities and audience communities are two outgrowths of this transformation. As media proliferate and converge, we can only assume that both types of community will increase in prevalence and influence. Anderson (1983) argues that all communities beyond the primal face-to-face are imagined, a process enabled by mass media. Rather than asking whether these new types of communities are authentic, he suggests that we look instead to "the style in which they are imagined" (p. 6). I suggest that one way in which to understand the imagination of community is through close examination of one of the most primal forces that ties people together—interpersonal interaction. It is in the details of their talk that people develop and maintain the rituals, traditions, norms, values, and senses of group and individual identity that allow them to consider themselves communities. Rather than judging from the outside, we need to listen closely to what members of new media communities have to say to one another and to those who ask. Only then will we understand their diversity and the opportunities and challenges they offer.

Notes

1. One example of this involved an *All My Children* participant who claimed that the character Aunt Phoebe was in fact his aunt. The fact that fictional aunts do not have real nephews was not lost on the other participants, who quickly ridiculed him out of the group.

2. The well-publicized study conducted by Kraut et al. (1998), which produced the finding that people became increasingly depressed as their Internet connection time increased, relied on a sample with many high school students using the Internet at home. The fact that these r.a.t.s. participants are primarily adult working women participating from their workplaces suggests the diversity of the Internet and the caution we should have about claims that collapse all users and uses.

3. This goes both ways. Scholars of interpersonal communication could benefit from considering the roles that mass media play in the construction and maintenance of our relationships and social groupings as well.

4. See Clerc (1996) for a particularly good scratching regarding *The X-Files*.

Appendix A: Surveys

Survey 1
(posted to the newsgroup in the winter of 1991)

1. How do we "define" rec.arts.tv.soaps (r.a.t.s.)?

2. How does r.a.t.s. compare to other newsgroups on Usenet or to soap groups on Prodigy, GEnie, or any others?

3. What are the r.a.t.s. standards of netiquette? How did you learn them?

4. How do we think of the people who post to r.a.t.s.? (obviously, not as housewives with their hair in curlers eating bon-bons!)

5. What do you consider your relationship(s) (if any) with people on the Net to be? Do you e-mail with other r.a.t.s. people?

6. What makes a r.a.t.s. posting or poster successful? Which ones do you like best and why?

7. How do the rest of you read r.a.t.s.? Where? How often?

8. Does your involvement with this group influence the way in which you watch the show? Which things you notice? Which characters you like? Other influences (like some people have said, the Net keeps them watching even when the soap gets dull)?

9. Does the form or content of the show influence the way in which you read r.a.t.s.? For example, how (if ever) does the show make you want to read or post? Or, make you not want to read r.a.t.s. or post?

I am also curious as to the age range on r.a.t.s., the jobs we hold, and how long you have watched your soaps and read r.a.t.s. If there are other important things I have neglected, please share your thoughts.

Survey 2
(posted to the newsgroup in the fall of 1993)

1. How do you describe rec.arts.tv.soaps (r.a.t.s.) to people who do not know what it is?

2. Why do you read and/or post to r.a.t.s.?

3. If you are a lurker, what are the reasons why you do not post?

Survey 3
(posted to the newsgroup in the spring of 1998)

1. When did you first begin reading rec.arts.tv.soaps (r.a.t.s.) or rec.arts.tv.soaps.abc (r.a.t.s.a.)?

2. What do you like most about r.a.t.s.a.?

3. What do you like least about r.a.t.s.a.?

4. In the time that you have been reading r.a.t.s. and/or r.a.t.s.a., what do you think are the most noticeable or important changes that have happened in the newsgroup?

5. What do you think are some of the reasons why r.a.t.s.a. has changed as it has?

6. In the time that you have been reading r.a.t.s. and/or r.a.t.s.a., what has remained the same?

7. What do you think are some of the reasons why these aspects of the group have remained more stable over time?

8. How has this group been changed by the World Wide Web?

9. Do you maintain or visit Web sites related to this newsgroup? If so, please describe how your soap newsgroup and soap Web use are related.

10. What types of relationships do you feel you have with other people who participate in this group?

11. How well do you think the term "community" fits this group now? Please explain why.

12. How do you think you would have answered Question 11 when you first got to know this group?

13. How (if at all) do you think participation in this newsgroup affects your offline life?

14. Do you have any other thoughts on this newsgroup, now or over time, that you would like me to consider?

15. What is your age?

16. What is your gender?
17. What is your occupation?

Survey 3
(version e-mailed directly to current and former participants in the spring of 1998)

1. When did you first begin reading rec.arts.tv.soaps (r.a.t.s.) or rec.arts.tv.soaps.abc (r.a.t.s.a.)?

2. If you no longer read r.a.t.s.a., when and why did you stop?

3. What do/did you like most about r.a.t.s.(a.)?

4. What do/did you like least about r.a.t.s.(a.)?

5. In the time that you read/have been reading r.a.t.s. and/or r.a.t.s.a., what do you think are the most noticeable or important changes that have happened in the newsgroup?

6. What do you think are some of the reasons why r.a.t.s.a. changed as it has?

7. In the time that you read/have been reading r.a.t.s. and/or r.a.t.s.a., what has remained the same?

8. What do you think are some of the reasons why these aspects of the group remained more stable over time?

9. If you have been reading since the advent of the World Wide Web, how do you think this group has been changed by the Web?

10. Do you maintain or visit Web sites related to this newsgroup? If so, please describe how your soap newsgroup and soap Web use are related.

11. What types of relationships do you feel you have with other people who participate in this group?

12. If you no longer read the group, have you maintained any relationships with people from the group? What types of relationships (if any) do you consider these to be?

13. If you still are participating in r.a.t.s.a., how well do you think the term "community" fits this group now? Please explain why.

14. How do you think you would have answered Question 13 when you first got to know this group?

15. If you are not participating in r.a.t.s.a. anymore, how would you have answered Question 13 at the time you stopped?

16. How (if at all) do you think participation in this newsgroup affects/affected your offline life?

17. Do you have any other thoughts on this newsgroup, now or over time, that you would like me to consider?

18. What is your age?

19. What is your gender?

20. What is your occupation?

Appendix B:
Genre Analysis

Method

To assess which genres were named in the subject line, I sampled 2 complete weeks of posts discussing *All My Children* (*AMC*). Drawing on a range of 41 weeks, I selected the week with the most traffic and the week with the least traffic from the weeks for which I had every single post. By selecting the 2 weeks with the broadest range, I expected to be able to see what genres appeared each week and also to gain preliminary insights into which genres contributed to the considerable difference in quantity between the 2 weeks. In the light week (ended September 7, 1992), there were 110 messages posted about *AMC*. In the heavy week (ended October 19, 1992), there were 280 messages about *AMC*. For each week, I looked at the subject lines, searching for indicants of category that were used by more than one person (either within the 2-week spans or elsewhere in the corpus). Because of the decision to look for genres open to more than one participant, the genre of FAQ (frequently asked questions) was excluded. I also calculated the number of responses to posts in each genre, recognizing that a response to a post within a genre might not itself be within that genre. For both sets of these categorizations, I calculated the number of posts in each genre, the number of lines in each genre, the average length of a post in each genre, and the percentage of the total posts and lines accounted for by each genre in each week. Despite the search for difference, the 2 weeks were proportionately nearly identical; only 3 of 14 categories differed by more than 5% of the total posts between the 2 weeks, and even those differences remained slight. Therefore, I combined the 2 weeks' results.

Categories of Genre

These were the categories of genre. Their frequencies are tabulated in the table that follows.

Trivia. Trivia posts use the term "trivia" in the subject lines. These are posts that raised questions from *AMC* history in game form.

Unlurkings. Unlurkings, marked by the use of the terms "unlurking," "unlurk," and "lurker" in the subject lines, are posts in which new or rare posters introduce themselves to the group.

Sightings. Sightings, marked as such in the subject lines, are reports of having seen current or former soap opera actors in other contexts.

Spoilers. Spoilers, indicated with the word "spoiler" in the subject lines, involved the sharing of previews culled from magazines, sightings, and other computer networks.

Updates. Updates, marked by "update" and the shows' dates in the subject lines, are retellings of daily episodes.

Tangents. Tangents, marked by "TAN" in the subject lines, are a default category into which falls all discussions no longer directly related to the soap operas.

New threads. New threads are posts that first raise topics related to the soap opera. Subject lines usually identify the topics by character or characters (e.g., "AMC: Tad/Ted") but can contain any of a range of components. The category of new threads includes many individual genres such as "predictions" (which guess at the shows' futures) and "comments" (which offer evaluations of the shows). None of these more precise genre titles is employed consistently in subject lines.

TABLE B   Genres of *All My Children* Posts

Genre	Number of Posts and Percentage	Number of Lines and Percentage	Average Number of Lines
Trivia	1 (< 1)	6 (< 1)	6
Re: Trivia	1 (< 1)	13 (< 1)	13
Unlurkings	2 (1)	40 (< 1)	20
Re: Unlurkings	5 (1)	101 (1)	20
Sightings	7 (2)	126 (1)	18
Re: Sightings	7 (2)	111 (1)	16
Spoilers	9 (2)	344 (3)	38
Re: Spoilers	23 (6)	842 (6)	37
Updates	12 (3)	2,067 (16)	172
Re: Updates	50 (13)	1,336 (10)	27
Tangents	30 (8)	1,861 (14)	62
New threads	43 (11)	1,211 (9)	28
Re: New threads	190 (50)	5,042 (38)	27
Total	380 (100)	13,110 (100)	37

NOTE: Percentages are in parentheses. Percentages do not add to 100 due to rounding.

Appendix C:
Analysis of Agreements and Disagreements

Coding Procedures

I narrowed the data to a coherent but manageable subset by analyzing all the disagreements and agreements in the discussion of one story line on the soap opera *All My Children* (*AMC*). That story line was mentioned in 524 messages. An agreement initially was defined as any post that was explicitly responsive to a prior message and that took the same position as that message (although agreements could, and often did, go beyond stating that shared position). Disagreements were defined as those posts that were explicitly responsive to other messages and took positions incompatible with the prior messages. Disagreements were not necessarily directly contradictory but stated positions that could not logically be held if one held the prior positions.

In all but one case, agreements and disagreements were explicitly linked to prior messages through embedded quotations. Such quotations contained automatically generated reference lines indicating the prior writers and usually were edited down to the particular section to which the posts responded. These quotations with reference lines were used in all of the disagreements and in all but one of the agreements (which was linked through the phrase "as others have pointed out"). Thus, there could be no question that the authors of these messages were oriented to the prior turns. Although these posts also might have done more than agreed or disagreed, because they directly referenced and either affirmed or contradicted prior turns, they were considered to be agreements or disagreements. This is consistent with the notion that messages are multifunctional and that a single segment can involve multiple activities (O'Keefe, 1988).

A trained coder and I began by independently coding all of the messages about this story line as involving either agreement, disagreement, or neither. Disagreements between coders were resolved through discussion. The very few cases in which we could not agree on a post's status as agreement or disagreement resulted from ambiguous similarity or dissimilarity between the prior and posted positions. Those messages were not counted as agreements or disagreements. Of the 524 messages, most (77%) were categorized as "neither." Of the remaining 121 messages, 70 (58%) were coded as agreements and 51 (42%) as disagreements. Thus, agreements constituted 13% of the total story line corpus, and disagreements constituted just under 10%.

Because posts often cover many topics, the disagreement and agreement responses often were only part of the posts. As in Mulkay (1985, 1986), the analyses presented here look only at the paragraphs immediately relevant to the topic of disagreement and agreement. I analyzed those sections of posts in which participants agreed or disagreed with previous positions, including all those components of speech that positioned messages as agreements or disagreements and those that framed these activities. Whereas this move pulls these responses from the full messages, it situates them in the temporal thread of talk in which they were embedded.

I developed a detailed coding scheme for these 121 segments by analyzing them repeatedly to determine which features appeared in multiple messages, a process that involved continual turning from data to categorical scheme, the latter being refined with subsequent rereadings of the former. The resulting scheme had 17 categories, 2 of which (quotation with reference and reference to another's talk) I have already discussed as methods of demonstrating explicit linkage to previous messages. The remaining 15 were: expression of the need to respond, other ways of linking to a prior message, explicit indication of agreement or disagreement, assertion that affirmed or contradicted the prior message, partial agreement, qualifier, elaboration, provision of reasoning, expression of gratitude to the previous poster, apology, explicit acknowledgment of the other's position, use of the other's name, smiley face(s), framing as nonoffensive, and a catch-all "other" category. I will elaborate on these categories in a moment.

Once this scheme had been generated, the agreements and disagreements were coded for each feature separately by each coder. Messages were coded for the presence or absence of each component rather than for quantity or sequential ordering (although at times sequences were apparent). There were several differences in our initial codings. To some extent, this was due to misunderstandings about the definitions of the categories. In other cases, this resulted from difficulties in distinguishing among categories (this was especially true of separating reasoning from elaboration). In some cases, the problems stemmed from focusing on different agreement or disagreement responses within the same posts. However, despite our initial divergences, we were able to resolve our coding differences remarkably easily, and there were no cases in which we still disagreed after discussing the logic of our choices. Although this categorical scheme is not the only way in which one could analyze the message components of these posts, it did account for nearly all of the agreement- or disagreement-relevant segments. Only 8 messages contained a message component categorized as "other."

Message Components of Agreements and Disagreements

Expression of the need to respond: Phrases such as "I had to reply to your post" that framed the author's post as necessary

Other ways of linking to a prior message: References to prior talk such as "we've talked about this already"

Explicit indication of agreement or disagreement: Use of the phrase "I agree" and strong agreement tokens such as "indeed" and "you said it," or use of the word "disagree" or its synonyms and disagreement tokens such as "but"

Assertion that confirms or contradicts the prior message: Assessment that affirms or contradicts the claim of the quoted message; considered an indicator of the presence of agreement or disagreement

Partial agreement: Phrases such as "I thought so too" followed by disagreement tokens such as "but" and "though" or phrases such as "at the same time" positioning what followed as disagreement

Qualifier: "I think that," "that's only my opinion," and other phrases that lessened the extent to which the speaker could be held accountable for the veracity of a post's content (Goffman, 1981)

Elaboration: Extension of the talk from the immediate agreement or disagreement to a new but related angle or topic; operationalized as anything that made more sense as the second half of the sentence "I agree with the quoted utterance and..." than as the second half of the sentence "I agree with the quoted utterance because..."

Provision of reasoning: Presentation of a rationale to support the writer's perspective; operationalized as anything that made more sense as the second half of the sentence "`I agree with the quoted utterance because...`" than as the second half of the sentence "`I agree with the quoted utterance and...`"

Expression of gratitude to the previous poster: Phrases such as "`thank you for your post`"

Apology: Use of the phrase "`I'm sorry`"

Explicit acknowledgment of the other's position: Phrases such as "`I see your point`" and "`I know what you mean.`"

Use of the other's name: Using the first name of the quoted poster

Smiley face(s): Socioemotional cue built out of punctuation marks—usually a colon, a hyphen, and a right parenthesis `: -)`

Framing as nonoffensive: Explicitly framing the post as nonconfrontational (e.g., "`no offense`")

Topics of Agreements and Disagreements

Many of the agreements and disagreements dealt with more than one topic simultaneously. A total of 71 agreements and disagreements involved only one topic, 25 involved two topics, 20 involved three topics, 4 involved four topics, and 1 involved five topics.

Factual Topics

Narrative events: Retellings of what happened on the show

Sighting: Posts about seeing a soap opera actor in another role or at a personal appearance

Interpretive Topics

Character psyches: Interpreting the meaning of characters' behavior

Realism: Assessing how (un)realistic the show's events are

Emotional reaction: Explicitly sharing one's own emotional responses to the show's events

Story line suggestions: Projected story lines that the posters would like to see, which might or might not be what the posters think actually will happen

Story line worth: Evaluating the story line as a whole

Ideological messages: Evaluating the social value of the representations constructed in the story text

Character worth: Evaluating the overall quality of individual characters

Genre preference: Evaluating normatively what a soap opera should show using the posters' own pleasures as the criteria

Dialogue: Assessing the quality of the writing of the show

Story line influence: Assessing what other stories might have influenced the soap opera writers in constructing the story line

Actor appearance: Evaluating how the actors look

Crossover: The crossover between *AMC* and *Loving*

Soap quality: Assessing the quality of the soap opera *Loving*

Directing: Assessing the quality of *AMC*'s directing

Actor input: The extent to which the actor had creative input into the writing of the character

Sets: The use and reuse of sets, in particular, a recognizable cabin used earlier

Narrative device: Whether or not one needed an invitation to attend a party on a soap opera (one does not)

TABLE C Frequency of Topics in Disagreements and Agreements

Activities	Total Posts and Percentage
Factual	
Narrative events	13 (11)
Sighting	3 (2)
Interpretive	
Character psyche	53 (44)
Realism	20 (17)
Emotional reaction	20 (17)
Story line suggestion	15 (12)
Story line worth	14 (12)
Ideological worth	13 (11)
Character worth	13 (11)
Acting	13 (11)
Genre preference	7 (6)
Dialogue	4 (3)
Story line influence	3 (2)
Actor appearance	3 (2)
Soap crossover	2 (2)
Soap quality	2 (2)
Directing	1 (1)
Actor influence	1 (1)
Sets	1 (1)
Narrative device	1 (1)

NOTE: Percentages are in parentheses. Percentages total more than 100 because they indicate what proportions of the agreements and disagreements addressed each topic. Several of the messages contained more than one topic and, therefore, are counted more than once.

References

Adams, R. (1992). Total traffic through uunet for the last 2 weeks. *news.lists.* (Internet newsgroup)

Allen, R. C. (1983). On reading soaps: A semiotic primer. In E. A. Kaplan (Ed.), *Regarding television* (pp. 97-108). Los Angeles: American Film Institute.

Allen, R. C. (1985). *Speaking of soap operas.* Chapel Hill: University of North Carolina Press.

Anderson, B. (1983). *Imagined communities: Reflections on the origin and spread of nationalism.* London: Verso.

Anderson, J. A. (1996). The pragmatics of audience in research and theory. In J. Hay, L. Grossberg, & E. Wartella (Eds.), *The audience and its landscape.* Boulder, CO: Westview.

Ang, I. (1985). *Watching Dallas:* Soap opera and the melodramatic imagination. New York: Routledge.

Ang, I. (1989). Wanted: Audiences—On the politics of empirical audience studies. In E. Seiter, H. Borchers, G. Kreutzner, & E. Warth (Eds.), *Remote control: Television, audiences, and cultural power* (pp. 56-78). New York: Routledge.

Ang, I. (1991). *Desperately seeking the audience.* London: Routledge.

Arnheim, R. (1944). The world of the daytime serial. In P. F. Lazarsfeld & F. N. Stanton (Eds.), *Radio research* (pp. 34-85). New York: Duel, Sloan, & Pearce.

Babrow, A. S. (1987). Student motives for watching soap operas. *Journal of Broadcasting and Electronic Media, 31,* 309-321.

Babrow, A. S. (1989). An expectancy-value analysis of the student soap opera audience. *Communication Research, 16,* 155-178.

Bakhtin, M. M. (1981). *The dialogic imagination.* Austin: University of Texas Press.

Bakhtin, M. M. (1986). *Speech genres and other late essays.* Austin: University of Texas Press.

Baron, N. S. (1984). Computer mediated communication as a force in language change. *Visible Language, 18*(2), 118-141.

Basso, E. B. (1992). Contextualization in Kalapalo narratives. In A. Duranti & C. Goodwin (Eds.), *Rethinking context: Language as an interactive phenomenon* (pp. 253-270). Cambridge, UK: Cambridge University Press.

Bauman, R. (1975). Verbal art as performance. *American Anthropologist, 77,* 290-311.

Bauman, R. (1992). Contextualization, tradition, and the dialogue of genres: Icelandic legends of the *kraftaskald.* In A. Duranti & C. Goodwin (Eds.), *Rethinking context: Language as an interactive phenomenon* (pp. 125-146). Cambridge, UK: Cambridge University Press.

Baym, N. (1995). *American women writers and the work of history 1790-1860.* New Brunswick, NJ: Rutgers University Press.

Baym, N. K. (1993). Interpreting soap operas and creating community: Inside a computer-mediated fan culture. *Journal of Folklore Research, 30*(2/3), 143-176.

Baym, N. K. (1995). The performance of humor in computer-mediated communication. *Journal of Computer-Mediated Communication, 1*(2). Available on Internet: http://207.201.161.120/jcmc/vol1/issue2/baym.html.

Baym, N. K. (1996). Agreement and disagreement in a computer-mediated group. *Research on Language and Social Interaction, 29,* 315-346.

Blumenthal, D. (1997). *Women and soap opera: A cultural feminist perspective.* New York: Praeger.

Bourdieu, P. (1977). *Outline of a theory of practice.* Cambridge, UK: Cambridge University Press.

Bourdieu, P. (1990). *The logic of practice.* Palo Alto, CA: Stanford University Press.

Briggs, C. L. (1986). *Learning how to ask: A sociolinguistic appraisal of the role of the interview in social science research.* Cambridge, UK: Cambridge University Press.

Brown, M. E. (1994). *Soap opera and women's talk.* Thousand Oaks, CA: Sage.

Brown, M. E., & Barwick, L. (1986). *Fables and endless genealogies: Soap opera and women's culture.* Paper presented at the meeting of the Australian Screen Studies Association, Sydney.

Brunsdon, C. (1983). Notes on a soap opera. In E. A. Kaplan (Ed.), *Regarding television* (pp. 76-83). Frederick, MD: University Publications of America.

Brunsdon, C. (1989). Text and audience. In E. Seiter, H. Borchers, G. Kreutzner, & E. Warth (Eds.), *Remote control: Television, audiences, and cultural power* (pp. 116-129). New York: Routledge.

Cantor, M. G., & Pingree, S. (1983). *The soap opera.* Beverly Hills, CA: Sage.

Carpenter, T. (1983, September 6). Reach out and access someone. *The Village Voice,* pp. 9-11.

Castleman, C. (1982). *Getting up: Subway graffiti in New York.* Cambridge, MA: MIT Press.

Chaiklin, S., & Lave, J. (Eds.). (1993). *Understanding practice: Perspectives on activity and context.* Cambridge, UK: Cambridge University Press.

Cherny, L. (1995). *The MUD register: Conversational modes of action in a text-based virtual reality.* Unpublished doctoral dissertation, Stanford University.

Cherny, L., & Weise, E. R. (Eds.). (1996). *Wired women.* Seattle, WA: Seal.

Chiaro, D. (1992). *The language of jokes: Analysing verbal play.* London: Routledge.

Clerc, S. (1996). Estrogen brigades and "Big Tits" threads: Media fandom online and off. In L. Cherny & E. R. Weise (Eds.), *Wired women* (pp. 73-97). Seattle, WA: Seal.

Cody, M. J., Wendt, P., Dunn, D., Pierson, J., Ott, J., & Pratt, L. (1997, May). *Friendship formation and creating communities on the Internet: Reaching out to the senior population.* Paper presented at the annual meeting of the International Communication Association, Montreal.

Compesi, R. J. (1980). Gratifications of daytime TV serial viewers. *Journalism Quarterly, 57,* 155-158.

Connery, B. A. (1997). IMHO: Authority and egalitarian rhetoric in the virtual coffeehouse. In D. Porter (Ed.), *Internet culture* (pp. 161-180). New York: Routledge.

Contractor, N. S., & Seibold, D. R. (1993). Theoretical frameworks for the study of structuring processes in group decision support systems: Adaptive structuration theory and self-organizing systems theory. *Human Communication Research, 19,* 528-563.

Culnan, M. J., & Markus, M. L. (1987). Information technologies. In F. M. Jablin, L. L. Putnam, K. H. Roberts, & L. W. Porter (Eds.), *Handbook of organizational computing: An interdisciplinary perspective* (pp. 420-443). Newbury Park, CA: Sage.

Danet, B. (1993). *Books, letters, documents: The changing materiality of texts in late print culture.* Unpublished manuscript, Hebrew University of Jerusalem.

Dannefer, W. D., & Poushinsky, N. (1977). Language and community: CB in perspective. *Journal of Communication, 27*(3), 122-126.

Doheny-Farina, S. (1996). *The wired neighborhood.* New Haven, CT: Yale University Press.

Duranti, A. (1988). Ethnography of speaking: Toward a linguistics of the praxis. In F. P. Newmeyer (Ed.), *Language: the socio-cultural context* (pp. 210-228). New York: Cambridge University Press.

Duranti, A., & Goodwin, C. (Eds.). (1992). *Rethinking context: Language as an interactive phenomenon.* Cambridge, UK: Cambridge University Press.

Ebben, M. (1993, October). *Women on the Net: An exploratory study of gender dynamics on the soc.women computer network.* Paper presented at the annual meeting of the Organization for the Study of Communication, Language, and Gender, Tempe, AZ.

Edmundson, M., & Rounds, D. (1973). *The soaps: Daytime serials of radio and TV.* New York: Stein & Day.

Erol's. (1997, September 16-17). Usenet statistics. Available on Internet: http://thereisnocabal.news.erols.com/feedinfo.

Fernback, J. (1997). The individual within the collective: Virtual ideology and the realization of collective principles. In S. G. Jones (Ed.), *Virtual culture* (pp. 36-54). Thousand Oaks, CA: Sage.

Fiske, J. (1987). *Television culture.* New York: Methuen.

Gaskins, S., Miller, P. J., & Corsaro, W. A. (1992). Theoretical and methodological perspectives in the interpretive study of children. In W. A. Corsaro & P. J. Miller (Eds.), *Interpretive approaches to children's socialization* (pp. 5-24). San Francisco: Jossey-Bass.

Geraghty, C. (1991). *Women and soap opera.* Cambridge, UK: Polity.

Goffman, E. (1974). *Frame analysis: An essay on the organization of experience.* Cambridge, MA: Harvard University Press.

Goffman, E. (1981). *Forms of talk.* Philadelphia: University of Pennsylvania Press.

Gumperz, J. (1982). *Discourse strategies.* Cambridge, UK: Cambridge University Press.

Gumperz, J. (1992). Contextualization and understanding. In A. Duranti & C. Goodwin (Eds.), *Rethinking context: Language as an interactive phenomenon* (pp. 229-252). Cambridge, UK: Cambridge University Press.

Gurak, L. J. (1997). *Persuasion and privacy in cyberspace: The online protests over Lotus MarketPlace and the Clipper Chip.* New Haven, CT: Yale University Press.

Hanks, W. F. (1996). *Language and communicative practices.* Boulder, CO: Westview.

Harrington, C. L., & Bielby, D. D. (1995). *Soap fans: Pursuing pleasure and making meaning in everyday life.* Philadelphia: Temple University Press.

Hay, J., Grossberg, L., & Wartella, E. (Eds.). (1996). *The audience and its landscape.* Boulder, CO: Westview.

Hayward, J. P. (1997). *Consuming pleasures: Active audiences and serial fictions.* Lexington: University of Kentucky Press.

Healy, D. (1997). Cyberspace and place: The Internet as middle landscape on the electronic frontier. In D. Porter (Ed.), *Internet culture* (pp. 55-71). New York: Routledge.

Hellerstein, L. N. (1985). The social use of electronic communication at a major university. *Computers and the Social Sciences, 1,* 191-197.

Herring, S. (1994). Politeness in computer culture: Why women thank and men flame. In M. Bucholtz, A. C. Liang, L. Sutton, & C. Hines (Eds.), *Cultural performances: Proceedings of the Third Berkeley Women and Language Conference* (pp. 278-293). Berkeley, CA: Women and Language Group.

Herring, S. (1996). Posting in a different voice: Gender and ethics in computer-mediated communication. In C. Ess (Ed.), *Philosophical approaches to computer-mediated communication* (pp. 115-145). Albany: State University of New York Press.

Herzog, H. (1944). What do we really know about daytime serial listeners? In P. F. Lazarsfeld & F. N. Stanton (Eds.), *Radio research* (pp. 3-33). New York: Duel, Sloan, & Pearce.

Hobson, D. (1982). *Crossroads: The drama of soap opera.* London: Methuen.

Hobson, D. (1989). Soap operas at work. In E. Seiter, H. Borchers, G. Kreutzner, & E. Warth (Eds.), *Remote control: Television, audiences, and cultural power* (pp. 150-167). New York: Routledge.

Hobson, D. (1990). Women audiences and the workplace. In M. E. Brown (Ed.), *Television and women's culture* (pp. 71-74). Newbury Park, CA: Sage.

Hollingshead, A. B., & McGrath, J. E. (1995). The whole is less than the sum of its parts: A critical review of research on computer-assisted groups. In R. Guzzo & E. Salas (Eds.), *Team decision and team performance in organizations* (pp. 46-68). San Francisco: Jossey-Bass.

Hymes, D. (1975). Folklore's nature and the sun's myth. *Journal of American Folklore, 88,* 345-369.

Hymes, D. (1986). Models of the interaction of language and social life. In J. J. Gumperz & D. Hymes (Eds.), *Directions in sociolinguistics: The ethnography of speaking* (pp. 35-71). New York: Basil Blackwell.

Jenkins, H. (1992). *Textual poachers: Television fans and participatory cultures.* London: Routledge.

Jensen, J. (1992). Fandom as pathology: The consequences of characterization. In L. Lewis (Ed.), *The adoring audience: Fan culture and popular media* (pp. 9-29). London: Routledge.

Jensen, J., & Pauly, J. (1997). Imagining the audience: Losses and gains in cultural studies. In M. Ferguson & P. Golding (Eds.), *Cultural studies in question* (pp. 155-169). Thousand Oaks, CA: Sage.

Joe, S. K. (1997, May). *Socioemotional use of CMC: Self-disclosure in computer-mediated communication.* Paper presented at the annual meeting of the International Communication Association, Montreal.

Kalcik, S. (1985). Women's handles and the performance of identity in the CB community. In R. A. Jordan & S. J. Kalcik (Eds.), *Women's folklore, women's culture* (pp. 99-108). Philadelphia: University of Pennsylvania Press.

Kamberelis, G., & Scott, K. D. (1992). Other people's voices: The coarticulation of texts and subjectivities. *Linguistics and Education, 4,* 359-403.

Kielwasser, A. P., & Wolf, M. A. (1989). The appeal of soap opera: An analysis of process and quality in dramatic serial gratifications. *Journal of Popular Culture, 23*(2), 111-134.

Kiesler, S., Siegel, J., & McGuire, T. W. (1984). Social psychological aspect of computer-mediated communication. *American Psychologist, 39,* 1123-1134.

Kilguss, A. F. (1977). Therapeutic use of a soap opera discussion group with psychiatric inpatients. *Clinical Social Work Journal, 5,* 525-530.

Kramarae, C., & Taylor, H. J. (1993). Women and men on electronic networks: A conversation or a monologue? In H. J. Taylor, C. Kramarae, & M. Ebben (Eds.),

Women, information technology, scholarship (pp. 52-61). Urbana, IL: Center for Advanced Study.

Kraut, R., Patterson, M., Lundmark, V., Kiesler, S., Mukophadhyay, T., & Scherlis, W. (1998). *Internet paradox: A social technology that reduced social involvement and psychological well-being?* Preliminary draft. Available on Internet: http://homenet.andrew.cmu.edu/progress/HN.impact.10.htm.

Lave, J., & Wenger, E. (1991). *Situated learning: Legitimate peripheral participation.* New York: Cambridge University Press.

Lemish, D. (1985). Soap opera viewing in college: A naturalistic inquiry. *Journal of Broadcasting & Electronic Media, 29,* 275-293.

Lewis, L. (Ed.). (1992). *The adoring audience.* New York: Routledge.

Liccardo, L. (1996, April 30). Who really watches the daytime soaps? *Soap Opera Weekly,* pp. 36-38.

Liebes, T., & Katz, E. (1989). On the critical abilities of television viewers. In E. Seiter, H. Borchers, G. Kreutzner, & E. Warth (Eds.), *Remote control: Television, audiences, and cultural power* (pp. 204-222). New York: Routledge.

Livingstone, S. M. (1989). Interpretive viewers and structured programs: The implicit representation of soap opera characters. *Communication Research, 16,* 25-57.

Livingstone, S. M. (1990). Interpreting a television narrative: How different viewers see a story. *Journal of Communication, 40*(1), 72-85.

Lockard, J. (1997). Progressive politics, electronic individualism, and the myth of virtual community. In D. Porter (Ed.), *Internet culture* (pp. 219-232). New York: Routledge.

Mabry, E. (1997). Framing flames: The structure of argumentative messages on the Net. *Journal of Computer-Mediated Communication, 2*(4). Available on Internet: http://207.201.161.120/jcmc/vol2/issue4/mabry.html.

Macdonald, F. (1979). *Don't touch that dial.* Chicago: Nelson-Hall.

McLaughlin, M. L., Osborne, K. K., & Smith, C. B. (1995). Standards of conduct on Usenet. In S. G. Jones (Ed.), *CyberSociety: Computer-mediated community and communication* (pp. 90-111). Thousand Oaks, CA: Sage.

McRae, S. (1997). Flesh made word: Sex, text, and the virtual body. In D. Porter (Ed.), *Internet culture* (pp. 73-86). New York: Routledge.

Miller, P. J. (1994). Narrative practices: Their role in socialization and self-construction. In U. Neisser & R. Fivush (Eds.), *The remembering self: Construction and accuracy in the self-narrative* (pp. 158-179). Cambridge, UK: Cambridge University Press.

Miller, P. J., & Goodnow, J. J. (1995). Cultural practices: Toward an integration of culture and development. In J. J. Goodnow, P. J. Miller, & F. Kessel (Eds.), *Cultural practices as contexts for development* (New Directions for Child Development, No. 67, pp. 5-20). San Francisco: Jossey Bass.

Miller, P. J., & Hoogstra, L. (1992). Language as tool in the socialization and apprehension of cultural meanings. In T. Schwartz, G. White, & C. Lutz (Eds.),

New directions in psychological anthropology (pp. 83-101). Cambridge, UK: Cambridge University Press.

Miller, P., & Mintz, J. (1993). *Instantiating culture: Socialization through narrative practices.* Paper presented at the meeting of the Society for Research in Child Development, New Orleans, LA.

Mnookin, J. L. (1996). Virtual(ly) law: The emergence of law in LambdaMOO. *Journal of Computer-Mediated Communication, 2*(1). Available on Internet: http://207.201.161.120/jcmc/vol2/issue1/lambda.html.

Modleski, T. (1983). The rhythms of reception: Daytime television and women's work. In E. A. Kaplan (Ed.), *Regarding television* (pp. 67-84). Los Angeles: American Film Institute.

Modleski, T. (1984). *Loving with a vengeance: Mass produced fantasies for women.* New York: Muntheun.

Moores, S. (1993). *Interpreting audiences: The ethnography of media consumption.* London: Sage.

Morley, D. (1989). Changing paradigms in audience studies. In E. Seiter, H. Borchers, G. Kreutzner, & E. Warth (Eds.), *Remote control: Television, audiences, and cultural power* (pp. 16-43). New York: Routledge.

Morreall, J. (1983). *Taking laughter seriously.* Albany: State University of New York Press.

Mulkay, M. (1985). Agreement and disagreement in conversations and letters. *Text, 5,* 201-227.

Mulkay, M. (1986). Conversations and texts. *Human Studies, 9,* 303-321.

Mulkay, M. (1988). *On humour: Its nature and its place in modern society.* Cambridge, UK: Polity.

Myers, D. (1987a). "Anonymity is part of the magic": Individual manipulation of computer-mediated communication contexts. *Qualitative Sociology, 19,* 251-266.

Myers, D. (1987b). A new environment for communication play: On-line play. In G. A. Fine (Ed.), *Meaningful play, playful meaning* (pp. 231-245). Champaign, IL: Human Kinetics.

Newcomb, H. (1974). *TV: The most popular art.* New York: Anchor.

Nguyen, D. T., & Alexander, J. (1996). The coming of cyberspacetime and the end of the polity. In R. Shields (Ed.), *Cultures of Internet: Virtual spaces, real histories, living bodies* (pp. 99-124). Thousand Oaks, CA: Sage.

Nightingale, V. (1996). *Studying audiences: The shock of the real.* London: Routledge.

Nilsen, D. L. F. (1993). *Humor scholarship: A research bibliography.* Westport, CT: Greenwood.

Nixon, A. E. (1970). Coming of age in Sudsville. *Television Quarterly, 9,* 61-70.

Nochimson, M. (1992). *No end to her: Soap opera and the female subject.* Berkeley: University of California Press.

O'Keefe, B. J. (1988). The logic of message design: Individual differences in reasoning about communication. *Communication Monographs, 55,* 80-103.

Ochs, E. (1988). *Culture and language development.* Cambridge, UK: Cambridge University Press.

Oring, E. (1992). *Jokes and their relations.* Lexington: University of Kentucky Press.

Ortner, S. B. (1984). Theory in anthropology since the Sixties. *Comparative Studies in Society and History, 26*(1), 126-166.

Palmer, J. (1994). *Taking humour seriously.* London: Routledge.

Parks, M. R., & Floyd, K. (1996). Making friends in cyberspace. *Journal of Communication, 46*(1), 80-97.

Perse, E., & Rubin, R. (1989). Attribution in social and parasocial relationships. *Communication Research, 16,* 59-77.

Phelps, A. H. L. (1833). *The female student: Or, lectures to young ladies, comprising outlines and applications of the different branches of female education, for the use of female schools, and private libraries* (2nd ed.). New York: Leavitt, Lord. (Originally published in 1826)

Pomerantz, A. (1984). Agreeing and disagreeing with assessments: Some features of preferred/dispreferred turn shapes. In J. M. Atkinson & J. Heritage (Eds.), *Structures of social action: Studies in conversation analysis* (pp. 57-101). Cambridge, UK: Cambridge University Press.

Porter, D. (Ed.). (1997). *Internet culture.* New York: Routledge.

Press, A. L. (1996). Towards a qualitative methodology of audience study: Using ethnography to study the popular culture audience. In J. Hay, L. Grossberg, & E. Wartella (Eds.), *The audience and its landscape.* Boulder, CO: Westview.

Radway, J. A. (1984). *Reading the romance: Women, patriarchy, and popular literature* (2nd ed.). Chapel Hill: University of North Carolina Press.

Raymond, E. S. (Ed.). (1991). *The new hacker's dictionary.* Cambridge, MA: MIT Press.

Reid, B. (1993). Top 40 newsgroups in order by traffic volume. *news.lists.* (Internet newsgroup)

Reid, E. M. (1991). *Electropolis: Communication and community on Internet relay chat.* Unpublished thesis, University of Melbourne.

Reid, E. M. (1995). Virtual worlds: Culture and imagination. In S. G. Jones (Ed.), *CyberSociety: Computer-mediated communication and community* (pp. 164-183). Thousand Oaks, CA: Sage.

Rheingold, H. (1993). *Virtual communities.* Reading, MA: Addison-Wesley.

Rice, R. E. (1989). Issues and concepts in research on computer-mediated communication systems. In J. A. Anderson (Ed.), *Communication yearbook* (Vol. 12, pp. 436-476). Newbury Park, CA: Sage.

Robins, K. (1995). Cyberspace and the world we live in. In M. Featherstone & R. Burrows (Eds.), *Cyberspace/cyberbodies/cyberpunk: Cultures of technological embodiment* (pp. 135-156). London: Sage.

Rogoff, B. (1990). *Apprenticeship in thinking: Cognitive development in social context.* New York: Oxford University Press.

Rouverol, J. (1984). *Writing for the soaps.* Cincinnati, OH: Writers Digest Books.

Rubin, A. M. (1985). Uses of daytime television soap operas by college students. *Journal of Broadcasting & Electronic Media, 29,* 241-258.

Rubin, A. M., & Perse, E. M. (1987). Audience activity and soap opera involvement: A uses and effects investigation. *Human Communication Research, 14,* 246-268.

Savicki, V., Lingenfelter, D., & Kelley, M. (1996). Gender language style in group composition in Internet discussion groups. *Journal of Computer-Mediated Communication, 2*(3). Available on Internet: http://207.201.161.120/jcmc/vol2/issue3/savicki.html.

Schieffelin, B. B., & Ochs, E. (1986). Language socialization. *Annual Review of Anthropology, 15,* 163-191.

Seiter, E., Borchers, H., Kreutzner, G., & Warth, E. (1989). "Don't treat us like we're so stupid and naive": Towards an ethnography of soap opera viewers. In E. Seiter, H. Borchers, G. Kreutzner, & E. Warth (Eds.), *Remote control: Television, audiences, and cultural power* (pp. 223-247). New York: Routledge.

Selfe, C., & Meyer, P. (1991). Testing claims for on-line conferences. *Written Communication, 8,* 163-192.

Silverman, D. (1993). *Interpreting qualitative data: Methods for analysing talk, text, and interaction.* London: Sage.

Smith, C. B., McLaughlin, M. L., & Osborne, K. K. (1997). Conduct control on Usenet. *Journal of Computer-Mediated Communication, 2*(4). Available on Internet: http://207.201.161.120/jcmc/vol2/issue4/smith.html.

Stivale, C. J. (1997). Spam: Heteroglossia and harassment in cyberspace. In D. Porter (Ed.), *Internet culture* (pp. 133-144). New York: Routledge.

Stone, A. R. (1995). *The war of desire and technology at the close of the mechanical age.* Cambridge, MA: MIT Press.

Stratton, J. (1997). Cyberspace and the globalization of culture. In D. Porter (Ed.), *Internet culture* (pp. 253-276). New York: Routledge.

Susman, L. (1997, July 29). Why soaps get no respect. *Soap Opera Weekly,* pp. 12-14.

Sutton, L. (1994). Using USENET: Gender, power, and silence in electronic discourse. In S. Gahl, A. Dolbey, & C. Johnsons (Eds.), *Proceedings of the Twentieth Annual Meeting of the Berkeley Linguistics Society* (pp. 506-520). Berkeley, CA: Berkeley Linguistics Society.

Tepper, M. (1997). Usenet communities and the cultural politics of information. In D. Porter (Ed.), *Internet culture* (pp. 39-54). New York: Routledge.

tile.net. (1997, September 17). Internet newsgroup. Available on Internet: http://tile.net/news.

Tracy, K. (1997). *Colloquium: Dilemmas of academic discourse.* Norwood, NJ: Ablex.

Turkle, S. (1995). *Life on the screen: Identity in the age of the Internet.* New York: Simon & Schuster.

Viewing notes. (1998, September 8). *Soap Opera Weekly,* p. 10.

Walther, J. (1996). Computer-mediated communication: Impersonal, interpersonal and hyperpersonal interaction. *Communication Research, 23,* 3-43.

Walther, J. B., & Burgoon, J. K. (1992). Relational communication in computer-mediated interaction. *Human Communication Research, 19,* 50-88.

Werry, C. C. (1996). Linguistic and interactional features of Internet relay chat. In S. Herring (Ed.), *Computer-mediated communication: Linguistic, social, and cross-cultural perspectives* (pp. 47-63). Amsterdam: John Benjamins.

Whetmore, E. J., & Kielwasser, A. P. (1983). The soap opera audience speaks: A preliminary report. *Journal of American Culture, 6,* 110-116.

Williams, C. T. (1992). "It's time for my story": Oral culture in a technological era—Towards a methodology for soap opera audiences. In S. Frentz (Ed.), *Staying tuned: Contemporary soap opera criticism* (pp. 69-88). Bowling Green, OH: Bowling Green State University Popular Press.

Index

About the Author

Nancy K. Baym is Assistant Professor of Communication Studies at the University of Kansas, where she teaches courses in computer-mediated communication and interpersonal communication. She earned her doctorate in speech communications at the University of Illinois at Urbana-Champaign in 1994.